St. Louis Community College

Forest Park
Florissant Valley
Meramec

Instructional Resources
St. Louis, Missouri

GAYLORD

The Frost Family's Adventure in Poetry

The Frost Family's Adventure in Poetry

Sheer Morning Gladness at the Brim

Lesley Lee Francis

University of Missouri Press / Columbia and London

Library of Congress Cataloging-in-Publication Data

Francis, Lesley Lee, 1931–
    The Frost family's adventure in poetry : sheer morning gladness at the brim / Lesley Lee Francis.
        p.   cm.
    includes index.
    ISBN 0-8262-0945-9 (alk. paper)
    1. Frost, Robert, 1874–1963—Journeys—England. 2. Americans—England—History—
20th century. 3. Poets, American—20th century—Biography. 4. Frost, Robert, 1874–1963—
Family. 5. Frost family.
    I. Title
PS3511.R94Z6527   1994
811'.52—dc20
[B]   93-47473
                                                                                                CIP

For permissions to reproduce copyrighted material,
see the last printed page of the book.

∞ This paper meets the requirements of the American National Standard
for Permanence of Paper for Printed Library Materials, Z39.48, 1984.

Designer: Rhonda Miller
Typesetter: Connell-Zeko Type & Graphics
Printer and Binder: Thomson-Shore, Inc.
Typefaces: Times and Monotype Corsiva

To
"the children" (theirs and mine)

A leaping tongue of bloom the scythe had spared
Beside a reedy brook the scythe had bared.

The mower in the dew had loved them thus,
By leaving them to flourish, not for us,

Nor yet to draw one thought of ours to him,
But from sheer morning gladness at the brim.

—"The Tuft of Flowers"

Contents

Acknowledgments

This account of the Frost family would not have been possible without the kindness of many people and institutions who possess original source material and who assisted me in the preparation of the final manuscript.

Particular thanks are due the curators of the special collections who facilitated access to the Frost materials: Philip N. Cronenwett at the Dartmouth College Library, Hanover, New Hampshire; Howard B. Gottlieb at the Boston University Library, Boston, Massachusetts; Cathy Henderson at the University of Texas Library, Austin, Texas; John Lancaster at the Amherst College Library, Amherst, Massachusetts; Michael Plunkett at the University of Virginia Library, Charlottesville, Virginia; William E. Ross at the University of New Hampshire Library, Durham, New Hampshire; Helyn Townsend at the Plymouth State College Library, Plymouth, New Hampshire. In addition, special thanks are due my daughter Deborah Lee Zimic and sister, Elinor Francis Wilber, as well as Professors Earl Wilcox (Robert Frost Society, Winthrop College) and William H. Pritchard (Amherst College) for their advice and constructive comments on the manuscript in progress.

I am most indebted to the American Council of Learned Societies (ACLS) and the Virginia Foundation for the Humanities for grants to aid in the research and writing, and to the American Association of University Professors for grants of leave.

The support of many friends in England is gratefully acknowledged: Alan Martin and Richard Emeny of the Edward Thomas Fellowship, Myfanwy Thomas, Edward Eastaway Thomas, O.B.E., D.S.C., and R. George Thomas; the Rev. R. J. Legg, Barbara Davis, Penny Ely, and Joyce Hogg in Dymock; J. Robert (Robin) and Pam Haines in Gloucester; Peter Mair, Jan Marsh, Anne Harvey, and Gervase Farjeon in London; Robert Hogg in Newcastle upon Tyne; Henry Pantin in North Yorkshire; David and Mary Abercrombie in Edinburgh.

I cannot close without a dedicatory word to my three daughters—Deborah, Kristiana, and Melanie—who have with patience and understanding awaited the birth of their mother's book (much as I awaited the birth of my first grandchild). May they receive my tribute to their forebears as a celebration of the family in the very best sense: "But nothing tells me / That I need learn to let go with the heart."

The Frost Family's Adventure in Poetry

Introduction

Education by Poetry

Don't join too many gangs. Join few if any.
Join the U.S. and join the family—
But not much in between unless a college.
—"Build Soil—A Political Pastoral"

A professor of Spanish literature I once had, whom I admired as the quintessential Renaissance man, began our course of study by reminding us that there are two ways to approach the field: "Going round the world or stopping to examine the rose." I chose the English years as the topic of my biographical studies of Robert Frost—my mother's father—due in part to the possession of family journals from my mother's childhood, and in part to a personal journey on which I had embarked in search of understanding. I began my journey with the belief that the best in us as artists is present in our childhood: the freedom from conventional perspective trammeling the fantasy, the freedom of association, all are strongest in the child. This belief, along with the wealth of writings of the Frost children, led me to the hope of resurrecting the world of nostalgia and, within the stated parameters, of elucidating—synecdochically—the whole.[1]

I had come to my grandfather's poetry as any young person might; not in school, where I read Shakespeare, Milton, and the Romantic poets for the most part, but at home, where I learned about Robert Frost and even memorized "Stopping by Woods on a Snowy Evening," "The Runaway," and "After Apple-Picking," all among my favorites. I saw my grandfather quite frequently but never for long periods of time: in Ripton, Vermont (at the log cabin and with the Morrisons); in Cambridge, Massachusetts (where I spent four years at Radcliffe College when he resided on Brewster Street); on the road (at the University of North Carolina at Chapel Hill with his close friends Gladys and Clifford Lyons);

at Sweet Briar College (where I taught Spanish for several years); and in Washington, D.C. (where he often visited my mother, sister, and me, as well as my cousin William Prescott Frost and his family). Although his wife, Elinor, and sometimes their children, called him Rob or Papa, he came to be known affectionately by all of us as simply RF.

My encounters with my grandfather left an indelible impression on me at an impressionable age, but I would be the mother of three before I could articulate any coherent response. I recalled how we talked about "the sound of sense" and "the strain of rhythm upon a meter"; together praised Henley's line "I am the master of my fate; I am the captain of my soul"[2] as a high and demanding calling and praised Milton for the way he liked to face the harshness of our trial; and commented upon the apparent accessibility of Mother Goose or Longfellow, and of other "popular" poets scorned by academic scholars. RF spoke of the difficulty in knowing when one has had an idea as one passes enthusiasm through the "prism of the intellect" and dams back and harnesses emotions by discipline "to the wit mill"; how you can never tell what you have said or done till you have seen it reflected in other people's minds; the danger of "losing one's sensitive fear of landing on the lovely too hard."[3] We always came back to the need to just *do* it, in the face of fearful doubts and anxieties, by the braving of alien entanglements, in the best Jamesian tradition.[4]

For my grandfather, this was all part of the creative process, and part of engaging life head-on, risking the spiritual in the material. I was able to share with him an English translation of Miguel de Unamuno's *Del Sentimiento Trágico de la Vida,* which he read in one night with genuine excitement. He learned little, he confessed, from the turgid prose of my master's thesis on "The Don Juan Theme in Contemporary Spanish Drama" (and he was gone and thus spared my completed doctoral dissertation on "The Collective Protagonist in the Historical Novels of Unamuno, Baroja, and Valle Inclán").

It would be years later before I applied these random philosophical thoughts to the problems of the Frost biography. Academic scholars, I concluded, often lost sight of a life that was no less poetic than the poems it produced, poems addressed to all kinds, and reaching out to challenge us, to "rumple our brains fondly," as he would tell his students. Appreciation of Frost's poetry outside the walls of academe might be resented or patronized as simplistic, but if that is so, so must we accuse Shakespeare, whose plays and sonnets speak to all of us, or Homer, whose *Odyssey,* even in translation, moves and instructs us today as few poems can. In our search for an angle, a twist in the interpretation of the poet's life, we may overlook its essence, its unwavering commitment to art, to family, and to a few friends: "Poetry has to heighten . . . by perpetual play of every faculty of art, imagination and figurativeness that heaven bestows," the poet warns us.[5]

What stuck with me through my own formal education and college teaching (in Spanish language and literature) was how easy it was to abandon all touch with life as an adventure; life seemed to have purpose only when it achieved a tightly disciplined structure where I could feel safe, and perhaps a little smug and self-important. But wasn't I letting down my students by the lack of spontaneity and enthusiasm needed to be a good teacher? When I returned to the Frost biography, I was looking for answers to the questions, not only about the Frost family, but also about the meaning in my own life and the lives of my children. I wanted the answers to be accessible through the act of an open-minded scrutiny of the verses and the Frost archives. What I learned was what my grandfather had learned before me and then passed on to his children with Elinor's full complicity, that education by poetry is education by metaphor:

> I think young people have insight. They have a flash here and a flash there. It is like stars coming out in the sky in the early evening. They have flashes of light. They have that sort of thing which belongs to youth. It is later in the dark of life that you see forms, constellations. And it is the constellations that are philosophy. It is like forcing a too early mathematics on a child, to bring him to philosophy too young. We have system and we have plan all too soon now. You know too well and have convictions too well by the time you are forty. The flashing is done, the coming out of the stars. It is all constellations.[6]

Except for Lawrance Thompson and his three-volume biography of my grandfather, I probably would have stuck to my resolution, reached before finishing college, not to write about someone, anyone, in the immediate family. The pitfalls seemed obvious: being too close to the subject would inevitably lead to distortion, betrayal of bias, or, at the very least, too generous an interpretation of his motives.

I had never considered my grandfather to be a typical grandparent: he was seldom in one place long enough, even at his home in Ripton or Cambridge, to casually drop in on for jollying or the like. On the contrary, I always envisioned him in action: taking long walks, teaching, fulfilling his reading commitments, or trying to help often troubled members of his own family. Even as the recipient of adulation and honors, he never lost for me his rugged strength of character and independence of thought, or his uncanny ability to include me directly in his talk. He came to serve as a role model far more so than my mother, Lesley, who, although just as independent—and fiercely so, I might add—never fully overcame what had become a strained emotional relationship with her two daughters.

Just as I would never be entirely free of my mother's expectations, she was destined to remain in her famous father's long shadow; but *I* could look upon my grandfather, who had already achieved national recognition before I was born, with the luxury of the distance and detachment a generation brings.

It was Thompson's single-minded interpretation of my grandfather's life that led me to want to "read more about it," to come to terms in one way or another with the obvious discrepancies between the biographer's relentless and humorless portrayal and my own as yet unschooled awareness of a man who was always accessible for good talk and understanding, who presented an awesome yet human and humorous presence, and who gave unselfishly to both friends and family over the years. I knew from my own experience that he enjoyed domestic intimacy and the continuity of reassurance, essential to his art, that it provided him. He actively participated in shaping the young lives of his children and of his many students. He drew special strength from Elinor in joining together vocation and avocation, life and metaphor.

Despite these strong convictions, I approached (and still approach) the Frost biography with trepidation. In part due to my sense of inadequacy and in part due to my particular training as an academic, my interest took a scholarly direction, searching out discreet projects on matters I thought were significant lacunae in the Thompson biography.[7]

I was drawn in those early years of my grandfather's often frustrating search for recognition as a poet (since he wrote "La Noche Triste" while still in high school) to the peculiar dynamics of a literary family and the impetus to creativity in the symbiotic relationship between parents and children. I came to believe, with writers like Rollo May (in *The Courage to Create*) and Arthur Koestler (in his *Act of Creation*), that the artist—in this case the poet—albeit beset by despair and self-doubt and inexplicable feelings of guilt, displays the creative and moral courage of the nonconformist to move ahead in spite of his despair and his doubts. He delves into "the smithy" of his soul, into the chaos from which he extricates form, to provide a "momentary stay against confusion." Out of his imagination, in a process of bisociation, he identifies and develops ideas, using metaphors, images, myths, and other devices available to his craft. The poems are born of the heightened vitality and intensity of emotion as the poet gives himself in an act of total commitment and, through the complex interaction of insight and the occasional almost mystical breakthrough of the unconscious, takes part in a dynamic struggle to understand his own existence and the world around him.

In RF's case, he and Elinor formed a pact with their marriage to protect the integrity of his poetic talents, the subtlety and originality of his work, in spite of constant pressures from his grandfather and from Elinor's parents and siblings to make an "honest" living and to provide for his family. He would later point out to his public that he had sometimes wished he was a ready writer in prose, but never in verse. He had, he proclaimed, "never rhymed for parlor games or for exercises or from a sense of duty to keep the wolf from the door." Elinor knew he "hated to know he *must* write," and she was prepared to sacrifice to whatever extent proved necessary to shelter him from outside pressures and to vindicate her belief in him as a genuine poet. In July 1913, with the appearance in London of *A Boy's Will,* she wrote home: "How can they help seeing how exquisitely beautiful some of the poems are, and what original music there is in most of them?"[8] And she shared her husband's disappointment in W. B. Yeats's failure to put in writing his initial praise of the poet's first volume of verse.

Unlike Elinor, Robert saw no contradiction in the urge to go to market with his poems. He wrote his friend Louis Untermeyer that his wife "seems to have the same weakness I have for a life that goes rather poetically; only I should say she is worse than I. . . . She always knew I was a good poet, but that was between her and me, and there I think she would have liked it if it had remained at least until we were dead. . . . She's especially wary of honors that derogate from the poetic life she fancies us living."[9]

The rich yet faded tapestry that emerged from the record of the early years helped me to better understand my mother's apparent anxiety on this subject. She loved both her parents—in differing ways, of course—but Thompson and others were placing the blame on her father for the seeming deprivation experienced by the Frost family until well after their return from England in 1915. Rather than confront head-on the unrelieved attack on Frost the man, my mother chose to provide greater balance in the overall assessment by publishing her childhood journals (as *New Hampshire's Child*) and by lecturing and writing about the care-free and loving days on the Derry farm, a place *her* mother had cherished, and about the children's "education by poetry" there. She had planned, prior to her final illness and death (in 1983), to write more about the time in England. Her Derry journals, however, are very revealing as a contemporaneous account of everyday life on the farm and, more important, in providing insight into the relations between family members during the critical period of her father's search for recognition.

Thompson was, to a degree, correct in his observation of the many moods and nonconformist attitudes that seemed to prompt a certain defensiveness and self-protectiveness in the poet. RF's jealousy of other poets, his occasional flare-ups of temper, and his general disorganization whether functioning as farmer, teacher, or something else are, I believe, legendary. But, I had to ask myself, how could Thompson succeed in his use of a single theory of neurosis and neurotic behavior to explain this remarkable life, and the poems that had reached "all sorts and kinds"? Would the record support his thesis that RF systematically and ruthlessly disregarded his family in a selfish and self-centered drive to achieve his own ends? There can be little doubt that genius and psychosis have common identifying features, and the line drawn between them is often blurred; the artistic temperament all too often lives on the perilous edge. There were, after all, already signs of mental instability in the Frost's family history. It is also true that to embark on a life as a poet, the artist and members of his family will be expected, especially where there is no financial security, to sacrifice collectively to reach the goal of public recognition.

But the issue of motive is a tricky one. I had come by now to realize how risky it is to seek definitive psychological explanations for events or for the dynamics of personality, a weakness, I believe, in many current biographies of public figures. The complexities and intangibles are themselves the warp and woof of the subject's life, as of his art.

We know (from his notes) that Thompson relied heavily on Karen Horney's *Neurosis and Human Growth: The Struggle Toward Self-Realization* to explain RF's artistic and moral temperament as it evolved over a long lifetime.[10] The problem with such an after-the-fact selective approach is its almost immediate and inevitable breakdown when applied to a real subject. Those of us who knew the poet were asking ourselves in dismay: Where has all the humor gone, the irony, the wordplay, the double entendres? Where, also, the rough and tumble, the chance everyday encounters and decisions, the need to act on limited knowledge? And where the acknowledgment of the artistic heroism of the nonconformist, with its inevitable bouts with despair and feelings of guilt?

Thompson himself recognized the problem of this approach and admitted its dangers: "The ultimate problem of a Frost biographer is to see if the biographer can be enough of a psychologist to get far enough back into the formative years of RF to try to understand and explain what forces were operative, back there, to create the curious forms of neurosis which RF had to struggle with throughout most of his life. Of course such an approach, on the part of the biographer, is dangerous—very dangerous."[11]

Because few if any of us are free from one form of neurosis or another, Thompson's analysis cannot be discounted altogether. But when events are being observed through the haze of time, as in this case, compassion is an essential biographical tool. More so, I would argue, in light of scientific advances in pinpointing genetic predilections, making assessment of motive or responsibility for personality traits more difficult. Where biographers have relentlessly pursued a particular angle, to the exclusion of others and with no apparent sympathy or affection for their subject, the experiment inevitably falls of its own weight.

It became apparent that the official biographer's crudely psychoanalytical interpretation had silenced the brilliant and humorous voice of the living poet and seriously misrepresented his relations with family and friends. Thompson's obsessive treatment of RF's personality reduced to an absurdity the wonderfully complex and sensitive nature of a man who made friends easily and whose generous devotion to family was exemplary among the struggling artists of his day.

In applying the psychoanalytical overlay to his subject, Thompson seldom includes the uninterrupted voices of the participants in the great adventure that, if included, would assuredly reveal the lighthearted play and inherent self-contradictions and ambiguities their immediacy and contemporaneousness would have ensured. Reginald Cook's book, *Robert Frost: A Living Voice,* gives us the poet's unadorned script, but without biographical context; Thompson, on the other hand, while he gives us context, unabashedly adds his own deadening analysis and destructive selectivity. Earlier, Elizabeth Shepley Sergeant had captured the poet's spirit (in a flawed biography), and more recently others—Cook, Poirier, Pritchard, Burnshaw, and Walsh, to name a few—have provided important reassessments.

Instead of characterizing—as I believe Thompson did—my grandfather's unwavering (but doubt-ridden) ambition for poetry as a dark regression in the service of the ego, in a selfish act of self-indulgence, I came to look upon RF's quest for recognition as a positive force inseparable from his and Elinor's efforts to awaken the world of the imagination in their children (and grandchildren). Despite the Frosts' isolation from the cultural mainstream in America prior to 1915 and their straitened circumstances, there is an Alice-in-Wonderland feeling to the family's passionate encounter of the spirit in an extraordinary feat of prowess and courage.

In studying the available bibliography, including the wealth of unpublished and as yet unexamined sources in my possession, the English years assumed for me a decided shape and texture. The years that preceded my grandfather's departure for England from Plymouth in 1912—years that included his completion of high school in Lawrence, Massachusetts, his two forays into a college education, and the critical years with his family at Derry—formed part of the whole, a solid background from which Robert Frost the poet could take full advantage of literary opportunities and contacts unexpectedly presented to him in England and later upon his return to America. Still suffering from excessive shyness, but increasingly confident as poet and teacher, he surprised even himself as to just how prepared he was for the breaking forth from the professional isolation of the earlier years; his wife and children, while cheering him on, shared his astonishment upon his emergence as a successfully published poet.

Although unaware of it at the time, my personal journey into my grandparents' past (and, indirectly, into my own) may have started when, in December 1953, I received a letter from my grandfather thanking me for a packet of my poems: "Your present," he wrote, "was the best mail I got for Christmas. You'd think I might be weary of poetry and the ambitions of poetry after all I have seen and known of both in the last sixty-five years since eighteen eighty nine when I wrote my very first poem and named it La Noche Triste in the language of your adoption."[12] Or it may have begun when I joined my grandfather in London in June 1957, from Madrid, where I was employed in the American Embassy. I was privileged on this occasion to accompany RF when he received his honorary degrees from Oxford and Cambridge universities, the first American since Henry Wadsworth Longfellow in 1868 and James Russell Lowell in 1873 to be so honored.

Or perhaps it began as I learned more about the remarkable friendship between Robert and Edward Thomas (which had extended to members of both families). 1914 was their year. There is general agreement among biographers with regard to the depth of Robert's love for the man about whom he wrote, "The closest I ever came in friendship to anyone in England or anywhere else in the world I think was with Edward Thomas."[13] John Wain and John Lehmann are among those who have written movingly about the significance for modern British poetry of their brief encounter. But for me it had more of an emotional resonance in the Frost family biography:

> . . . the obstacle that checked
> And tripped the body, shot the spirit on
> Further than target ever showed or shone.[14]

Edward Thomas would enlist in the Artists' Rifles in 1915; after being commissioned a Second Lieutenant and volunteering for service overseas, he would be killed at Arras on Easter Monday 1917, foiling plans to bring the families together on one side of the Atlantic or the other when the European conflict was decided; but the friendship survived in the hearts of the living and on the written page.

I also became increasingly aware, in my research, of the role of women, in general—and family members, in particular—in the shaping of the poet's life and work. Susan Hayes Ward accepted "My Butterfly: An Elegy" from the unknown teenager for publication in *The* (New York) *Independent* in 1894; she went on to become no less a source of moral support and affection for the whole Frost family. Following her retirement to Berwick, Maine, she suggested the story (from her own childhood) for "Wild Grapes" as a parallel to "Birches" but for girls, a contribution RF gratefully acknowledged. Harriet Monroe, at Pound's urging, came openly to admire Robert's poems, which she would publish in *Poetry* over the years; although never close to the Frosts, she, too, reached out to family members. While the Frosts were still in England, Amy Lowell had been the target of much controversy and ribald comment by the poets and their critics who frequented the London cafés. But upon landing back in New York, the Frosts were pleased to discover on the newsstands the extraordinary tribute from Amy in the *New Republic* (February 20, 1915). Despite Amy's at times overbearing manner, relations between her and RF remained friendly in the name of poetry and of the dramatic voice they both enjoyed. While at Wellesley, my mother was invited to Amy's home in Brookline, and Amy (together with her constant companion, Ada Russell, and an entourage of servants) spent several days in the Frosts' home at Amherst. Mrs. M. L. Nutt, the widow of David Nutt's son, was a neurotic and suspicious Frenchwoman who jealously guarded the rights to Robert's published and yet-to-be-published work, yet it was she who accepted the manuscript for *A Boy's Will* and *North of Boston* from the little-known poet. In America, it would be Florence, the wife of Henry Holt, who, like Amy in London, read a copy of *North of Boston* and sang its praises; with her encouragement, Alfred Harcourt invited Robert to join her husband's publishing firm, with which he remained throughout his lifetime.

The Frost family, close-knit and at times isolated, would survive the insecurity and financial distress of those early years, caught up as they were in "a life that goes rather poetically." Family members who scattered following their return to America from England in 1915 would maintain a degree of identity through the strong parental involvement that lasted at least until the death of Elinor in 1938.

Upon the death of *my* mother, Lesley, in 1983, I found among her things a small canvas suitcase containing a number of notebooks prepared by the Frost children for their parents: "Many Storys" ("by Irma Frost to mama and papa, Christmas 1912"); "An Important Year" ("by Four Children, Dedicated to Papa & Mamma, 1913"); "On the Road to Fleuraclea" ("by Lesley Frost, Dedicated to Papa on Christmas morning, December 25, 1913"); and Lesley's 1912–1913 and 1914 untitled composition notebooks. With the children's notebooks, I found six of some twelve or fourteen issues of a little "magazine" she and the other children had "published" as *The Bouquet,* at The Bungalow and Little Iddens in England and, for a brief period, upon their return, in Franconia, New Hampshire. "*The Bouquet* represents the closing chapter of our combined authorship," Lesley remembers. "It had all begun on a small (30-acre) farm in Derry, New Hampshire, *just* north of Boston. It was there that the several loves—of nature, of poetry, of God, of each other—had been nurtured."[15] Only recently, I discovered four composition notebooks from this period belonging to Carol Frost (and preserved by his widow, Lillian LaBatt Frost); one of them, written in Beaconsfield, is "dedicated to mama and papa, Christmas 1913," and is all about "our old farm" at Derry, New Hampshire.

What struck me was how the accomplishments of the Frost children in England were a natural sequel to the journals Lesley kept on the Derry farm from the age of five. The trusting, childlike view of life and freshness of response, the inebriation and "imagination thing" that reduces the distance between reader and writer and the real world in the journals are carried on in the writing of the Frost children in England and are evidenced in the work of their father. The romance and the reality mixed in a heady brew in those halcyon days, and the family's closeness contributed to a sense of "sheer morning gladness at the brim."[16]

1

A Literary Family on the Verge

Derry and Plymouth

Most lives are meant to be lost. At least any that are found have to be lost first.[1]

*I*n revisiting the Derry years (1900–1911), capped by a year in Plymouth, New Hampshire, where Robert Frost taught at the Plymouth Normal School, I was able to identify the root cause of the Frost family's persistent nostalgia and homesickness while in England, as well as the root in experience that informs the poet's verses and distinguishes them from his fellow poets on both sides of the Atlantic. The contemporaneous record from the time in New Hampshire (flowing directly into the record for the English years) demonstrates, beyond any doubt, the inseparable, seamless nature of the Frost family's life in and of poetry until shortly after their return from England in 1915.

Living on the Derry farm in New Hampshire with her parents, my mother (Lesley)—together with her sisters (Irma and Marjorie) and brother (Carol)—received an "education by poetry." "I learned," she wrote in the introduction to the published facsimiles of her Derry journals, "that flower and star, bird and fruit and running water, tree and doe and sunset, are wonderful facts of life. The farm was enough of a world for learning." She learned that the natural thing is always the adequate symbol, that the reality around her and the "imagination thing" are inseparable. Here is how she described the microcosm of the Frost children's world in 1908, at the age of eight:

journeys On The Farm

Our farm has interesting places to travel to, just like the world, though you do not have to journy so far as in the world. We go to some place almost every day that it is good enough to go and that is only when it is nice, but when it snows we sometimes dress up and go tramping out to the gate. When it shines we go every where on our farm though we have been there a hundred times.

The alders is one of my favorit places to go, because it reminds me of the brook that said "I sparkle out among the fern to bicker down the vally," and the brook out there is just like it, though there isn't any fern, but it sparkles out among the woods to bicker down the vally. The next best journy I like is going over in the grove. That doesn't remind me of anything, but it is best to play in. You can make little houses and everything with the sticks and pineneedles that are over there and we go there very often, but we only go out in the alders once in three or four days.

The big pasture is my next favorite place because there is a little round grove out there of about six trees and they all touch together at the top and make a lovely shade to sit under as soon as it is warm enough and it is very comefortable. After the big pasture the field over across the road is next best. That is noted for it's checker*berrys*. We go there almost every day to get checkerberrys or checkerberry *leaves* whatever we find there both just as good to us. All these places that I am speaking of we travel to about every day and play in each one half an hour and play that half an hour is half a year at some far off place in the world. April 9, 1908.[2]

We know that *all* the Frost children "played school" and kept composition notebooks as part of their at-home education while living on the Derry farm, but that, from this period before the Frost family left for England in 1912, only Lesley's journals (published as *New Hampshire's Child*) have survived. It should be remembered, however, that the children's writings in England, mentioned earlier (Irma's "Many Storys," Carol's "Our Old Farm," Lesley's two untitled composition notebooks and "On the Road to Fleuraclea," "An Important Year" by the four children, and, above all, the little magazine *The Bouquet*) nostalgically recall important aspects of life in Derry and Plymouth and contribute to our understanding of the family dynamics.

The children's notebooks and journals, and RF's own stories written for his children, show strong and pervasive parallels. RF's verses are analogous both in terms of their subject matter and stylistic development: daily life is mixed with elements of fantasy, the close and affectionate observation of nature, and an awareness of the precarious human condition and moral imperatives. Family values, in this context, are fostered in unorthodox ways, through a loose educational philosophy suggestive of Thoreau, Rousseau, or Montessori, with whose experimental approaches my grandparents were familiar. We will see, as well, the close parallels (and significant differences) with other literary families from this and earlier periods, with whom the Frosts also enjoyed at least a passing familiarity.

Two important areas in the poet's life are reflected in both the children's notebooks and in his own poetry from the Derry years: his teaching experience at Pinkerton Academy in Derry Village and at the Plymouth Normal School, on the one hand, and, on the other, his experience working the Derry farm and interacting with his family, now grown to six (Robert, Elinor, Lesley, Irma, Carol, and

Marjorie). It would be his young audience, at school and at home, that helped shape RF's early verse, as becomes especially clear through a careful reading of the journals.

RF would have, in fact, a considerable body of verse (and some important pieces of prose) in the marketplace before the Frost family left for England. His poetic idiom had matured (as was evident already before leaving Harvard College in 1899 in his second year there), and he would carry with him most of the poems that were to appear in his first two volumes, *A Boy's Will* and *North of Boston*, published in London to favorable reviews and the beginning of public recognition both there and in America. He understood the strain between rhythm and meter and the importance of intonation, of mood and moment in creativity, of technical mastery. He understood the psychology of sound, and the images of sound conjured up through the imagination, as well as the sophistication and amplification of the proverbial turns of speech that already distinguished some verses in his first published poem, "My Butterfly: An Elegy," which appeared on the front page of *The Independent* on November 8, 1894, a hundred years ago.

Too little attention has been given in the biography, I believe, to RF's growing confidence as a teacher and colleague prior to the family's departure for England, a downplaying explained, in part, by the absence of almost any reference to these experiences in letters or journals from this period. We know, however, that besides helping his mother in the classroom in Salem up to the time of her death in 1900, and employment as principal of the Shepard Evening School while at Harvard, he would come to devote more and more time to teaching and related activities than to "farming" as the Derry years progressed. Furthermore, while at the Pinkerton Academy in Derry Village, he was developing both a keen ear for dramatic speech and stage production and a greater ease in relating to his peers. We will see how the interest in dramatic dialogue is given full expression while in England.

Former students at the Pinkerton Academy and the Plymouth Normal School in New Hampshire provide a retrospective look at the poet and his family, reminding us of the maturity already achieved by 1911–1912. The author Meredith Reed remembers "a youngish-looking man with ruffled hair, deep-set blue eyes, and lips that looked as though they might be going to break into a smile—yet might not." His eyes, which seemed to be looking straight at her, were "curiously amused and even more blue than I had thought." She said she had never heard a voice like his, as when he read Shelley's "Ode to the West Wind": "There was a sort of music to it, only music wasn't the word. It was light, like an open field; it was dark like mountain woods; sometimes it would break up into a lot of colors like glass hit by the sun; and sometimes it made you think of a violin when the strings were stretched too tight and tones jumped out from under the bow all rough and quivery-like."[3] Margaret Abbott, who met her husband, John Bartlett, while they both were students at Pinkerton Academy, wrote that she was "carried aloft" by Robert's readings from Palgrave's *Golden Treasury* and other literature. Students considered him chummier with them than with the faculty: he skipped chapel, and he was interested in all sports and liked to hunt in the woods and fish in Beaver Lake. While still at Derry, he would invite the "boys down at his house for talks and games on Saturday mornings and it was always deemed a great pleasure to be invited." He mingled with the students, playing football and "Ten Step."[4]

At the Plymouth Normal School, where Robert taught psychology and child growth and development, he was regarded as dreamy and soft-spoken, "wont to gaze into space and discourse more to himself than to the class." His students found him exceptionally kind and gentle, someone who "always seemed to be [so] much interested in *each* of us as an *individual* that we soon felt . . . he was a real friend." They were never bored in his classes because he always had ideas to present and was not confined to a text. When the Titanic sank (April 14–15, 1912), for example, the whole class was given over to discussing the newspaper accounts of the tragedy. He was easily distracted by stories about nature's creatures, and he would ask endless questions. He was enchanted when one of his students took him to see two bunnies hidden in the upper branches of a small hemlock, where she had fed them carrots and bits of apples. He was shy, the student observed, and she "could understand why his wife looked so adoringly at him and worked so hard for him."[5]

Elinor was well liked, too. At Derry, the other grangers helped her in many ways to prepare a small garden. "She did what little out-door work was done but she was unequal to it at that time having small children to care for." The students enjoyed talking to her, and they admired her quiet concern for and devotion to her husband. At Plymouth, a student remembers spending "one of the pleasantest evenings" in the Frosts' living room with a group of girls from the school. "I think it must have been before Christmas for the room was bright with decorations. A big fire in the fireplace, someone popping corn. Mrs. Frost, saying little, but making everyone comfortable and homey, and looking like a lovely madonna. The children were all there, quite young then and Mr. Frost entertained us with his stories and poems and just being himself." Students got to know the Frost family well, it seems. On Mondays, the days the students were free instead of Saturdays, they would go together on "an all day's hike to Mt. Prospect with [their] lunches provided by the School. These were very pleasant times."

Nine-year-old Irma Frost would recall in her "Many Storys" (Christmas 1912) climbing a mountain in Plymouth she couldn't remember the name of "with some of the nomole school grils." They made their way to a spring for their picnic, and then went on up the mountain with the girls, while "Marjorie and mama did not go to the top." One girl put a feather from her hat in "papa pocket when he didn't no it." Elinor and her daughters got a ride home "in the otermobl . . . and we had a good supper."

Robert may have been the only teacher at the time with a family, and the Frosts often came to the dining hall for their meals; on these occasions, he was, the students recall, "attentive in his manner toward his family and would listen to the children's prattle, occasionally breaking in with an amusing incident which would make the children giggle." There were neighbors at Derry who thought Robert was a lazy farmer, which he was, and Mr. Silver, with whom the Frosts took lodgings in Plymouth while there on a one-year appointment, commented on the absence of routine in the Frost household. He remembered their late hours and the sight of the children going off to school, grabbing a bite of food left on the table from the previous evening.

Elinor did not talk about the past, and her tendency to silences may have dated from the death of her first son, Elliott, who died on the Derry farm from some type of influenza at the age of four in 1900. Although she and Rob exchanged harsh words at the time, they were never estranged.[6] She soon renounced any belief in a Supreme Being, distancing herself from her mother and oldest sister, Ada, who had become Christian Scientists; they had urged the Frosts not to call the doctor, who, when eventually summoned to the Derry farm, said it was too late to save the child. Elinor's sister Leona and her father, Edwin White, continued to visit the Frosts at the Derry farm, and her father died of a heart attack while at their home in Derry Village in 1909.

RF told family members that he had never written a poem without having Elinor in his thoughts. Every one of them, he said, pertained to her in some way. He also said she had the best ear for sound in poetry of anyone he ever knew: she would tell him when a vowel sound needed to be changed. Her daughter-in-law, Lillian LaBatt Frost, remembers Elinor as a quiet gentlewoman, whose silences disturbed her husband but seemed natural to her. She had a good sense of humor, with a sweet, shy giggle, Lillian recalls. She enjoyed reading and watching and listening to the evening card games, and she liked to play croquet. She made all the children's clothes when they were young, and she never thought of herself if there was RF or her children or grandchildren to think about. A college friend, from her St. Lawrence University days, agrees. She never thrust herself forward, he remembers; she was unassuming and unostentatious: "In other words, she was in no way a mixer. Her real life was an inner one. She was always and everywhere demure, quiet, contemplative, serious and thoughtful."[7]

Part of the reason for this distancing may have been Elinor's fragile health: she tired easily—perhaps because of a heart condition that gradually worsened as a result of childbirth and personal loss, perhaps because of a tendency to melancholia, we simply don't know. She found it difficult to complete household chores, which she detested, and she leaned on her more energetic husband and eldest daughter to pick up the pieces when she became ill. An editor of the family letters adds perceptively to this impression of Elinor and the pale reflection of this intelligent woman's inner life we find in her correspondence: "Elinor Frost—seldom as relaxed or revealing as Robert—is beside and a bit behind her husband in [her] letters, just as she was in life. No liberationist, however, should be too quick to misunderstand. She was no less opinionated than her husband, and their views frequently collided. Hers was an enormous influence—both in family matters and in the shaping of Frost's poetry."[8] A growing sense of fatigue and sadness, as family tragedies mounted, would overshadow Elinor's final years, but that was a future no one in the Frost family could foresee in 1912.

Life and poetry were so intimately related at home, in fact, that only Elinor was fully cognizant of her husband's personal ambition. In her Derry journals, Lesley recalls that her father, "after exposing me to a variety of narrative and lyric poems (some of which I quickly learned by heart) and after getting me to write brief critical essays [in her journals by the age of seven] never so much as hinted that he was frequently writing poems of his own, at the table in the kitchen of our farmhouse, long after we children had gone to bed."[9] Lesley summarized these roles in her introduction to the published journals:

> It was to Mama we returned with full accounts of our adventures, adventures encountered on our own or out walking with Papa. The house was her castle, her province, and she *was* home. Going home from anywhere, at any time of day or night, meant returning to her. . . . By the time we had divided up the time of day, even the time of year, there was very little time left over to worry about. . . . Reading (by the age of four) and being read aloud to (until the age of fifteen!), I unconsciously heard the warp and woof of literature being woven into an indestructible fabric, its meaning always heightened by the two beloved voices going on and on into the night as a book was passed from hand to hand. We children could linger to listen until we were sleepy, however late.

Elinor Miriam White and Robert Frost had shared valedictorian honors, and Elinor had given an address on "Conversation as a Force in Life" at their graduation from high school. She had contributed to the Lawrence High School *Bulletin* an essay on "A Phase of Novel Writing," and there is strong evidence that at least two of her poems also appeared in the *Bulletin*. As a child, in 1888, she had been mentioned as a "good drawer" in a newspaper report of a school exhibition, and at least one of her paintings hung in the Frost family home in later years. Elinor Frost's sister, Leona White Harvey, was a skilled painter in water-colors and oils, and she made a living as a portrait artist after leaving her husband in 1915. Elinor only reluctantly admitted having written poems for a brief period in high school and being fond of painting as a girl.

Whether because of the burdens of raising a family and teaching the children at home, or because Robert conveyed, through displays of jealousy or more subtle means (as has been suggested by his biographer), the sense that "one artist in the family is enough," Elinor appears to have given up any serious pursuit of artistic self-expression even before she agreed to marry Robert. There is no evidence to suggest she consciously chose to dedicate herself exclusively to her family to avoid competing with her husband: they both viewed Robert's poetry writing as a collaborative effort, and they both were passionately committed to nurturing the world of the imagination in their children. During the years in Derry and England, at least, the collective impression of creative energy and the resourceful life of the imagination emanating from the Frosts as a family is generously documented.

Except in preparation for this book, it had not occurred to me to sit down and read straight through my mother's Derry journals, although I had heard my mother read from the notebooks at the dedication of the Robert Frost Farm as a New Hampshire State Historic Site in 1977 while standing on its piazza surrounded by friends, including the state's governor. Today I am convinced that anyone wanting to understand RF as poet and craftsman, or simply what made him tick as a human being, should include a close reading of *New Hampshire's Child*.

Lesley's journals are an indispensable source for our understanding of what motivated the struggling poet at the moment of the big forward movement and push toward success in England. On almost every page, my mother's notebooks reveal how RF the poet benefited from the routine activities that allowed her father to ruminate on and to mull over the constant flow of impressions; to respond in subtle and thoughtful ways to the natural phenomena, whether out botanizing, caring for the farm animals, or mundanely enriching his literary yearnings through close interaction with family members; and to apply in a nonacademic setting, with all kinds and types of talking companions, his by now carefully thought out philosophical and psychological orientations.

Life on the Derry farm was relaxed and varied. While there was little money for the extras we take for granted today, by contemporary standards the Frosts enjoyed a happy and healthy existence, one they certainly looked back on with nostalgia. Activities divided up the day: tending to the farm animals (chickens, a cow, and a horse), writing and "playing school," chasing the cow or a stray bull (or even a stray hunter), going into town to shop (and, on one occasion, to church) with mama or papa, or, in the evenings, playing games (dominoes, a civil war game with dice, "puss-in-the-corner," bobbing for apples) and reading aloud. In one family scene, mama is raking up the yard, papa is cutting with the scythe, and Carol and Irma are sitting on the hay cart, while grandpa (Elinor's father) is preparing a bonfire. Irregular hours, exacerbated by RF's and Elinor's differing biological clocks—RF was a late riser, Elinor a morning person—and the at-home school arrangements permitted a great deal of flexibility in the daily activities.

The Frosts did not go hungry. We know, from the journals, that meals, prepared by one parent or the other, were haphazard, and not surprisingly were high in dairy products and poultry produced on the farm. They were supplemented by the abundance of nuts, berries, and fruits gathered by family members throughout the year. Lesley and Carol, we learn, grew green beans, but vegetables are seldom mentioned in the journals. Descriptions of a breakfast that included eggs and toast or toast and cream, followed by bunches of grapes or a peach, or of the first turkey for a Thanksgiving dinner that included mince and squash pie, cran-berries, and other delicacies, convince the reader that the Frosts did not feel deprived. Although there was a great deal of moving of household furniture and sprucing-up projects, neither parent liked to cook, and there seems to have been at best a minimal understanding of nutrition. Candy of all kinds were consumed by the children, sometimes without their parent's knowledge, but often as a reward.

The Frosts also enjoyed a life beyond the family configuration. They made friends at Pinkerton Academy and in Derry Village; there were frequent visitors to the farm (neighbors, relatives, and academy students), and we know that the family attended an occasional concert or theatre production, and on one occasion took a boat to New York City, where my mother accompanied her father to the zoo and the theatre.

The family walks (usually on Sunday or after picnics, often just on the paths near home) included Elinor, whose protective, more gentle voice is heard through-out the journal pages as the person to whom the children and Papa told of their adventures at the end of day. Elinor's favorite spot, the alders on the "corduroy path" beside the bridge at Hyla Brook, is an emotional centerpiece, and the place where one day Elinor would ask that her ashes be scattered. Both Lesley and Carol describe the family's picnic area as "our park," a place where Papa would transplant the rose pogonias and hobblebush, and that featured the many paths to and from the smaller circumference of their mother's ventures outdoors when the children were too small to walk far. Elinor was gentler in her ways than her husband, rarely disciplining the children with conviction, preferring to pass the hours reading to or with them, making and mending their clothes, or, in warm weather, sitting on her special "seat" nailed between two pines at the alders.

As early as 1905, Lesley wrote about how "papa and i took a long wake [long walk]," and her father memorialized the importance of their late evening walks in his poem "The Fear": "Every child should have the memory / of at least one long-after-bedtime walk." As we can surmise from such poems as "A Time to Talk," there was a close association between their walks and talks, and the poetry these activities inspired.

The wildness and excitement my mother sensed in her father (his genius, she and I would surmise) came out in these long walks, sometimes with all the children, to gather checkerberries or play house or store in the grove, but more often with Lesley alone. Although Irma sometimes went along, Marjorie was still too small: "Generally we go in and play school and then we take a walk," Lesley wrote. Walks with "the children" were more carefree; with Papa, the talk was more focused, about what is "generally" true, dreams, make believe, fairies and goblins, inventing word games, or more serious botanizing in the cranberry bog or orchard. They loved to hunt for orchids from the bog to bring to Mama. The number of birds, flowers, and animals identified in these journals is astounding, and Lesley boasted of knowing "most of the birds songs." In almost every journal entry, my mother is not only learning from her natural surroundings but, equally important, absorbing her father's peculiar receptiveness to those surroundings: considering a pasture with groves of pine, maple, or chestnut trees; swinging birches; sitting on stone walls; chatting for hours with friends in town; imagining the neighbor's woods with goblins and fairies; or following Papa's lead in dealing with her fears—of the cold nights, the dark cellar, sudden movements of animals in the woods, the sound of gunfire, or too much snow, too fast, from a snowstorm coming on.

The bonding that occurred in these walks, at the deepest level, would be responsible, I believe, for a great deal of the tension between RF and his eldest daughter in later years. My mother had had the seemingly undivided attention of an admiring father, as manifest in her journals, from the time she took her first steps until she left the home environment upon the family's return from England in 1915–1916. She had already become, unconsciously and in indelible ways, her father's alter ego, revealed later by her public pronouncements as writer and lecturer. In between, she fought to resist his well meaning but often meddlesome influence in her daily life, with only mixed results. With children of her own to support, she had come to champion the importance of family ties in unselfish and constructive ways.

Though the Frost children "played school" with their mother up until the time of their move to Derry Village in 1909, the journals give no suggestion that Elinor minded the burden she had assumed in teaching the children at this early stage in their lives. In fact, she would resist the move into town, where the children could be placed in public school, as her husband urged. In Plymouth, Beaconsfield, and in Franconia (in other words, after 1911), the nature of the argument over the children's upbringing would alter significantly. The children were older, in need of playmates and a more structured classroom, and, just as important, Elinor was having increasing medical problems that overwhelmed her at the same time that RF was being drawn out of the home into the beginnings of his public career as teacher and poet.

In my mother's notebooks, we can trace her father's hand in developing the skills of his children as writers. We know that Lesley had begun writing, as part of her at-home education, in 1905, before the age of six. She told me that her journals were the result of her father's way of teaching writing—by *writing*—and that learning to write, from his viewpoint, was learning to have ideas. He taught the writing, she said, and her mother the reading. The reading was prehistoric in the sense that she felt as if she were "born reading." The writing came a little later. She understood that every notebook entry should have a date, a title, even a sort of plot, or at least a shape. Indeed, they were *called* stories ("The hunting story," "The cow story," or "Meeting a Fairy — A Story," for example). In her journals, Lesley occasionally refers to the process itself: "i do not like to rit a story when I go out doors because I want to pant [paint] and I sho mama and papa them after I pant them"; "but just then papa called me to rite my story." As Lesley explains, she would go upstairs for quiet, then her father would carefully scrutinize everything she wrote, as soon as she wrote it; she would play until it was "time to right my story and then when i have ritten my story papa and i talk a frew minints and then I go down stairs and go out doors again."

Through their journal entries, RF expected the children to convey the excitement of discovery on the farm: the fun and laughter, the startling and sometimes scary events, and the overcoming of fear. Both Lesley and Carol describe one such challenge, when Papa placed four ten-cent pieces on a box down the road near a pine tree and each child, alone and in the dark, had to go down and bring back the coin.

While the scary moments stuck in the children's minds, as they do for most children, and were ready subjects for their journals, other emotions, of joy and wonder, anger and love, strike an equally genuine note. The natural speech of children at play gives the little stories an immediacy and charm: the children "spanking" the cow that escaped or chasing a bull or one of the horses (of the three they would have at Derry: Billy, Eunice, and Billy II); "playing school" with mama in the front room on the sofa, then marching out into the kitchen to show papa what they had learned; watching deer or a crow at the window; a row between the children; Papa's April fool's joke; collecting nuts or quartz stones.

Lesley's compositions reach further into the world beyond the farm: she imagines life on Mars ("O what are those things") and she looks for sunspots with a piece of glass painted black. Called out of bed by Papa to see the northern lights, she "wondered and wondered" what caused the "queer" happening. Exciting too are other natural phenomena: changes in the seasons or a thunderstorm coming on.

Telling psychological details include those that provide insight into Papa's temperament, an analysis he apparently encouraged. But even when we see him getting angry at the hunters shooting in the pasture, or spending hours looking for a lost cap (until it is too late to go after the cow), his impatience is a telling part of a story plot and is conveyed to the reader with affection. The children's own foibles are no less the source of teasing and good humor.

Under their father's tutelage, the children learned to change the narrator, to develop plot and dialogue; they could soon distinguish between prose and verse. In the later entries, Lesley and Carol include tentative attempts at dramatic dialogue, reflecting, it seems, their father's emerging interest in the theatre. For the children, the love of drawing and painting competes with writing (as will be especially evident in *The Bouquet,* the little magazine they "produced" while in England 1912–1915), and the farm comes alive in color: the color of the leaves (on the oaks, walnuts, chestnuts, birches, pine, and quince), the horses, the birds, and the many species of flora that were gathered into bouquets to take to mama— even the colors of the home decoration.

As the eldest, Lesley's writing surpasses that of her sisters and brother in stylistic awareness. She notes when a thought "strikes" her. The dreams at night are terrible, she says, but in the daytime she takes "a walk in the fields thinking of birds and flowers" and enjoys "lovely half fairyland dreams." Sometimes her thoughts are interrupted or she is distracted. She is always looking for what is pretty or lovely: the "pretty sky" or "the two loveliest autumn nights." Sprinkled here and there are the natural expressions of disbelief and wonder: "and it is fun getting them dont you think so yes"; "and I bet he will be sorry dont you"; "we got so excited"; "but what do you suppose it did"; "was too surprised to laugh"; "we all shouted and had a good time." Throughout the text, one senses how much of every waking day, even doing the farm chores, is spent in activities "just for the fun of it."

Even the literary allusions and attempts at dramatic dialogue and verse are woven in as part and parcel of the constant bustle of activity. Undoubtedly influenced by their parents' taste in literature, the children would choose from among the 125 or so volumes in the front room bookcase, a small but highly selective library (which remained with the Frosts wherever they moved—from Derry to Plymouth to England). The favorites were read aloud evenings even after the family had settled in Franconia upon their return from England in 1915.

A perusal of Lesley's journals gives us a fair idea of her literary preferences. Besides her struggles with Cicero's *Orations* and Caesar's *Commentaries,* and the family readings from Palgrave's *Golden Treasury,* Lesley was familiar with other family favorites: Homer, Shakespeare, Wordsworth, Longfellow, Emerson, Shelley, Arnold, Scott, Burns, Tennyson, Synge, and Yeats. She tended to focus on individual poems rather than the poets. She found Wordsworth's "Lucy Gray or Solitude" too sad when sweet Lucy is lost in a snowstorm in the lonesome wild. She understood the image that flashes "upon the inward eye" in "I Wandered Lonely as a Cloud," and the voice of the solitary Highland Lass whose strains "were tenderly melancholy, and felt delicious long after they were heard no more," in "The Solitary Reaper." She was more excited by the story poems, such as Tennyson's "The Lotos-Eaters" or "The Morte d'Arthur," but especially by the warlike sound in "The Revenge," named for an English ship that sank five Spanish vessels in a fifteen-hour battle near the Azores in 1591. She mentioned the mortal combat between father and son in Arnold's "Sohrab and Rustum," and she thrilled at the exploits of Wallace and Bruce or Sir Patrick Spens in the early verse romances and ballads that were collected by Scott. She shared with her grandmother, Belle Moodie, a love of Jean Ingelow (a love not shared by her father), who, like Belle, wrote fairy tales, and such sad poems as "The High Tide on the Coast of Lincolnshire (1571)."

Lesley was blessed with a robust constitution and remarkable energy. Despite an often hectic pace, and the many obstacles thrown in her path as a single mother working and raising two children (of whom I was the youngest), she would continue to write and to publish up to the time of her death in 1983. Her father and others in England openly praised Lesley's early reading in Virgil and Caesar, as well as her many compositions. In 1929, she edited an anthology of poems entitled *Come Christmas,* which she dedicated to my sister, Elinor, on her first birthday. A novel, *Murder at Large,* followed in 1932. Two volumes of imaginative and rollicking children's stories, *Really Not Really* and *Digging Down to China,* in which my sister and I are featured, were published in 1962 and 1968, respectively. A book of humorous poems, *Going on Two,* dedicated to a grandson, appeared in 1973. She even ghostwrote a biography of the Brontë sisters.

Irma would try her hand at sculpture (while raising two sons), and Carol would dream of becoming a published poet (while working a farm with his wife and son

in South Shaftsbury, Vermont), before sister and brother succumbed to the rav-
ages of mental illness. Marjorie, plagued by poor health and nervous fatigue, died
in childbirth, leaving behind some finely crafted poems that her parents had
printed privately with the title *Franconia* (1936). Only recently, "Spring," one of
Marjorie Frost Fraser's poems from this collection, was anthologized (in a book
entitled *Imaginary Gardens*) beneath a reproduction of Andrew Wyeth's *Christina's World.*[10]

Late in life my mother confessed that she felt haunted as a child by a sense of
kinship with the Brontës, inspired, no doubt, by her prolific reading and study
from an early age. Living in similar isolation, but with more precarious finances
and a much smaller library, the Frost children, especially Lesley, became aware
of the parallels with the five Brontë sisters and their brother, from among whom
Charlotte, Emily, and Ann emerged in their tragically short lives as the creators
of surprisingly intense and mature novels. The story of the Brontë sisters and
brother, as told by their biographers, emphasizes the "habit of writing" by all
family members: the fact that two of the daughters became renowned as authors
after their mother succumbed to an early death does not detract from the influence of the surviving parent, Patrick Brontë, on his children's literary production:

> However insignificant, pedestrian or trivial the critics may find Patrick's books,
> they have an undeniable importance in the story of the Brontë family's literary
> development. Even their mother had made at least one attempt at literary composi-
> tion and a respect for literature and an understanding of the discipline of writing
> permeated the whole of their lives. Whatever their intrinsic worth, Patrick's books
> were available to his children: they saw them in his study and in shops; they would
> read them and handle them; but above all, the fact that the books *existed* and that it
> was *their* Papa's name on the title page was to engage their imagination. At a
> remarkably early age, the Brontë children set out to "print" their own books, albeit
> as miniatures and copies of Papa's. As Charlotte tells us, the idea of being authors
> was as natural to them as walking and one they never forsook.[11]

The Brontë children indulged in an almost spontaneous scribbling of prose and
verse, which derived from the games they played and led to the production of an
astonishing library of small handmade books. Under strong Romantic influences,
of Scott and Byron, domestic reality and the world of make-believe were closely
interwoven, but the games of authorship were less an escape into fantasy to avoid
loneliness or sadness than an expression of naturalness, joy, and excitement.
Thrown back—as were the Frost children—on their own resources, receiving
scant formal education, in close companionship at home, encouraged and abetted
by their father, the Brontë children achieved discipline of invention and composition, capturing style and atmosphere. Unlike Robert, Patrick became increasingly

cheerless, espousing harsh evangelical doctrines and suffering from increased morbidity upon the death of his wife. Kept at home while the other children tramped to the wool mills, Charlotte, displaying extraordinary proficiency and maturity for a girl of thirteen, spins the words in the sunny air of the moor, "delighting in the sheer joy of invention":

> We have a web in childhood
> A web of sunny air;
> We dug a spring in infancy
> Of water pure and fair;
>
> We sowed in youth a mustard seed
> We cut an almond rod;
> We are now grown up to riper age—
> Are they withered in the sod?[12]

Her brother Branwell had, by the age of 12, branched out into journalism, imitating the *Blackwood Magazine* in his creation of the *Great Glasstown Confederation,* a series of journals, chronicles, and literature of the African kingdoms of his imagination. Like the Frosts, the Brontë children savored all kinds of writing, devouring newspapers, magazines, annuals, children's books and their father's library as source materials for their own creations. They enjoyed the pleasures of parody and the use of nonsense words and advertisements for verisimilitude in their children's magazines—just having fun in writing. And, like the Frosts, they added the dimension of drawing and painting to illustrate their work.[13]

Correlations with the lives of other artistic families, while not necessarily the ones that came to Lesley's mind, are obvious: the Lowells, the Alcotts, the Adamses, and the Stephenses are examples.

The parallel with the Alcott family is striking on several counts. We know that the four Alcott sisters, encouraged by their parents—friends and neighbors, in Concord, Massachusetts, of Emerson and Thoreau—wrote journals and produced plays as part of their childhood education. Louisa's sister May became a portrait artist, working in charcoal, ink, and oils; she excelled as a still-life painter and copyist. After moving from Concord to Boston, the four daughters instituted yet another family entertainment, a secret club named the Pickwick Club in honor of their favorite author, Charles Dickens. Louisa described the meeting of this club in her great domestic novel, *Little Women* (1868). The children ascended to the club room where they tied badges round their heads and took their seats with great solemnity: "Meg, as the eldest, was Samuel Pickwick; Jo, being of a literary turn, August Snodgrass; Beth, because she was round and rosy, Tracy Tupman; and Amy, who was always trying to do what she couldn't, was Nathaniel Winkle. Pickwick, the president, read the paper, which was filled with original tales, poetry, local news, funny advertisements, and hints, in which they good-naturedly reminded each other of their faults and short-comings."

We know that, in 1849, when Louisa was seventeen years old, the Alcott children, with Louisa as "publisher," had produced their own family newspaper. Very similar to the Frost children's magazine, *The Bouquet,* but without contributors from outside the family, the Alcott paper, variously titled the "Olive Leaf," the "Pickwick Portfolio," and the "Portfolio," continued until about 1853, featuring romances, autobiographical narratives, and poetry by the Alcott sisters.[14] Another chapter in *Little Women,* "The P.C. and P.O.," contains a revised sampling from the "Olive Leaf," in which stories with a moral—overcoming selfishness, anger, greed, vanity, or the like—reflect Dickens's propensity to create each character as a caricature of some virtue or vice.

The Alcott daughters would read their newspaper out loud or rehearse their plays, while, as in *Little Women,* they would await the return of their mother, the heart of the family. Their father, Amos Bronson Alcott, suffering occasional bouts of alienation from his family, understood the humanizing influence of his children: "their fears, their hopes, their loves, their purposes and wants," their "glad joyousness and their lively sense of beauty and nature."[15]

A recent item in *Diarist's Journal* describes the childhood journals of Louisa May Alcott on display at Orchard House, the family home in Concord. Interestingly, included in the paper is a discussion of Lesley Frost's Derry journals as another example of the use of the genre as an educational tool:

> Like Louisa Alcott's Fruitlands Journals, these give us an idea of what extraordinary fathers felt their children should be taught. It is also of interest because it gives a picture of the five-year-old farm child who was encouraged to give vent to her imagination, encouraged to tell stories, to write her observations of the things she saw on the farm and on country walks, even to describe her dreams. Again, in no sense was this a private document; it was to be shown to, and even in a manner of speaking, to be criticized by the parent.[16]

Keeping apart from society, with parental reinforcement of a philosophy of independence and the development of self-taught skills of observation and expression, may very well have strengthened the genetic endowment of these artistic families.

Well before the Frost family departed Plymouth for England (in late summer 1912), Lesley had assumed the role as mentor to her siblings. Elinor's frequent pregnancies and more fragile condition were offset by her eldest daughter's seemingly endless energy. Lesley was viewed early on in the Frost family as fiercely independent and adventuresome. At the age of nine, in her Derry journals, she writes unconsciously but perceptively about these relationships that would continue into adulthood:

The children's Ideas About The World

The children think it is very curius about all the things in the world that I tell them about, they hardly beleave it and keep saying "how do you know" "how do you know." When I tell them how big the world is Irma always says "O I don't beleave that" and then I tell her to go and ask mama but she says no, because she knows mama will say yes and then she will have to beleave it, but she doesn't want to think it is true so she doesn't ask her. Once after we had taken quite a long ride Carol said "that we had been clear around the world," but I told him "that we hadn't at all" and then he said almost around it and I said "no" and he said "yes". Then I told him that we had only been just a tiny bit of a way compared with the world and to wait till he got older and see if we had gone around the world. I will ask him when he gets my age. June 30 1908

This and other essays in Lesley's journals reflect her reading and study in the fields of elementary astronomy, botany, geography, history, literature, and physics. Proud of her steadily accumulating knowledge, in this passage she gives us a pleasant glimpse of how "the children" (whom she views protectively) challenge her attempts to educate them. Her precocious reading would help her adjust to entering school and beginning her formal education.

The two schools my mother best remembered from her childhood were in Derry Village. The family moved there in 1909 to be closer to Pinkerton Academy, where her father taught and produced his first dramas, *Cathleen ni Hoolihan* and *The Land of Heart's Desire,* which made a deep impression on her. The other was a two-room grade school where she entered sixth grade when she was nine, staying through eighth grade when the family left for Plymouth.

In my mother's wonderful narrative reading for Folkways Records, *Derry Down Derry* (1961), she selects poems by her father from *You Come Too,* a collection for young people, linking each of them to life on the farm: "The Pasture," "The Cow in Apple Time," "The Runaway," "Stopping by Woods on a Snowy Evening," "The Last Word of a Bluebird," "Mowing," "The Tuft of Flowers," "Rose Pogonias," "The Quest of the Purple-Fringed," "After Apple-Picking," "October," "Mending Wall," "Blueberries," "Birches," "Evening in a Sugar Orchard," "Fireflies in the Garden," "Hyla Brook," "Good-By and Keep Cold," "Storm Fear," "The Onset," "Spring Pools," and "A Prayer in Spring," are those she illustrates for the listener with descriptions from her own experience as reflected in her Derry journals, with orchards, pastures, the cranberry bog, berrypicking, farm animals, and flowers, which were their constant delight; the poems reflect, as well, the fears and simple joys, the hard work, and the fleeting seasons, no less conveyed in her journals.

Lesley would recall that magazines for children—in particular *The Youth's Companion* and *St. Nicholas*—were in the house throughout her childhood, "even a pile of old-old ones in the 'attic,'" which was their playroom, over the kitchen in Derry. A family paper, *The Youth's Companion* offered its readers a weekly selection of serialized stories, cowboy and Indian lore, lessons on thrift, love of country, and other virtues, brief items of a topical nature, literary brevities headed "For the Companion," a children's page, and a sizable, if picturesque, advertising linage.[17] A number of Robert's poems appeared in the pages of *The Companion* before the Frosts departed for England, and, in a letter to its editor (written at The Bungalow in Beaconsfield sometime in December 1912) seeking permission to publish "Reluctance," "October," and "Ghost House" in *A Boy's Will,* he described his first volume as "a series of lyrics standing in some such loose relation to each other as a ring of children who have just stopped dancing and let go hands. The psychologist in me asked to call it 'The Record of a Phase of Post-adolescence.'"[18] We can see the influence of William James's *Principles of Psychology,* a text he used at the Plymouth Normal School in 1911.

While life on the Derry farm was relaxed, it was intimately associated with my grandparents' ongoing preoccupation with their children's upbringing. Because their parents were accredited teachers, Lesley and her sisters and brother were excused from the school in Derry Village. Lesley recalls that she was

> taught the alphabet on a typewriter, and by the age of three was writing, phonetically but legibly, on the machine. By five, I was writing longhand, also legibly, though highly misspelled. . . . My mother taught the organized subjects, reading (the phonetic method), writing (then known as penmanship), geography, spelling. My father took on botany and astronomy. They both went over our stories for criticism, though it was my mother who scanned them first for spelling and grammar. . . . Reading was most important.[19]

An entry in Lesley's Derry journals from this period explains how the Frost children were taught:

> playing school
>
> Almost every day about ten o'clock Mama calls us in the front room and we have to sit up on the sofa and tell storys then we have to count 1 2 3 4 5 and then we sing a song and then read and then do a b c d and when any one says a word right he gets the word and then we sing anouther song and then we do our exersizez and then we march around the room once or twis and then march out into the kitchen to show papa how we can do it. oct 4 1906[20]

In his teaching methods—or lack of them—in correspondence with students, and in verse, Robert would express his ideas on education: like Baptiste in "The Ax-Helve," he knew the

> Lines of a good helve
> Were native to the grain before the knife
> Expressed them, and its curves were no false curves
> Put on it from without.

In his pocket notebook jottings from this period, he emphasized the need of "reading for pleasure" in "families where the word improvement is never heard." It is preferable, he notes, "not to have children remember you as having taught them anything in particular. May they remember you as an old friend. That is what it is to have been right with them in their good moments."[21] He understood, and acted upon, his and Elinor's belief that reading and being read to are essential means of education. My mother would recall how her somewhat anxious dwelling upon fairies and goblins, and the use of her little "stories" to overcome real or imagined fears on the farm, was strongly stimulated by her Scotch-Celtic father, who liked to read aloud to the children from books of fairy tales, including Belle Moodie's published story, *The Land of Crystal, or, Christmas Day with the Fairies.*

Bruno Bettelheim, in his perceptive study *The Uses of Enchantment,* cites the need to spin out daydreams, ruminating and fantasizing about the story elements. He develops this theme in telling ways that I believe are applicable to all good children's literature, by providing structure and suggesting images in which both sides of human nature are revealed, not just the sunny side. The tales teach us that, although a struggle against severe difficulties in life is unavoidable and that a moral dilemma exists in which evil is as omnipresent as virtue, one meets unexpected and often unjust hardships, masters all obstacles, and at the end emerges victorious. And, in their original form, these stories reveal important poetic qualities.[22]

In the Frost family, the children in their formative years were exposed through their readings and writings from direct experience to the clarifying concepts of justice, fidelity, love, and courage, not as lessons imposed by their parents, but as discovery, as experience, as an organic part of the adventure of living. A surprising number of Lesley's journal entries from this period are about fairies: "A Big Flock of Little Fairies," "Meeting a Fairy," and "The Fairy and the Squirrel," where the fairies mysteriously leave gold rings and diamonds on the children's table. There is even a transcription of William Allingham's "The Fairies," memorized and recited by the Frost children. In her college treatment of Yeats—

another family favorite—and the Irish poet's almost obsessive preoccupation with fairies, Lesley asks that the writer use realistic, believable details when treating fairies and that there be a consistency of style. We should not be surprised, then, to find included in *A Boy's Will* the poem "Spoils of the Dead," with its strange association of fairies, elves, and death, and where, suggestive of Lesley's story, the fairies "eerily played with the glittering things, / And were not afraid."

As we have seen in the Derry journals, one consequence of this persistent concern for the children's "education by poetry" is that the creative genius of Robert Frost the poet was constantly enriched by his sharing of experience with his children. When *A Boy's Will* appeared in London in 1913, it contained a poem that was later dropped from the *Collected Poems*, "Asking for Roses." In its original form, the table of contents of *A Boy's Will* included a gloss for all but two of the poems; for this poem, it read, "[He is no dissenter] from the ritualism of youth which is make-believe." We know how Robert moved away from the make-believe in the dramatic eclogues of *North of Boston*. But the "imagination thing," the metaphor, the unforced natural thought, were the building blocks of the poet's nature and of his poetry. His mother before him, his wife, and his children were imbued with the romantic spontaneity and suspension of disbelief of their early readings.

Raised near the Golden Gate, Robert "was one of the children told / Some of the blowing dust was gold." And some of his poems, like "In a Vale," with its "misty fen" and "maidens pale" (*A Boy's Will*), retain the childlike sense of wonder, others the wonder of love, as in "The Telephone" and "Meeting and Passing" (*Mountain Interval*). The title of his first volume of poems was, as we know, a tribute to Henry Wadsworth Longfellow, who, in "My Lost Youth," wrote: "A boy's will is the wind's will, / And the thoughts of youth are long, long thoughts."

Like Edward Thomas and Walter de la Mare in England, RF was interested in reaching out in his poems to children. Many of his poems appeal to young readers, and they were collected by him in his volume entitled *You Come Too*, dedicated to Belle Moodie Frost, "who knew as a teacher that no poetry was good for children that wasn't equally good for their elders." Long after he had written them, RF added the words "as told to a child" to two poems: "Locked Out" and "The Last Word of a Bluebird" (*Mountain Interval*), the latter going back to Derry days, when Lesley's father wanted to reduce her anxiety by having the crow send her a message over the departure of the bluebird for the winter. The child's point of view is reflected in "Good Relief," "Out, Out—," "Birches," "The Bonfire," and "Wild Grapes," and by inference in "The Runaway" and

"The Fear." In two other poems, Robert delves more philosophically into the wonder years: in "The Black Cottage" (*North of Boston*), he comments on how it is

> Strange how such innocence gets its own way.
> I shouldn't be surprised if in this world
> It were the force that would at last prevail.

And on the effect of altering the Creed:

> But suppose she had missed it from the Creed,
> As a child misses the unsaid Good-night
> And falls asleep with heartache—how should *I* feel?

And, again, in "Directive" (*Steeple Bush*), he describes the broken goblet in the "children's house of make-believe," where it is "Under a spell so the wrong ones can't find it, / So can't be saved, as Saint Mark says they mustn't" (Mark 10:13– 16). He found evidence of the innocence "in the bubbling of children," a force that emerges in his poems as a leitmotif.[23]

In her Derry journals, Lesley includes two little stories written especially "for Carol" and "for Irma" that suggest she may have been mimicking her father's own made-up stories that he told to the children at bedtime. Recently edited as *Stories for Lesley,* the eighteen stories, never intended for publication, had been jotted by RF into notebooks sometime between 1899 and 1907, when Lesley would be seven, Carol four, Irma three, and Marjorie a little over one year.[24] Meant for (and about) all four Frost children, they place each child in different, often heroic or scary roles on the farm: Lesley being asked advice by the family dog, Snider (who, previously named Schneider, would die in 1907 after being attacked by another dog), or Lesley puzzled and thinking; Carol, "The Lord Protector" of his sisters with his "terrible smile," frightening the fairies down on the pasture wall or Carol up the Nut Tree with the three magicians, worrying about his lost cap; Irma running home to Papa and Mama after a fearful encounter, while gathering checkerberries, with Old-Stick-In-The-Mud, the big pasture fencepost; and baby Marjorie "reading" to the children from leaves a "bed story" about a butterfly.

The similarities between these little prose pieces and the children's journals are striking. Not only do the stories make reference to the same landmarks, such as the woodpecker tree, Hyla brook, and the cranberry bog, but they clearly attempt, with the animation of the familiar animals on the farm and with the natural turns of phrases and plays on words, to deal with some of the fears experienced by the children that are reflected in their notebook entries. They represent, as do the children's compositions, yet another way in which all the Frosts took part in looking for the fun and wonder in their lives in affectionate and reassuring ways.

In addition, RF's children's stories fit neatly into the tapestry of his developing poetic idiom. They are delightfully successful in their own right, offering a sharp contrast to much of the work from *North of Boston* onwards. Absent from these little stories is the bleak psychological insight or stoical severity of his blank-verse narratives. They offset the stark realism of his poultryman tales, which would have been out of place in stories for children, representing, instead, the trusting view of life and suspension of disbelief that constitute a foretaste of some beautifully idyllic poems from this period that appeared in *A Boy's Will*. Robert worked through these stories to catch the tones, strategies, and expressions of living speech: colloquial double negatives, hesitations, what we have come to call "the sound of sense." Mimetic mastery and a rich, unsentimental frankness add to the stories' expressiveness and intimacy of detail. The humorous, yet psycho-logically true, depictions of family situations—with a woodchuck, a squirrel, a cow, a monkey, and even a lion and a rhinoceros—capture our imagination. One story begins, "Fairies live in juniper bushes—you have to believe that"; another describes how the rabbit, scared by a raspberry picker, "cuddled down in a dark place just like a little lost ball that won't tell you where it is"; and, in another, poor Snider, chased by a cow down Derry road, "fell upstairs and got under a bed." RF takes the everyday happenings on the Derry farm and, interacting with his children's school playing, raises the level of artistic mastery in an exercise that enriched his poetic output in important ways.

We know, from an examination of Lesley's journals, that many of her father's poems—Walsh refers to as many as fifteen or twenty, the index of *New Hampshire's Child* to twenty-seven—coincide with specific topics or incidents treated in her daily compositions. Carol's notebooks reinforce several of these. He recalls happy times in the pasture, swinging birches, climbing stone walls, and hearing the gunfire of squirrel hunters; he gives us, as well, a detailed description of the cellar hole from a burnt house in the pasture, perhaps the subject of his father's poem "Ghost House." At least three other poems—"After Apple-Picking," a topic suggestive of Lesley's "Our Apple Orchard" (where she sees "in [her] mind" the picking with pail and ladder), "The Kitchen Chimney" (with its danger of fire), and "Spoils of the Dead," mentioned earlier—should be added to the list.

While it appears unlikely that Robert drew directly from the journals or composition notebooks to write such poems as "Birches" or "Mending Wall," there is no question but that the topics Lesley wrote about were those discussed in the tight-knit family during their walks and evening gatherings; the fact that Elinor and Robert read and commented on each journal entry would certainly have reinforced these mutual associations.[25]

The pattern of lifestyle described in these writings branched out in new directions during the Frost family's stay in England, through increased contact with the English literati in a period of intense flowering of the arts, a growing interest in the drama, and a greater sophistication in the contribution of the children to their education by poetry. But the underlying motif—displayed in outbreaks of genuine homesickness for life back on a New England farm—would remain intact.

Let us then look in on the Frost family members as they embarked for England, and we will hear in their own words (and those of their peers) what transpired during that fateful period in their lives. We will take part in the unique playing out of their great adventure: today, such "experiments" in learning (both indoors and out) have become exceedingly rare. Our growing dependence on technology and instant communication precludes the seclusion or undivided attention necessary to raise our children on reading, writing, and the art of direct observation. When we consider a family of a recognized artist—an Emerson or a Thoreau, the Brontës or the Alcotts—the educational philosophy carries with it a special weight. We may, as I do, share in the nostalgia for the sheer wonder and innocence left behind on a New Hampshire farm; the Frosts—parents and children alike—would seek to recover, in Franconia, as elsewhere, some of the excitement of discovery and disbelief of the years at Derry and in England, but they were gone, replaced by the complexities that accompanied the emergence of Robert Frost the poet as a highly sought after public figure.

2

The Trip

The SS Parisian

*I*n the ongoing search for time to write and to mull over and to go ever more deeply into things through metaphor and the free association of ideas, Robert's decision to leave Plymouth, New Hampshire, where his teaching career was on an upswing course and was proving a serious distraction from his poetry, coincided with his wife's own desires and expectations. Two former students of Robert's at Pinkerton Academy in Derry, John Bartlett and Margaret Abbott, had married and moved to Vancouver where John could pursue a writing career; Robert in particular was strongly drawn to the wild, natural beauty of British Columbia. Elinor had suggested England: she longed to live under thatch, as near to Stratford as possible. Robert not only wanted to please his wife but also saw the added pleasure of returning to the cradle of English lyric poetry. The matter was settled by the toss of a coin: they would sail for England!

At the time of their departure from Plymouth, August 1912, Lesley had turned thirteen, Carol ten, Irma nine, and Marjorie seven. Almost a year after the Frost family arrived in England and were settled in the rented cottage in Beaconsfield outside of London, the four children put together a small composition notebook (running 120 pages in length) for their parents. On the cover they wrote: "An Important Year by Four Children, Dedicated To Papa & Mamma, written in The Bungalow, Reynolds Road, Beaconsfield, Buckinghamshire, England." While Lesley has indicated that the notebook was prepared during late spring and summer 1913, only a few of the entries are dated. A table of contents lists the entries by author, some of which must have been transcribed by Lesley for her younger sisters and brother. A map with a drawing of the SS *Parisian* crossing the Atlantic from Boston to Glasgow and a map of Beaconsfield are a part of the notebook; included also are lists of shopkeepers in Derry, Plymouth, Beacons-field, Ledbury, and Newent. Under the heading "Different Feelings," Lesley wrote:

> Excited! If we children were not ex[c]ited the last week or two before we left "The Cottage, No. 8 Highland Avenue, Plymouth, N.H." I don't know who ever gets excited. It seemed all like a dream. First came moving's share of deciding, then packing, getting information about England and a hundred other things, then say-ing goodby to Plymouth freinds [*sic*], finally getting dressed the last morning after a tossing night on mattresses on the floor, and going to the train. At last all was over though and we rolled out of the Plymouth station, maybe forever.

With their precipitate departure, leaving behind most of their possessions in Plymouth, Lesley and the others clearly sensed the enormous import of the adventure before them. Since leaving the farm in Derry, first, in the fall of 1909, to move into rented lodgings in Derry Village (near Pinkerton Academy, where Robert taught full-time), and from there to Plymouth, where Robert assumed a teaching position at the Plymouth Normal School, the children were aware of significant changes taking place in their and their family's lives. Lesley's journal entries tapered off; Robert gave up farming altogether; and the children entered school for the first time, attending a one-room schoolhouse in Derry Village. By accepting temporary quarters in the home of the Normal School's director, Ernest Silver, who, as principal of Pinkerton Academy, had persuaded Robert to accom-pany him to Plymouth, the Frost family was anxious to know where all this uncertainty was leading. Robert had confided to Susan Hayes Ward that the "long deferred forward movement . . . is to begin next year"; but nothing suggests that the children were aware of their father's determination to be a published poet. "It became increasingly clear," Lesley would recall, that her parents "wanted a dramatic change of scene together with a time, away from the burdens of teach-ing, for getting more poetry written. . . . All that had been contemplated was fresh scenery, peace to write, the excitement of change."[1]

Although another move was imminent by the end of the 1911–1912 academic year, with the choice having by June commencement narrowed to Vancouver (British Columbia) or England, the timing of the decision (after the coin flip brought up England and "living under thatch") took the children by surprise. Even the announcement of their departure placed by Mr. Silver in *The Plymouth Record* stated somewhat evasively that "Professor Robert Lee Frost, Mrs. Frost and four children sailed . . . for England for a two years' stay. Mr. Frost has been a member of the Normal school faculty for the past year, and he goes abroad at this time for his health and observation."[2]

Elinor Frost was no less surprised at what they had done: "[T]wo weeks from the day of our decision, we were on our way out of Boston Harbor," she wrote Margaret Lynch in Franconia. "We stored our furniture, and brought only bed-clothes, two floor rugs, books, and some pictures." It should be added to her account that shipped with the few belongings was the all-important Blickens-derfer ("Blick," for short) typewriter and two chairs, one of which served as Robert's writing "desk." The children were allowed to bring next to nothing.[3]

Making their way to Boston from Plymouth, Lesley saw the lights of the city, "made brighter by the dust having just been washed off the globes by rain" and "reflected from the lamps and the lit windows of gay hotels. . . . All was light rush noise and confusion down between the great rows of high buildings," in contrast to the dark, silent sky above. "We slurred around corners and slid along streets until we finally drove up to a hundred eyed hotel, alighted, and went in." Carol provides us with a description of "Boston Harbour," after the family arrived at the wharf by car from the railroad station: "We looked down on the boat. It was dirty and wet. The water was green and deep." While Papa was off looking for the luggage, "mama asked a man when the boat sailed. He said it went the next morning. We were surprised at that. When papa came back he said the blue chest was gone and the great big white one too. We were mad but we looked for a place to get on the boat. We found it. It was like a chicken's stairs, and two men stood on each side of it, and we started down."[4]

The SS *Parisian,* scheduled to leave Boston Harbor heading for Glasgow on Friday evening, August 23, 1912, was delayed until five o'clock Saturday morning due to the late arrival of some of her freight. Her cargo included 211 barrels of apples and 46,665 bushels of wheat, and she carried a full list of passengers, among whom were Robert and Elinor Frost and their four children.[5]

Elinor mentions the ocean trip only in passing: "We sailed from Boston to Glasgow, and enjoyed the ocean trip on the whole, though Mr. Frost, Lesley and I were quite seasick for a few days. The younger children escaped with only a few hours discomfort."[6]

Lesley already had a passionate love of the sea and its mysteries through poetry, and she later crossed the Atlantic out of Gloucester, Massachusetts, on the *Wanderbird,* a motorless, wireless sailing ship that took her around the British Isles to Scandinavia. But she would never forget the feeling of seasickness on this, her first sea voyage:

Rose, sunk! up, down! high, low! back, forth. I woke with a horrible feeling in my stomach and a whirling head. Great green waves went over the port-hole, a wind roared outside and I shut my eyes at every sinking of the ship. How far down is she going? When will she start to rise. Then suddenly she would be caught at the bottom of [a] steep moving green gulf between two waves and would start her ascent. Up, up, up and the higher she went the more I dreaded the next drop. This was a storm and I knew it. ("An Important Year")

Having returned to America in 1915, Lesley finished high school in Amherst, Massachusetts, before entering Wellesley College in the fall of 1917. She wrote a series of compositions for her freshman English class, several of which touch upon the stay in England. In one, she remembers being seasick: "I came up on deck early in the morning to try to overcome the first attack of sea-sickness by breathing and swallowing the strong wind and rain that were sweeping across the ship." In another, she romanticizes the experience in describing her responses to the moods of Nature:

When on board ship out upon the sea, sandwiched between grey waves and grey clouds, I have exulted in nature's mood. I have stood on the windward deck and let the fine cold rain beat against my face as it was beating upon the glassy waves and beating up along the deck so furiously that it whitened as it struck. Just as the wild dismal fog-horn blowing out into the grey answered to the wildness of the day, so I responded. A white gull wet its wing tips in a near wave. By the curve and dash of its flight I imagined that it, too, felt and gloried in the storm.[7]

Her contemporaneous description in "An Important Year" lingers over the ever-present seagulls:

There were three or four different species of seagulls which we saw on our way over here from America, but the most common kind and the one we could be almost sure of seeing every time we looked over the edge of the boat, were purly [pearly] white birds. They might possibly have had a tinge of grey on the center of their wings and head, but I have forgotten. The others were more rare kinds. . . . These small white ones by which we were surrounded were always in flocks, either propelling themselves through the air with gracefull wingstrokes, or dropping like stones, which are sharp a[t] both ends, from some high airy perch, where they had been going around and around, down to the water or shooting over the water like lightening, first bearing to the right then to the left. . . . All the way over I never saw any kind of gull catch a fish, although once I saw one at the top of the mast with one under his foot, if I didn't dream it. (June 23, 1913)

The gulls formed a mass trying to get food thrown overboard from the lower deck, "and the water around it would become in a few seconds simply white with gulls. Where they all came from I don't know, but there they were." Lesley could see a speck on the ocean where the gulls balanced on a box or barrel that would go out of sight whenever a large wave rose between them. They would come flying back to the ship "one by one" and wheel around waiting for more food.

"As we came in sight of Ireland they became thicker and thicker, and as we sailed up the rocky coast the air was full of gulls shreiking and circling around our masts." During the day and a half they steamed up the coast, gulls with nests on the shore would take turns sitting on the two masts, and they were always polite in relinquishing their perch. The description in "An Important Year" includes an ode by Lesley "To the Seagull" and a drawing in color of a gull floating on the water.

Lesley's brother, ten-year-old Carol, contributed to "An Important Year" his impressions of his shipboard experiences. In his entry "The Storm on the Parisian," he describes the big waves and violent wind. He and his seven-year-old sister Marjorie decided to make windmills. Unable to find sticks, they made paper horns with a pin through them and tied them to a string. Carol wanted a windmill so badly he went down into the trunk and found Mama's hat pin, but she wouldn't let him use it, so he found some wire and used it instead. Out on deck, he and Marjorie let the makeshift windmills blow out over the ship, but they kept catching on the ship's side; Marjorie's got caught in somebody's porthole for a while before she got it out, a little torn. The waves were washing over the deck, and Papa told them to come up to the front of the ship to feel the spray. But the wind was too strong. "I couldn't go any further, it was too much for me. So I went back," Carol writes. He and Marjorie went down in the dining room to watch the waves that came against the window: "We thought we were going down. The storm lasted all day."

We can expect to find in the children's writings a reflection of the Frost family's interest in Scotland, her land and her people, an interest stimulated by early exposure to their Scottish grandmother, Belle Moodie. In "An Important Year," Lesley includes a wonderfully humorous and imaginative piece entitled "The Three Scotchmen," depicting three very different personalities from among the many Scotch on board the SS *Parisian:* it was the time of the year when the natives were coming back from their vacations visiting relatives in America or their American compatriots were visiting their homeland for Christmas.

The first of the three was a high-school teacher in Edinburgh, returning from a brief vacation observing American schools. "He was one of the most thourough Scotchmen there, and he looked it. He had a rather blond red mustache which he kept damp and very sharp at the end by incessantly twirling it," Lesley writes. Well educated, his brogue was less pronounced than others gone to America, but he felt "very deeply" the rule of Scotland by England, and thinking about "Scotland's trials of the past" made him a little hard to get along with. He would suddenly awake from a reverie if the subject of British rule arose. "Then you would either have to correct yourself, and that probably made him feel triumphant, or else be very evasive and change the subject quickly, but this was very hard to do."

A second character, the captain of the SS *Parisian,* was a very disagreeable fellow. "He never talked to anyone of the passengers, except at table, where he sat at the head of one of the long tables in his coat of office covered with coloured silk badges, either sewed on or pinned on. Then all he did was to crack jokes, some old and some new, and laugh about them himself more than anyone else." He was jovial only at table, however. At all other times, when he wasn't asleep— he slept more than half the day—"he was the crossest man" she had ever seen. The officers, sailors, deckhands, or kitchen help were "forever doing something that he didn't like." When he was furious, he would stamp the deck and shout orders and scowl, "with his eyebrows hanging away down over his eyes and the creases in his forehead." He got worse and worse. Once when the "little boy who blew the bugle for dinner" stopped to laugh and talk a moment, the captain came along and grabbed him by the arm and gave him a rough shove toward the companionway. He was last seen the morning they went ashore. "We children had come on deck about five o'clock," Lesley explains. "It was still dark, but we were so crazy to see a little of Glasgow harbor we had got up early and come on deck before anyone else. As we walked up to the railing in the fore part of the ship a voice up in the look-off said, 'You little kiddies get below. What be you doing up here at this time o'day.'"

The last Scotchman Lesley describes "was not really a Scotch*man,* but a Scotch boy," who was very mischievous. "There was a swing on the ship and whenever he was on deck there he was hugging my knees or tugging at my dress and saying 'Come and swing me I say.'" At first she played with him, but once she began to be seasick, it was a different matter. The boy became a "perfect bother." The two chief words used in Scotch conversation are *yonder* and *kiddie,* and his mother, who was caring for his baby sister, more than twenty times a day would tell him, "'Now Jackie go and play with the kiddies,' and he would answer, 'I won't go and play with the kiddies. Their bad. Lesley won't swing me. I want some chocolates mama. Go and get me some chocolates.' And then again he would come up and bury his face in his mother's lap whinning, 'The kiddies won't be nice to me mother.'" The last time she saw him was on the Glasgow wharf, being dragged along in a great hurry by his father. "He was trying to look back at me all the time, and he kept bumping into trunks and suitcases and trucks. His mother with the one hand that was free from the baby she was carrying would smooth out his clothes after one of these bumps and say, 'Now Jackie walk along, and don't try to look at the kiddies.'"

Elinor would recall how, on the last day of the voyage, they "skirted along the

north coast of Ireland, and thought the dark, wild looking headlands and blue
mountains very beautiful."[8] In her college composition on W. B. Yeats's *Land of
Heart's Desire,* Lesley conveys the mystery of the rugged Irish coastline as they
headed for Glasgow:

> I remember the day when we sailed up the northern coast of Ireland on our way to
> England. The blue bare hills with no trees on them, not to mention a house, nothing
> but heather and flying gulls, rose out of a bare sea against a bare sky. Cutting into
> the hills was a bay where lay some warships as lonely and deserted if not more so
> than they would have been out of sight of land. The increased swell off the land that
> rocked the boat sideways added to the wildness of it all. It certainly was a place for
> fairies
>
> > . . . to ride upon the winds
> > Run on the top of the dishevelled tides
> > And dance upon the mountains like a flame.

It is Carol who gives us a view of "The Glasgow Harbour" as the SS *Parisian*
approached it by night:

> The first sight of land we saw were some mountains. Then we began to get nearer
> and nearer land. Pretty soon we saw seven English war-ships going down to
> Tobomory bay. Those sailed away. After some time we saw big rocks beside us.
> There were light-houses on the hills, but they were not lit up. Pretty soon it came
> night and they were lit. Some were pink and some were white. We watched them
> until we had to go to bed. When we went to bed I stood up in my bed and looked out
> the port hole. In the Clide river the boat went smooth. You could see little ripples.
> The shore just twinkled with light-houses. Then pretty soon I lay down to sleep. . . .
> When I woke up we were at Glasgow Wharf. The children dressed and we all went
> on deck. We saw a train on the wharf, but the captain said to go right down stairs.
> He didnt say to go down but he said "You four little kiddies to go down," so we went.
> Pretty soon some men came to get our baggage. We had the steamer trunk to be taken,
> and the suit-case. Then we all went up and said goodby to every-body and went.

Writing home the following January, to Harold Brown, assistant to the state
superintendent of public instructions in New Hampshire, Robert tried to explain
their situation:

> What do I mean [by reaching England]? I have been asking myself. Did I reach
> England when I went on board ship? Of course the ship was English—all ships
> are—and I could have been arrested there by English officers for any crime done in
> England (such as writing a bad poem) . . . . Or did I reach it when I first saw the
> coast of Galway which, peaceful though it looked through the haze, is where the
> wild and fascinating Irishman still snipes the deputies of the absentee landlord? Or
> did I reach it when I nearly got myself thrown overboard by a Scotchman for
> innocently calling the fleet I saw off the Mull of Cantire English instead of British?

(I was finding out that if Ireland loves England in one way Scotland loves her in another.) Or did I reach it when I set foot in 'Glasgie mud and dirt'? Or when we picniced, the six of us by ourselves, in the snug compartment of the toy train for eight hours on end straight across the counties to Euston station in London?[9]

The all-day train ride from Glasgow to London inspired several entries in the children's notebook, "An Important Year." Carol chose "The Cannals," Lesley "The Heather Hills." The canal Carol tells us about is "curly" and more prevalent in England than in Scotland. It went "under the railroad and then behind a hill." They would see it way off in a valley and then close to the tracks before curling off again:

> This cannal was too curly. It just curled right along. It curled behind hills. It curled just like hair. Once it curled behind a monstrous hill, and we didn't see it for a long time. Pretty soon it came back on a very flat place. There we saw a donkey pulling a boat. A man was driving them. We watched this, but it soon went out of sight behind us. That cannal curled under the track behind hills and out on the plains under bridges. That curly cannal curled every way. Pretty soon it curled to London, and that was all we saw of the curly cannal.

Lesley's description of "The Heather Hills" betrays a thirteen-year-old's unusual sensitivity to the symbolic importance of the terrain:

> On the train to Glasgow into England, there were many hills purple with heather, and it all grew so evenly that it looked like purple ground. It grows so near together, and into such knotted masses, that no other plant, tree or weed has time to get started. Scotland is very hilly and often we would see quite large steep hills sloping down to long sweeping valleys, and hill behind hill all blazing purple in the sunlight from the heather. I thought of the people who in the wars with England had crouchingly crept among that heather and over those hills to escape from either the Scottish or English. It looked very hard to lie down and hide in, for it looked close to the ground, and level with no places higher than others, but it might have been very high and only level on top, with plenty of room to crawl along underneath. I have never had any heather in my hands, in fact I never saw it until we came over here. No heather grows in England that I know of except, as I suppose up near the Scottish boundary, where the soil is about the same as in Scotland. We are staying in England so I may not see any more until we go up through Scotland again.

The contemporaneous "An Important Year," a notebook prepared by the four Frost children during the family's first year in England, is illustrative of the children's developing writing skills as part of their at-home instruction. The world as it is observed in the notebook's pages helps explain the family's responsiveness to its surroundings and to the extraordinary events unfolding before its eyes: we are carried back nostalgically to Derry and Plymouth in New Hampshire and forward along the precarious path in an unchartered adventure of the spirit.

In their decision to follow "a life that goes rather poetically," leaving the security of the Plymouth Normal School to cross the Atlantic to a country where they knew no one, Elinor and Robert had shown both courage and imagination. On the day of their arrival in Glasgow on the SS *Parisian* (September 2, 1912), the Frosts caught the train to London. Once settled in a cottage in the London suburb of Beaconsfield (Buckinghamshire), their shared excitement and anticipation soon found expression in the gathering together of a few poems into two small, typewritten manuscripts.

3

Beaconsfield

"At a Christmas Window"

"*I*t was perhaps the boldness of my adventure among entire strangers that stirred me up to my appealing from the editors of magazines to the publishers of books." Thus did RF try to explain, years later, the fateful events of 1912, while with his family in Beaconsfield, England, that led to the publication of *A Boy's Will* and *North of Boston* in London. And thus did the Frost family awaken to a new chapter in their lives that would take them back to America with the outbreak of World War I and to public recognition of Robert Frost the poet.[1]

In the fall of 1912, as the Frosts entered the recently leased Bungalow on Reynolds Road in Beaconsfield (Buckinghamshire), they had no inkling of the far-reaching outcome of their journey. By Christmas the following year—having completed their jointly written notebook they called "An Important Year," and Lesley and Carol having prepared creative notebooks for their parents entitled, respectively, "On the Road to Fleuraclea" and "Our Old Farm"—all four children would be aware that something momentous had occurred in their lives since their arrival in England. But, as they walked down Reynolds Road from the train station toward The Bungalow, they were eager only to get settled and to enjoy their new surroundings.

The search for the cottage had been "tiresome," Elinor said, and the rent was higher than they expected. Robert, with his genial ex-bobby companion from *T.P.'s Weekly* as a guide, had been forced further and further into the suburbs until, around September 10, 1912, they had reached New Beaconsfield, a forty-minute ride from Marylebone or Paddington stations. What they found was a densely populated town, more agricultural than industrial, that was just beginning to interest commuting Londoners as a pleasant place of residence.[2]

Writing for "An Important Year," Irma describes "Our New House," giving us a firsthand glimpse of the family's arrival by train at Beaconsfield station and the walk up the road through the town, stopping for groceries along the way. Having finally reached the cottage, she

> saw people putting "fernercher" in our house. The others had gone in already. Papa unlocked the side door, and he put the key on a nail. We went through that room into the hall. Then we went into a big bedroom and then into a small one, and then into the sitting room where the furniture was. Then we went out through the hall into the kitchen. There were some men washing the room. It was awfully dirty. Mama and the children had gone out in the garden, so we went out too. There was a hot-house, a summer house, and some dead flowers. We looked around and then we went in and placed some of the furniture around.[3]

Built in 1909, the attractive stucco and shingled cottage was leased to the Frosts for twenty dollars per month for one year. In her 1912–1913 diagram of The Bungalow, included at the back of "An Important Year," Lesley takes us across the "piazza" through the front door and into the "parlour" to the left off a narrow hallway. Continuing to the left along the T-shaped passageway, we come to the little bath, beyond which we enter the kitchen with its coal-burning stove. A door leads to a small shed attached to the kitchen with its own entrance from the garden. Returning to the house and following to the right along the hallway (which, in Lesley's drawing, ends in a tiny room, from which a French doorway opens outdoors at the side of the cottage), Lesley shows us the three bedrooms, the first and smallest with her and Carol's initials; the second assigned to Mama and Papa; and the third and largest, at the front of the house, occupied by Irma and Marjorie. The four fireplaces are not shown. Outside The Bungalow are the high laurel hedge facing the side entrance, the gate onto Reynolds Road in front, and the "hothouse" set well back in the spacious garden, where the children would play and prepare the first issues of the in-house magazine, *The Bouquet,* and other "books" for their parents. While today the hedges of red-osier dogwood mentioned by Robert in a letter home have disappeared, the leafy, thick-limbed "fifteen-foot hedge of American laurel" still provides privacy between the houses on Reynolds Road.[4]

To help fill the cottage, the Frosts went to High Wycombe and bought enough used and new furniture "to get along with for about $125," with plans to sell it again when they left. They bought the cheapest furniture they could find: "a kitchen table that we covered and put in for the living room table, some of those wicker chairs that bend when you sit in them, some beds in the rooms around the living room. That was all. We just camped." The household furnishings were, indeed, spartan: "You ought to see how few pieces of furniture we keep house with," Robert wrote his young friends in Vancouver. "It is cosy enough, but it would be a lesson to you in plain living."[5] Most important, of course, were the books, a few paintings, the Blick typewriter, and the two wooden chairs brought from America. The chairs were reassembled in The Bungalow and placed close to the fireplace in the parlor: Elinor's favorite rocking chair and Robert's Morris chair, where he wrote with a board laid across the broad arms. (The Morris chair and the board have survived.)

Although preoccupied with trying to make ends meet, and experiencing with the children occasional bouts of homesickness, Elinor was nevertheless pleased with their new surroundings:

> But it is a dear little cottage, built low, of some kind of stucco, with beautiful vines growing all over it, and there is a grassy space in front nearly large enough for a tennis court, and behind is a very large garden, with pear trees, strawberry bed, and a great variety of beautiful flowers. Red and yellow roses have bloomed in it since we came. Around it all is a high hedge, so thick and high that we are quite hidden from view. The town is very pretty and has plenty of historical associations. Edmund Burke, the statesman, and Edmund Haller the poet are both buried in the churchyard here. William Penn's home and burial place is about two miles from here, and Milton wrote Paradise Lost in a village only four miles away. There are stretches of fine old beech trees lying outside the town, and we have had many delightful walks. There are no wooden houses here. The English houses are all built of stone, brick or stucco, and that gives a very different and picturesque effect to their towns. . . . We find everything most interesting. The people are very polite, but they *are* very different from Americans. I would say that the majority I have had an opportunity to observe seem inferior to me, if I was not afraid of being prejudiced.[6]

While realizing that adjustment to their new surroundings would not be easy, Robert was no less pleased with The Bungalow as a place in which to write poetry. Having "proved myself as a teacher in two departments of learning without benefit of college, my soul inclines to go apart by itself again and devise poetry," he confided to Susan Hayes Ward. Neglected by editors in America, including Miss Ward at *The Independent,* he hoped to gain inspiration from the closeness to the cradle of English lyric poetry. "If there is any virtue in Location—but don't think there is," he added, "I know where the poetry must come from if it comes."[7]

In fact, without the demands of teaching and other distractions, the first few months in The Bungalow at Beaconsfield were extremely productive for Robert. There were few visitors, and little attempt was made to get acquainted with neighbors, who included G. K. Chesterton, author of *Heretics,* a book Robert had previously admired. Lesley put Chesterton's initials on her map where his house was located near Reynolds Road, but there is nothing to suggest he and RF ever met. In correspondence, Robert acknowledged the Milton connection, and he mentioned that they were within "a mile or two of where Grey lies buried . . . and within as many rods as furlongs of the house where Chesterton tries truth to see if it won't prove as true upside down as it does right side up." But he resisted sightseeing of any kind, showing little enthusiasm for exploring these Beaconsfield associations.[8]

Until Robert decided to attend the February 8, 1913, opening of Harold Monro's Poetry Bookshop in London, he seems to have shunned company outside the family. Instead, he concentrated on his own writing. Romantic and impractical, he had never promoted his poems in America through contacts with other poets or coteries of literary critics and editors. And, once settled at The Bungalow, as Elinor pointed out, he was "busy doing some writing which he has had in mind to do for a long time."[9]

For the fun of it, he indulged in casual play with thirty-some poems laid out on the floor of the parlor. Lesley helped her father by typing the manuscript for two volumes of verse on the family's Blick typewriter, and Elinor was an active participant in the selection of the poems. Robert soon chose, almost at random, W. E. Henley's publisher, David Nutt, overseen in 1912 by Mrs. M. L. Nutt, the widow of David's son, Alfred Trubner Nutt. When Robert entered the publisher's office with the manuscript for *A Boy's Will,* "a woman dressed all in black, as if she had just risen from the sea, came into the office."[10]

Mrs. Nutt, who never revealed her full name, was a severe and suspicious Frenchwoman. Her obsessive and bitter nature not only proved a serious irritant to Robert and to his future American publisher, Henry Holt & Co., but also in all likelihood contributed to her own impoverishment and lonely death. The end of 1912 was a boom time for publishing, however, and Mrs. Nutt, who liked to promote new writers, wrote to Robert on October 26, offering to publish his poems. The negotiations that followed were interminable, dragging out until December 16, when a contract was signed, committing the poet to four books. In the end, Robert was delighted to be accepted by the first publisher he had approached, thereby avoiding the vanity press to which many English poets had turned in desperation.[11]

The freshness and surprise shared by the whole Frost family just before Christmas 1912 are revealed in Lesley's recollections of the historic moment:

> But actually it was not until a morning in 1912 when a card came to a cottage (it was named The Cottage on the gate in the hedge) in Beaconsfield, that we knew *A Boy's Will* had been accepted for publication. That was splendid. We were pleased because our elders seemed pleased. We couldn't comprehend, because we had been given no foretaste of them, what resolve, what hope, what patience in waiting, had

gone into that first book; what a climax, what a beginning, was signified by such a recognition coming at last.[12]

All this excitement and euphoria in the Frost household did not, of course, translate into any income, either before or after Mrs. Nutt accepted *A Boy's Will* for publication.

Robert and Elinor had agonized over the school situation for their four children. The school year had already begun when the Frosts reached Beaconsfield, and, with no income, they hoped to be able to place the children in the government schools. However, it took only one visit by Robert to a public school for their plan to be scrubbed. Entering the rambling brick structure from the earthen yard, he was cordially greeted by the school principal, Arthur Baker, who escorted him to a partitioned classroom with tiled floors and an open fireplace. Robert noted the backless benches, like those he had known at Harvard, and two or three battered pianos, one used on this occasion to accompany "the lads in broad white collars [who] sang 'Odd, bobs, hammers and tongs' for me." He complained about the scarcity of textbooks in the school and about the small library, of "perhaps 200 volumes, absolutely non-literary and non-educational." While favorably impressed by the school's principal and the teachers whom he met, he was most troubled by the children:

> I should have said that the school takes care of all the poor children of the town for as many years as any of them go to school, say five or six at most. The teachers have classes of about forty apiece. [The children] were well enough when one considers what they were. One would have to go to the slums of the city for their like in face and form in America. I did not see the sprinkling of bright eyes I should look for in the New England villages you and I grew up in. They were clean enough—the school sees to that. But some of them were pitiful little kids. Mr. Baker stood them on their seats for me to inspect like slaves in the market—cases of malformation and malnutrition. Too many of these in proportion, I thought. But you have to remember that no one here sends his children to the government schools if he can possibly send them elsewhere.[13]

It was soon agreed that Lesley and Irma would be sent to St. Anne's, a private dame school located (according to Lesley's map in "An Important Year") nearby on Baring Road, while Carol and Marjorie would be taught by their mother at home. Elinor acknowledged to friends that housework was easier than in Plymouth (in part because of the availability of "a great variety of well-baked, wholesome bread and cake at the bakeries"), but, she reminds us,

> I am teaching the children myself, and of course that takes time. We cannot afford to send them to good private schools, and it is quite out of the question to send them

to the free County Council schools, for it would be too awful to take them home speaking Cockney English, wouldn't it? Either kind of school would be bad for our children, for one kind would influence them to look down on a certain part of humanity, and the other to look up to the other part of humanity. I think our American school system very much superior to anything there is in England.[14]

On her map of Beaconsfield, Lesley lists the names of her homeroom classmates, and of her teachers, Miss Edwards and Miss Cox. One of her twelve classmates, May Ribbons, lived with her family in a cottage called Greenhill, just down the street from the Frosts, at 22 Reynolds Road. She and Lesley would continue to correspond long after the war separated them.

No mention is made of the school in the children's notebooks. Lesley recalls that their schooling was carried on at home. The Bungalow was home, and at the time it "did not *seem* cramped," she explains: "The Frost family always made its kitchens into living rooms. My mother never worked *alone* in the kitchen, as women do nowadays. We all congregated around the stove or the ironing board or the sewing basket, and *talked*. Also, in Beaconsfield, the charming gardens at front and back were as good as rooms, since they were deeply hedged-in, English style, for privacy."[15]

Carol's entry in "An Important Year" on "Repairing our House" suggests that an effort was made to redecorate the cottage's interior. As Carol describes it, a man came to the Bungalow who said the ceiling and hallway needed plastering, the walls needed papering, and the woodwork needed painting. The man returned with his cart and paint and "blue distemper" to put on the kitchen wall, and a stepladder to whitewash the kitchen ceiling. Big heaps of white powder accumulated in the corner. He mixed the whitewash with the blue distemper, which he applied with a great big paintbrush, before rolling out the wallpaper. The paper "wasnt very pretty," so Mama went to "wicom" (Wycombe) and brought back some she liked. While the old man's brother prepared the plaster and whitewash, Irma and Carol took the paper cutters and started to scrape off the paper; but Carol wouldn't let Marjorie have the chisel. Stripping the paper was "dreadful hard work for us but we kept it up until we were done."

In good weather, a favorite pastime for the Frost family, beginning shortly after their arrival in England, was to take long walks out into the country: "There are stretches of fine old beech trees lying outside the town," Elinor wrote home, "and we have had many delightful walks. . . . The fields are all smooth, the pastures are a vivid green, and the woods all cleared of underbrush centuries ago, I suppose." By the following summer, the family had had "a number of pleasant picnics. We pack a lunch into several different bags," Elinor explained, "so that we can share the load and tramp off two or three miles through the lanes and paths."[16]

In an entry she called "Our Picnic," Irma describes one such outing with the family: "One day papa said to mama let's have a picnic and mama came out in the yard and told Marjorie to go down street to get some thing for the picnic." After changing her dress, Marjorie got meat and a lot of bread, and Papa went into the kitchen to make some sandwiches for lunch—some cake had already been cut. The children watched Papa make the sandwiches and get water for Carol to carry "because it was awfully hot and we always needed plenty of water." Everyone had something to carry. They went across the field, by the hedge, and down the hill between the clover and up the other side between the wheat and over the other stile and around the corner, a long way along the road, past a little pond, and then "we went through a gate across two fields and then we were there." The children threw themselves on the ground to rest and asked Mama if they could eat; but Papa said to wait just a little while. So they went to climb a tree for acorn balls. Lesley and Carol went off together, "so of course they have to call us 'miss sisybells', yes, they all[ways] have to do that you know, and so we have to call it back to them." After collecting the acorns and some stones, they ate lunch. When they had got their fill, they went to swing on the gate, "but Papa said we better not." They played in the sand until Mama said it was time to go home.

Lesley includes a more "learned" essay on "Lanes and Paths" in "An Important Year": "It is more fun to go to walk in England than in America," she wrote. "English fields and woods are a tracery of paths and hedged lanes." She compares the lane to an English country road, shut in, and laced with hedges. "Each new walk is a guessing game . . . like those you play indoors only much better." She observed that the word "Lane is only used in poetry in America and I once thought it was a made up word partly for the rhyme and partly because it has a poetry sound like glade and glen." Because the hedge may line a lane or may demarcate a person's land, there is a question of right of access: "If a path on which people have been used to walk on goes through some person's property, I think the person who owns the land has to get special permission to stop people from crossing." Farmers have to be careful not to disturb the paths and must build stiles where a path enters or leaves their fields. "The farmers must get mad sometimes," she writes, "especially when the children who pass through the wheat fields pull out the stems and eat off the ends or pick off the ears and eat the kernels."

Elinor and the children discovered that their moods fluctuated with the changes in the English weather and the passing of the seasons. Elinor was buoyed, as spring 1913 approached, by the sound of birds that filled the air. "For the last week or two," she wrote Margaret Bartlett, the larks have been back from the South, and quite a flock of them stay in the field that lies over the hedge on one side of our house. I can understand now why the lark is the subject of so much English poetry. Every few minutes one will rise from the ground, as if overcome by emotion, and soar straight up in the air until one can scarcely see him, singing all the while such a sweet, rapturous song, and then let himself straight down again, singing until he reaches the ground. I never heard such a lovely bird song.

Family members agreed that while the "many weeks of rain and cloudy skies were very depressing, . . . England is certainly a charming place in summer."[17]

Conceding that the children "do not like England as well as America"—following that first winter in The Bungalow, with its "many weeks of gloomy skies"—Elinor observed how their spirits were lifted as winter gave way to spring and spring gave way to summer: "Beaconsfield is a pretty town," she wrote Sidney Cox,

and there are delightful walks in all directions, across smooth fields separated by hedge-rows, and through stretches of beautiful old beech woods. All through May and June we have had charming weather, and the country has seemed very lovely after the many weeks of gloomy skies during the winter. The birds which we have never seen before, the skylark, the cuckoo, and the English blackbird, have been very entertaining to us.[18]

She delighted in "all sorts of wild flowers, masses of cherry and apple blossoms, and singing birds everywhere. The song of the lark has been a revelation to me," she wrote her friend Marie Hodge in Plymouth, "and the cuckoo and English blackbird are both interesting and charming. If only we might have more sunshine, but even now the sun rarely shines out brightly." Even as she wrote these words home, Elinor remarked, "Irma has been sitting beside me, writing you a little letter on the typewriter."[19]

From her uncorrected notebook (called "Many Storys" and presented to her parents at Christmas 1912), we learn of nine-year-old Irma's love of flowers, a love she shared with her mother. Irma and Papa had planted morning glories near the back wall. While she waited for them to bloom, some three weeks later, she kept busy "because we had a lot of viserters, and I like viserters." One day she found the flowers halfway up the wall: little pink and white flowers were coming out, "and I was very proud of them." Of course, Mama and Papa had much prettier ones, she wrote, but she liked hers best. She had learned from Papa that the vines out in the woods—which she liked to wrap around and around herself "until I was all green"—would kill the trees.

In mid March 1913, when Irma's mother wrote to Margaret Bartlett, who was recovering from appendicitis and a miscarriage, Irma added a note of her own: "England is difrent then America," she wrote. In England there were hedges, and she hadn't seen a pine tree; the trees in front had blossomed and the leaves were coming out on the trees in front and back. In the backyard they had a "storber bed" (strawberry bed), and they were digging the ground as she wrote; "Mama is going to have a radish garden and a letes [lettuce] garden, and she is going to have some flowers to[o] I think papa is going to plant something. Marjorie and Carol and I are going to have some flowers, too. Lesley has a sprand anckl for five weeks and isnt well yet. She got it in school."[20]

As Irma's comment indicates, Lesley's first winter in Beaconsfield was especially trying. In early May 1913, Elinor wrote her friend in Plymouth, thanking her for the letters she wrote the children:

> It was very kind of you to write to each one of them. . . . We have had considerable anxiety and care since Christmas. About the middle of January Lesley sprained her ankle during the gymnastic exercises at school. It proved to be a very bad sprain, and for eight weeks she did not stand on that foot. For five weeks of that time she wore a splint and for one week a plaster bandage around the ankle. At first our doctor thought there might be a fracture and advised our taking her to London to have it X-rayed. We did so, and determined in that way that it was not a fracture. You can imagine Lesley's nervous and weak condition during those weeks of pain and confinement. For three weeks now she has been able to walk around the house and garden, and it is a great pleasure to us all to see her on two feet again.[21]

While her father observed that "Lesley had a chance to see her own bones in the x-rays," he agreed with Elinor that she suffered from the confinement and inactivity, and that the situation was "hard on a mother." As the weather improved toward summer, Elinor reported, "We are all feeling ever so well except Lesley. Her ankle is well again, but there is a tendency to flat-foot after the severe strain, and her general health is not very satisfactory. She is growing very fast this year, and somehow she hasn't much strength for anything except growing."[22]

In all likelihood, Lesley took this opportunity to drop out of St. Anne's school, along with Irma. By February 1914, Robert was reporting to John Bartlett, "The children all keep well but as they have found the schools impossible here they come pretty heavily on Elinor. She has not been at all well this year. I may have to give up my wilder schemes and turn to money making for the family. Not that I am ever asked to. On the contrary."[23]

We do not have a record of Lesley's view of these weeks of invalidism, but we do know that she, like her father, was "very very homesick in this English mud." During her second winter in Beaconsfield, she wrote to her friend Beulah Huckins in Plymouth: "Although it has hardly snowed it is very cold, and it seems more cold than it really is because the English houses are not built with the purpose of keeping out winds and bitter frosty air. Everyone says it is an unusually cold winter while last winter was unusually rainy, muddy, and misty. We seem to have encountered the two most extreme winters." Both winters the Frosts spent in Beaconsfield the weather—the cold rain and mud—had a depressing effect on them, and they came to realize that they couldn't "hope to be happy long out of New England."[24]

It was during their third (and final) winter in England, 1914–1915, after the start of the war, that the cold and draughts began to make the Frosts sick, a fact that may have been a factor in the timing of their departure. But, in the summer of 1913, Lesley made the best of the topic by writing a short essay on "English Soil" for "An Important Year." She again describes apparent differences between England and America. Unlike America, there "are few boulders, but small stones called gravel," she writes. After a piece of ground has been plowed, "it is practically white from the number of stones turned up." The colors are lovely, and the mix of the soil is clay and much chalk, "both in the ground and water." One can find fossil shells in the milk-white chalk pits: "Papa found one once, or what we thought to be one, in a pit near here." Unfortunately, there is the mud: "The rainy season or winter keeps the ground muddy for a good many months, and deep sticky mudd [sic] it is too. . . . When the ground is muddy, mudd sticks to mud . . . and when a little collects on your rubbers you soon are walking two or three inches above the ground." When it dries in spring, it turns gray brown and "hard as stone, and is all cracked as if a fire were burning underneath it," turning the ground into layers of stone.

In her story "Passing Away Time . . . True," which appeared in the June 1914 issue of the children's magazine, *The Bouquet,* Marjorie recalls running with Carol across a bridge, fences, ditches, and a field, and then trying to get over a muddy gate with a slippery log. She slipped and the mud came up to the top of her high boot. She wiped it off in the grass and went home. "And this is only carols and my adventure of passing away time. I mean one of them We have a good many."

Rain was a problem when they played in the greenhouse, as Marjorie explains in her story called "The Summer-House." The little house in the back garden of The Bungalow was sometimes called a hothouse, sometimes a greenhouse or summerhouse, but by the time the family moved to Ledington in Gloucestershire, it had been renamed The Bouquet House after the in-house magazine. In Marjorie's story, the children opened a play store in the summerhouse. They took a board from the dirt path, nailed some rope on it, hitched it up and "hung some store things on it. Then we hung up a blanket to dress in." Another board was used for a bookshop, and the hen's dust bath that Irma found "kicking around" was used for a soda fountain. Marjorie went to get the dolls' clothes and saw Lesley getting things out of "her secret place." It had started to sprinkle, and by the time Lesley got in the summerhouse, "it just poured." Pretty soon the summerhouse began to leak, and everything got "drinchin." They put some things under the board, but Carol's blouse got awfully wet on the back, and Marjorie's feet were wet. Carol offered to take each of them up to the main house with the umbrella that Irma had brought back with newspapers on her head. They all got "sopping" wet. "We changed our shoes and stockings. When it stopped raining we went down after the things, and brought them all up as fast a[s] we could and made a store in the little shed, but it took too long to play that night."

I gather from Carol's account in "An Important Year" of "The Only English Snow-storm" that snow was unusual even in winter. It came at night, but "Papa said we could go out and play in it, so we did." Carol said, "Let's make a snowman," and he got his done first. Marjorie tried but the stomach broke, so the children used part of hers for the head. They named him "Bonar Law, and then we smashed him down for a sliding place. Lesley made one by pushing the snow along with the brush broom until she had a big pile." But "we had no time to play. Papa called us right in to bed. In the morning Marjorie said she heard the snow come off the roof crash on the ground. We went out to see our sliding places and the[y] were all melted."

It was Carol's job, as he explains in another entry entitled "Trying to Kill the Weeds," to help Papa pull up the dead flowers and weeds that Irma had noticed in the big garden the day they arrived. While some came up easily, Carol reports, most broke off in the ground. Papa had him bring an axe and dig them up; they threw away a big pile of long weeds. But pretty soon they started up again, and Carol and his father had to cut them down over and over again.

Robert, it seems, derived little pleasure from the English flower garden. Writing to Sidney Cox in early May 1913, he acknowledges that he likes flowers, "but I like em wild." He says he may "yield a little to others for one spring in the cultivation of one form of the beautiful. Next year I go in for daffodils [in Ledington]." It appears that, while he and Irma planted morning glories and he and Carol dug up the weeds, he never got around to planting flowers to supplement the roses. Elinor writes of "quantities of roses in our garden," but that "we didn't plant anything. Rob didn't feel in the mood to bother with it, and I haven't had any time, what with teaching and sewing and housework. But there are so many fruit trees in the back garden that it is a pleasant spot anyway. The currants and raspberries are just getting ripe."[25]

Marjorie contributed a short piece to "An Important Year" on "How our Fruit Comes Out." The eight-year-old's handwriting is difficult to decipher, but one can make out her descriptions of apple trees and raspberry and loganberry bushes. Apparently, each child was assigned a different tree to take care of.

The children's notebooks give us an even broader view of the activities enjoyed by the Frost family while at Beaconsfield. The garden referred to frequently in their entries became the home of at least two rabbits and five hens. In "My Rabbit Story" (included in her notebook "Many Storys"), Irma describes two bunnies, one gray, the other black. She likes to see them standing on their hind legs, scooting together behind the door, and jumping up on the windowsill, where they "cuddle down in the corner." The gray one, she writes, is the tamest and has better manners; the black one is more fearful and puts his feet in his water and food. They look funny when they wash their faces. Irma has never seen them sleep: "I think I go to bed before they do. I have never seen them shut ther eyes." If you whistle or trill, they get scared, their eyes get very big, they prick up their ears, and they stop eating.

Lesley was curious about the rabbits, too. She inquired of her friend Beulah, in Plymouth, about their habits:

> One of our two bunnies, I am almost sure is going to have babies. They have dug a hole in the ground floor of the hot-house in which they live, and the black and white one has carried down a lot of hay, as Irma has said yours did. I am longing to see them. We never have had rabbits before, so we don't know their ways. Did your mother rabbit bring her babies out of the hole immediately or did she keep them down until they were a few days old?[26]

In the introduction to her Derry journals, Lesley mentions two baby bunnies as having been named "Marcus Aurelius and Uther Pendragon—Mark and Penny for short!" but she and Irma do not mention names in their contemporaneous accounts of the Beaconsfield rabbits.

Lesley *did* name her buff Orpington hen, however. In "The History of Molly," included in "An Important Year," she explains,

> Molly is a hen. You will have to know that first, for you might think she was a person or a cow. She is a buff orpington. She has a dark buff neck and head, breast, and a little of her back is buff. . . . She was bought with five other hens, two buff orpingtons, like herself though not so pretty, and three black hens. She was the first hen to be named. I set the example of naming them all by naming her Molly. She is my pet hen so this is why I tell her history rather than the others.

The other Orpington is named Betty. After describing her laying habits, Lesley says she is tame enough to eat out of her hand; "she is a very quiet refined hen, and not jumpy and nervous and timid." She comes to the call of a hen. "Finally she got so she would follow me, call or no call, about the back yard whenever I went out." One Sunday, Lesley had stayed home when the other children had gone to the beech woods with Mama. Having been chased by a big white dog, Molly disappeared. Lesley "cried for I thought [the dog] might have killed her or she might have flown off over the back fen[c]e and gone off into the woods." After the others came home, Carol found Molly wedged into a crack in the rubbish heap. "She was hot and trembling, and her heart was beating hard, but she soon got better after drinking and eating and being held and patted." These hens have a good life in terms of food and space, so they "cannot complain if their house roof does leak a little." Molly, unlike the others, "is very quiet and submissive."

The Frosts enjoyed playing games, and like many other Americans in a foreign land, they improvised a game of baseball. Irma describes "Our Ball Game" in "An Important Year": "I will play a ball game with you now said papa," she wrote. So Irma went to get Marjorie and the racket (bat). Lesley and Marjorie were up first. Lesley gave a great hit; Irma ran and got it. Lesley got a run. "Safe" cried papa. Marjorie hit a little one right in Papa's hand. "Out" cried Carol. "What is the score" asked Papa. Nine to nothing. Irma hit the ball and got a run. Carol got a hit and a run. "We went on in this way until I got out. and they wan."

Indoors, at night or in bad weather, playing cards with the children was a favorite diversion, and Lesley's red composition notebook for 1912–1913 carries in the back the vocabulary in French necessary to play "Whist," followed by several pages keeping score, some of it in French. One of her more ambitious entries in "An Important Year" is a one-act play about "A Game of Cards," which captures marvelously the mock-serious interactions between the various family members and must have pleased her father for its psychological perceptiveness.

A Game of Cards

Scene. A sitting room in an English Bungalow. Two large chairs confront the fireplace. One of wood and cloth. The other of wicker and cloth. [P]apa sits in the wooden one. Mama sits in the wicker. In wooden dinning chairs which are scattererd about sit Irma, Carol, Lesley, and Marjorie.
Papa begins the conversation.

Papa. "I'll play a little game of cards tonight if you want to children."
Different personages. "Sure," "Yes," "Alright."
Lesley. "Where are the cards."
Mama "Look in the drawer."
Table drawer is opened. Shuff[l]ing of papers and books ensues. Mama and papa talk (together)

Irma. "Found them?"

Two or three no's follow.

Lesley. "Who had them last."

Carol. "Marjorie did."

Marjorie. "I didn't. I gave them to Irma last."

Irma. "I've got them."

Papa. "Hurry up. Havn't you found those cards yet. I can't wait all night."

Lesley. "Yes. Where did you find them Irma."

Irma. "Behind the books in the bookcase."

Carol. "Who put them there."

Marjorie. "O! I remember putting them there." She picks her fingers bashfully.

Carol. "I told you you had them."

Papa. "Get the board."

Marjorie. After looking for it. "Where is it."

Lesley. "O! Carol had it in his room. Go and get it Carol, and hurry up.["]

The board is found, after some hunting, in Carol's room, shoved under the bed. It is put on the arm of papa's chair.

Papa. "Who'll play the first hand with me."

Marjorie. "I will." Brings up a chair

Irma "I will." Taking the seat.

Papa. "You can shuffle first, little Irma, if you want to."

Irma. "Alright. I've been wanting to."

Irma shuffles. Shuffles, shuffles, and shuffles.

Papa. "I think thats enough. Deal now."

Irma. "Cut Carol."

Lesley. "Come on Carol. Tend to your business. Cut."

He cuts.

Marjorie. "What's cut."

Papa. "Never mind about that. Deal Irma."

Irma deals a little way.

Lesley. "*Stop.*"

Irma. "What is it."

Lesley. "I thought you gave too many to papa, but I guees [guess] you didn't. Go on."

She finishes dealing

Irma. "Hearts is trump."

Marjorie. "Whew. Ace too."

Irma. "Now look at that. I'm not going to show it to you again."

Lesley. A little irritated by there having the ace. "Whose play is it. Come on. O! Its mine. I forgot."

Papa. "Clubs is called. Is it my play?"

Two or three yeses.

Lesley. "Now Carol can't you go higher than his jack."

Irma. No he can't.

Lesley. "Then we know Irma's got the queen, king, ace of clubs."

Irma. "I don't care."

Papa. "Well you ought not to tell. Whose trick is that. Take it. O! Its ours, is it."

He takes up the trick and slowly puts it down, as if thinking.

Lesley. "Play, Irma. Its your turn."

Irma. "I'm thinking"

Lesley. "It doesn't do you a bit of good to think."

Marjorie. Leaning over Irma's shoulder. "Play that."

Papa now, as at every pause, begins to talk to mama

Papa. Awakening from a revery. "Play. Irma I'm tired of waiting.["]

Irma throws down a card in despair. Papa comes back to himself.

Papa. In astonishment "Trumps!"

Irma. Snatching it from the board quickly. "I didn't know that was trumps."

The game goes on in this way. Finally the hand is ended.

Lesley. "I forgot to get my score book and pencil. Get them marjorie Will you."

Marjorie looks about on the table windowsills, and in the drawer.

Marjorie. "I've got a pencil, but I can't find your score book."

Lesley. "Get any old scrap of paper then. Hurry. Its my deal. Hurry."

The paper and pencil is brought.

Lesley. "You got one point. Didn't you."

Papa. "Yes."

Lesley shuffles and deals, and Irma cuts, while the same exclamations and things are said. Irma still stays in her seat. Finally Irma becomes aware of bashful pokes and meaning looks and low whispers of "Irma" from Marjorie.

Irma. "What do you want, Marjorie. Stop looking at me that way. What does she want Lesley."

[F]or Marjorie grows too bashful to speak.

Lesley. "It's her turn to play you know"

Irma. "O, yes, but why can't she say so instead of acting that way. I knew it was her turn."

The game goes on, and is the same all through. Here and there bettween the acts sombody has to go for a drink, or Carol has to go and lock up the hens, or a door is banging. At the end of the game.

Lesley. "You beat us 10 to 8."

Papa. "Yes thats a very good score, but get your nightgowns and hurry to bed now. It's nearly nine."

Lesley Frost

July 9, 1913. Wendsday.

As Irma mentioned at the time, she enjoyed visitors to The Bungalow; but there appear to have been few of them, at least until Robert began to meet other poets and critics in London following the opening of Monro's Poetry Bookshop in January 1913. The infrequency of visitors is reflected in the children's notebooks, which do not include compositions about persons outside the immediate family. An exception is Lesley's description of "Another Old Old Man" in "An Important Year." This colorful character, perhaps one of the itinerant peddlers common in the area, was a "real old man" who walked the road between Beaconsfield and Penn:

"Got any matches or 'baccy' today," Is always the first words you hear when he gets within hearing distance. Then "sigh, sigh", while pulling off one grey glove. "So stiff, can't hardly move it, reumatics." I guess he would stand and talk to you all day if you didn't hurry on. . . . He has seen us many and many a time, but each time has not seemed to know he has seen us before. Papa has said every time, "I neither smoke nor carry matches," but every time we meet him he asks us if papa carries tobacco or matches. It must take him 3 or 4 hours to walk from the group of houses at the top of the hill on the way to Penn down to the beech woods and back.

In winter, he wore a large old gray shawl and a cane; on his head was an old felt hat "with a few holes in the brim and covered with dust." His baggy trousers were patched and soiled and his shoes were caked with mud. "I think this old man said he was 78 years old. . . . I haven't seen him for quite a while lately."

There is little in the record to suggest that the Frosts, while at The Bungalow, took part in local festivities. Elinor and Robert did go to London for an occasional play, and just before Christmas 1912 (on December 20), the entire family went to see King George V, who came to Old Beaconsfield to greet Lord Burnham on the ancient common at the annual Drag Hunt. There is no record of the Frosts taking part in some of the other town activities—bazaars, flower shows, dances, some Shakespeare and Gilbert and Sullivan, an annual Wild Beast Show, or concerts by the town band.[27] However, the "Great Performances" described by Irma in "An Important Year" may have occurred in Beaconsfield rather than in the zoological gardens in London, about which there are a number of other entries. In Irma's account, girls and boys on horseback galloped around a band of men with trumpets. After they went in the barn, a little girl came out with a lot of sticks. Then a man came out with a whip. While the girl held the stick, the man gave a lash and cracked the stick. He did it over and over again. Then two ponies came out; two men tried unsuccessfully to mount them, but each time they would "fall off backwards."

By the following Christmas—December 1913—Robert and Elinor were taking the train into London on occasion, to see a play or to attend some social function to which they had been invited. Robert wrote to Frank Flint about "gadding" at a party in Kensington, where friends (probably the Mairs and Adamsons, whom the Frosts had met in Scotland and who will be introduced later) lived and whose children had befriended his children. Elinor seemed to enjoy the "high life" opened to her on these occasions, and she even took up smoking cigarettes with the other women with whom she came in contact.[28]

We know also that at around this time Lesley and Carol spent several nights with the Mairs at their home in Campden Gardens (Kensington) just before Christmas, and Irma wrote to Beulah Huckins in Plymouth, probably not long after, to describe a lively New Year's Eve party the whole family attended either in Beaconsfield or, more probably, in London: "I danced too," she wrote, "and then we had a big party and the children sat down and the grown-ups stood up with cups of tea and cookies. We had cakes and candies and everything. I did not eat much cake because it was too rich at night about eight o'clock we went home in a automobile. Marjorie was rather sick that night."[29]

The Frosts realized that, in order to husband their resources and to avoid distractions from Robert's writing, they would have to curtail these social extravagances: "Our means forbid," Robert wrote John Bartlett just before Christmas. "Wander not from the point I keep making that we are playing a rather desperate game with our little wealth."[30]

Through it all, Robert stoutly maintained that, compared to other struggling artists in England before the war, the income from his grandfather's estate provided them with the bare necessities and a nourishing diet: "But we had, with our extra American pennies, eggs, meat, milk. I ought to know—I did a great deal of our cooking!"[31]

Lesley, however, years later would recall the genuine hardships they had endured in Beaconsfield, especially around the Christmas holidays. She would write movingly about the importance of Christmas to the Frost family as a child: getting the tree and decorating it; reading the Christmas poems by Palgrave, Blake, Rossetti, Stevenson, and Longfellow; exchanging simple gifts, often no more than a composition notebook or a hand-carved toy. She assures us that her father "*was* a religious man . . . if his way of bringing up his children can be said to bear witness."[32] She cites her father's poem "A Prayer in Spring" as an example of the Christmas spirit instilled in the children, of expressing gratitude for what we have today. In her Derry journal, the then eight-year-old Lesley described the few gifts each child received on Christmas Day, 1907: "After we had looked at them all a minute we dressed and ate breakfast and had a happy time all day long playing with our toys." Looking back, she admits the passage "proves we were poor—we were—but it also proves we were happily unaware of being so."

While that may have been true in 1907, I believe that by Christmas 1913, Lesley (and probably the other children, as well) were far more aware of the precariousness of their situation. Walsh correctly suggests that the lines in Robert's poem "Good Relief"—beginning with the words

But the two babes had stopped alone to look
At Christmas toys behind a window pane
And play at having anything they chose

—provide a portrait of Frost with his children in High Wycombe at Christmas 1913, doing the little shopping they could afford and enjoying the festive atmosphere. "For purposes of the poem the four children have been changed into two lone waifs, a boy and a girl."[33] The poem, which Robert never collected, is believed to have been written in the fall of 1912, and its original title was "At a Christmas Window." It was included in manuscript facsimile as the frontispiece to the 1935 special edition of an anthology, *Come Christmas* (1929), that Lesley edited for Coward-McCann in New York City.[34]

Eleanor Farjeon, who befriended the Frosts after they had moved to Dymock from Beaconsfield in 1914, observed later in Ledington, at Little Iddens, how sparse the furnishings and how resourceful the Frost children were on meager resources. In one of Lesley's stories in *The Bouquet,* "Inconsist[e]ncy," Willie tries to get his little sister Molly's penny—"which Mama gave her while the other children were outdoors to get candy without telling the others"—away from her by trickery. This and many of the children's descriptions of their games and other activities convey a sense of making do with whatever they could find lying around: boards from the path to make a store in the summerhouse; barrel staves to make a tree house; crushed berries to make colors for paints; a makeshift windmill. How true the lines from their father's poem "Directive":

> First there's the children's house of make-believe,
> Some shattered dishes underneath a pine,
> The playthings in the playhouse of the children.
> Weep for what little things could make them glad.

Lesley's poems and imaginary stories from this period are contained for the most part in her composition notebooks, in her notebook entitled "On the Road to Fleuraclea" that she presented to her father at Christmas 1913, and in the children's magazine, *The Bouquet.* The notebook "On the Road to Fleuraclea," which was written at Beaconsfield between November 5 and December 24, 1913, according to the cover, contains poems and stories rather than journal entries. One such story, "Something Queer," is at least a strong psychological reflection of the sentiment in "Good Relief," and, in its explicitly autobiographical detail, underscores the Frost family's financial distress come Christmas 1913. The story begins:

Far away in a little town by the great city of London with its red tiled roofs kept bright by the winter rains, and with its houses of stucko and brick surrounded by hedges and rain-darkened fences lived a family of six people, four of whom were children. Long before Christmas they were spending what money they had for presents for each other. As each one had such a small amount they separated into two parties, the two oldest together and the two youngest. The youngest (Irma and

Marjorie) were still quite interested in dolls so their brother and sister (Lesley and Carol), who were the oldest ones, decided to make toy furniture for the corn[e]r behind the fireplace in the sitting room. With most of their money they bought boards and small boxes from the one grocery store of the town which stood between the one postoffice and the one of two dry-good stores. The second time they went there to spend their next to their last four cents a queer thing happened, one of those things which moves something away behind your ribs, something you like and yet dont like.

They had passed through the "real store" filled with bright Christmas foods "wrapped in bright tissue paper" and through the dark and unnoticed corners of the shop (with its dull canned and jarred goods) to "a tiny store-house at the back." Here the broken boxes with their straw, split boards, and nails were tossed. From here they went through a narrow alley to a light cement-floored area. While an errand boy was showing them some boxes, a man snatched hurriedly at the girl's arm and mumbled, "Come with me, come along, come, come with me." Following him, they came to a little wooden shed; the man unlocked the padlock, and there the man told the children that they could choose the boxes they wanted. The shed was piled with kindling, a chopping block and axe, and tiny boxes nailed to the wall with nails and screws and tools. "I thought of Quilp's shop on a dirty wharf of the Thames and of men like Quilp, and you can imagine why I thought of such things and what they led to." The children picked out what they wanted and then asked the man, "How much are they?" The man was deaf, so they repeated the question louder. He waved his hand toward the store: "Ask the guv'nor inside, ask the guv'nor, he'll tell you." "The children picked up the boxes said thank you in a voice much too low for him to have heard and left the shed." The story ends without providing an answer to the children's question or indicating the significance of the Dickensian character.

In fact, just before Christmas 1913, with no down payment on the recently signed contract with David Nutt, and with no other income in sight or extra cash for presents, the children descended upon the grocer's back room, to barter with their three or four pennies each of spending money, for old wood to make one another presents.[35]

Isabelle (Belle) Moodie Frost (Mrs. William Prescott Frost, Jr.), 1876.

Robert and Elinor Frost at Plymouth, N.H., 1911.

The Frost children at the Derry farm, 1908 (Marjorie, Lesley, Irma, Carol).

The Frost children at Plymouth, N.H., 1911 (Lesley, Carol, Marjorie, Irma).

The Frost children in front of the Beaconsfield cottage, spring 1913. (Courtesy of Plymouth State College Library)

Little Iddens, home of the Frost family in Ledington, Gloucestershire, April–September 1914.

The Gallows Cottage, home in Ryton/Dymock of the Abercrombies where the Frosts resided September 1914–February 1915. The photo was taken in 1912–1913, with what appears to be the estate manager standing in front. (Courtesy of David J. Oldman)

Edward Thomas, in 1914, after In Pursuit of Spring *and shortly after he met RF. (Courtesy of Myfanwy Thomas)*

Robert Frost in a publicity photo made at High Wycombe, June 1913. The picture appeared in the London Bookman for August, the first photograph of RF as poet ever published.

Helen Thomas (Mrs. Edward Thomas) and Myfanwy, c. 1913–1914. (Courtesy of Myfanwy Thomas and the University of Wales Library)

Bronwen and Merfyn Thomas, c. 1910. (Courtesy of Myfanwy Thomas and the University of Wales Library)

Wilfrid and Geraldine Gibson, c. 1914, in front of the Nailshop, their home in Greenway, Gloucestershire, and the site of "The Golden Room." (Courtesy of Michael Gibson)

English friends and acquaintances of the Frosts in a photo of May 1914 (l. to r. John Drinkwater, Wilfrid Gibson, Edward Marsh, Lascelles Abercrombie, Geraldine Gibson, Catherine Abercrombie.) (Courtesy of Jeffrey Cooper)

Catherine and Lascelles Abercrombie with their sons David and Michael at Ryton/Dymock, c. 1914. (Courtesy of Jeffrey Cooper)

Eleanor Farjeon, c. 1914. (Courtesy of Gervase Farjeon)

Edward Thomas as a Second Lieutenant of the Artillery, c. 1916. (Courtesy of Myfanwy Thomas)

Robert Frost writing on his homemade board laid across the arms of his Morris chair, both lifelong possessions carried to England and back. (1915 photo)

J. C. Smith, RF's Scottish friend (whose wife, Edith Philip, was Jessy Philip Mair's sister), in a photo sent to Lesley by Amy Smith in 1913.

Jessy Philip Mair in 1918, outside Buckingham Palace after receiving her O.B.E., with her four children: Ethel Marjory, Elizabeth Christian, Philip Beveridge, and Lucy Philip. (Courtesy of Philip Mair)

Robert and Elinor in 1928 passport photo at time of return trip to England.

The Frost family (Elinor, Robert, Lesley, Irma, Marjorie, Carol) in Bridgewater, N.H., 1915. (Courtesy of the Plymouth State College Library)

Robert and Carol Frost in Franconia, N.H., 1916–1917.

Lesley Frost engaged in Greek games while a student at Wellesley College, 1917.

Lesley Frost in 1938.

Lesley Frost in 1971, in a photo taken in front of a painting of her mother by James Chapin. (Photographed by David Powers)

Robert Frost in a field in front of Little Iddens during his visit to England in May–June 1957. (Howard Sochurek, Life magazine, © Time Warner)

4

London and the Poetry Bookshop

$\mathcal{B}$efore leaving the United States for England, Robert and Elinor had hesitated between going to Vancouver (British Columbia) or to England. When the choice had been made, they celebrated not only the opportunity to live under thatch, but, more important, the chance to enjoy the land of Palgrave's *Golden Treasury,* and to see performed the poetic dramas they had read aloud and admired from afar. In the years preceding World War I, London was the center for English literary and theatrical activity, and it proved a powerful influence in the lives of all the Frosts. Fortunately for those who would come to appreciate his poetry, Robert gravitated toward those places in the city where writers and poets gathered; his decision to attend the opening of the Poetry Bookshop (on January 8, 1913) would have major repercussions for him and his family. While his first two volumes of verse, *A Boy's Will* and *North of Boston,* had already been accepted for publication by David Nutt, and he was inwardly confident of his poetic idiom and had achieved popularity as a teacher, it was here, in the Poetry Bookshop and elsewhere in London, that he would develop easy relations with his literary peers, losing, in the process, much of the shyness that had characterized his appearances during the Derry years.

Robert had come to England to write poetry away from the distractions of teaching and disappointed relatives. The as-yet-unrecognized American poet only slowly came to the realization that making such literary contacts might actually help bring his verse wider and more favorable critical recognition, while providing needed friendships for the whole family. The time the Frosts spent in the capital, upon their arrival in England from America, and later during their visits from Beaconsfield, would prove instrumental in furthering these ends.

From the moment she arrived at Euston Station by train from Glasgow, after the sea voyage from Boston, Elinor was enchanted by the city: "London is splendid," she wrote home a few days later. "The absence of elevated railways and surface cars make it a far more beautiful city than New York, I think. The streets are full of motor buses, which glide along, hooting and tooting and which find their way miraculously through the crowded streets. They are two-storied affairs, and it is fun to sit on the upper story out in the open, and to watch the fine streets and the crowds from that height." And the children were enchanted, too. While Robert was "busy looking for a house in the towns about," Elinor "took the children about the city" as much as she was able during the day.[1]

It is no surprise that, in preparing their notebook of "An Important Year," the children's recollections of those first few days in England center on London's Zoological Gardens. Eight-year-old Marjorie writes about "The Zoologicl Bird-house." She recalls, "One day when papa was off looking for a house mama took us to the zoological gardens, and we went to a place where there were some big and little birds in a bird-cage. . . . We brought some food to give to them." The colorful birds—goldfinches, cuckoos, and sparrows—were scared and noisy, picking Marjorie's finger and leaving a mark with their bills. She and her sisters and brother went home when Mama told them to stop feeding the birds. In an untranscribed entry, Marjorie describes "The Elephants" at the zoo. Having bought tickets for the elephant ride, they each had to wait a long time for a turn: and then, she writes, her elephant "went giglee goglee and a waa he went." When they had all had a turn, they went home "and wated fo papa." Ten-year-old Irma writes about "The Bear," one of four in a big cage. People gave them sugar, and if it didn't quite come in the cage they "would put out ther pose [paws] to get it." One bear, when the sugar went in the water, would "put in his par and get it out (gost [just] like hands) and put it in his mouth." Another sat and pulled his toe with a grunt. Then a man came in and cleaned out the cage. "The bears were having a gret time."

Irma and Lesley both wrote about "The Monkey-House." Irma counted one big cage and several smaller ones, and she remembered how a child screamed and had to be taken out of the house when "a monkey darted towards her and caught hold of her finger." Lesley describes, in "One Old Old Man," a particular monkey she saw as they came in the door of the monkey-house:

a poor little thing in a small cage. . . . [H]is fur was of a dark almost black brown, but on his face he had a short soft beard that extended up his cheeks and eyebrows of a light brown, and this looked so white against the darkness of the rest of his fur, you would think he was an old old man with white beard and hair. . . . His half-burried eyes looked as if they had tears in them. . . . [S]uch a look of pleading came into his eyes that it made me feel terribly sad.

For Robert and Elinor, however, the great attraction of London initially had been its richness in theatrical productions. On their first day in England—September 3, 1912—having made their way by cab from the train station to the Premier Hotel at Russell Square, a modest annex to the stately Imperial Hotel and finding themselves very excited and all alone, "without a single friend, in the biggest city in the world," they quickly made plans to go to the theater. Leaving thirteen-year-old Lesley in charge of the younger children, who had been put to bed, Elinor and Robert went to see Shaw's *Fanny's First Play*, which was enjoying a record-breaking run at the Kingsway on Great Queen Street, close to the hotel. Despite their fatigue from the long train ride from Glasgow, they undoubtedly got a kick out of the play's maliciously witty attack on middle-class values.

Elinor and Robert went to the theater "nearly every evening" during the ten days Robert spent searching for a rental property they could afford. Later, while residing at The Bungalow in Beaconsfield, Elinor would "go into London occasionally" with Robert, most often to take in a play.[2] There are few specifics concerning these trips into the city. In one letter, Robert mentions that "Mrs. Frost and I were at a play on Saturday in which we were asked point blank to profess our faith not only in fairies, but in devils and black art as well." Accepting the challenge, he asked only "to be allowed to define in what sense. But that is another story and a lifelong one."[3] Perhaps they had gone to see a play by Yeats. Not long after, in sending John Bartlett a Christmas present of the December 1913 issue of *Poetry and Drama*, with the first printings of his "The Fear" and "A Hundred Collars," Robert's marginal notes on Hardy's poem "My Spirit Will Not Haunt the Mound" mentions that "Elinor and I saw a terrible little curtain raiser (hair-raiser would be better) called The Three Travellers [based on a short story] that he made."[4] The plot of the play, involving the identity of an escaped sheep stealer and the hangman, may have provided inspiration for Robert's play *A Way Out*, which he would publish in 1917.[5]

Elinor and Robert's interest in drama was not new. While at Pinkerton Academy in Derry, Robert had produced five plays representing four different literary periods within a two-week period, an experience that tested his theory that "talk" was the most dramatic and poetic when sentences were lean and sharp with the give-and-take of conversation and helped him focus on certain aspects of his technique that would find full expression in the *North of Boston* eclogues. He had become proficient in the expressive reading aloud of Irish plays, including Synge's *Playboy of the Western World* and Shaw's *Arms and the Man*. He was drawn to the playwrights who moved the theater away from its current artificiality by infusing their plays with contemporary social and moral problems, debated with wit and intelligence. Robert characterized his own rhymed one-act play, *The Cow's in the*

Corn, as his "sole contribution to the Celtic Drama." He had shown his friend Edward Thomas a draft of a play entitled *An Assumed Part* when they first met in 1913, which was published as *A Way Out.* Two other plays, *In an Art Factory* and *Guardeen,* did not appear in print until 1985. We know that Robert hoped to bring out, with David Nutt, a third book of "out and out plays" to follow *North of Boston,* but that the war and his own insecurity as a playwright prevented him from seeing his goal to completion.[6]

Given his personal interest and ambition to write poetic drama, Robert quite naturally sought opportunities to meet the living playwrights whom he had admired from afar. Although Hardy, he wrote John Bartlett in Vancouver, "is almost never seen in a public place," this was not true of either Shaw or Yeats. Having commuted into London by himself from Beaconsfield, he soon caught up with Shaw at a meeting at Caxton Hall, near Buckingham Palace. He reported that he had "heard G. B. Shaw tease the Suffragettes at one of their own meetings till they didn't know whether he had come to help (as advertised) or hinder them."[7] RF came to view the Fabian freethinker as something of a plutocrat with arrogant manners, who offended his sense of social equality.

No less important than the contact with the London theater were the people he met while in the city. At the time the Frosts set sail for England in late summer 1912, most of their friends were neighboring farmers and special students whom they had mentored at the Pinkerton Academy and Plymouth Normal School. Robert was happiest when engaged in casual talk and storytelling, and the aspiring poet had never mixed with the literati with whom he might have come in contact in New England. Settled in Beaconsfield, he and Elinor had sought primarily the solitude Robert needed for his writing.

When, on an impulse, he decided to attend the opening of Harold Monro's Poetry Bookshop on January 8, 1913, he met for the first time other aspiring and successful poets and writers, some his artistic peers. His excessive shyness and sensitivity made it difficult for him to initiate these relationships, and his inexperience proved a hindrance initially. However, to his own surprise and delight, he soon found acceptance by an expanding group of friends in the various literary circles then enjoying a small renaissance in London.

What Robert had encountered, unexpectedly, was to be a short-lived revival in poetry the two years before the War. As Eleanor Farjeon explains,

> Poets had grown tired of poetic language, of huge indigestible slabs of blank verse, of *In Memoriam* and *Sohrab and Rustum* and all they stood for; and it became fashionable to write poetry in the idiom of everyday speech and to celebrate the little things rather than the great, the world-shaking. . . . Once again men talked about poetry in pubs, instead of only in drawing-rooms and studios. There were

more people writing verse, and more people reading verse, in the two years before the War than there had been for many decades.[8]

The community of poets growing in London was increased with the preparation of *Georgian Poetry* and the opening of the Poetry Bookshop at 35 Devonshire Street, under the auspices of Sir Henry Newbolt, professor of the Royal Society of Literature and a supporter of young poets. The cosmopolitan Harold Monro, who directed the Bookshop and whose catholic tastes and love of walking endeared him to the poets, had abandoned the editorship of *Poetry Review* in favor of the quarterly review *Poetry and Drama*.

But Monro's great contribution may well have been operating the Poetry Bookshop. He had leased the handsome eighteenth-century building located on a shabby, dark street in the Holburn slum, and the district provided a Bohemian and colorful background for poetry activities: those entering the property were in danger of being hit by flying kipper skins and bombarded by the hammering from the workshops of the gold beaters who had the neighboring house.[9]

The actual bookshop, where poets and poetry lovers were encouraged to browse, was housed on the ground floor of the house; the offices for editing *Poetry and Drama* were on the first floor; and rooms above, on the second floor and in the attic, were made available as bed-sitting-rooms for needy poets and artists. Wilfrid W. Gibson was one of the first tenants to move into his tiny box of a room, over the door of which was posted: "In case of fire, access to the roof through this room."

At the back of the house was a large room for poetry readings. There had been until then no tradition of poets reading their own work, but the readings in the back room, to the accompaniment of the hammering next door, were increasingly popular the two years before the war; by the time the Frosts left for America over two hundred readings had been held, making poetic history. (It would not be until October 1928, during the Frosts' return visit to London, that Robert would at last feel confident enough to give a reading of his own at the Poetry Bookshop.)

While attending the Bookshop opening, Robert met Frank S. Flint. His first letter to his newfound friend betrays an underlying insecurity mixed with genuine excitement: "I was only too childishly happy in being allowed to [laugh] in a company in which I hadn't to be ashamed of having written verse. Perhaps it will help you understand my state of mind if I tell you that I have lived for the most part in villages where it were better that a millstone were hanged about your neck than that you should own yourself a minor poet." He goes on to provide lengthy comments on the volume of verse he had purchased at the opening, Flint's *Net of the Stars*. He mentions that Mrs. Frost wanted Flint to choose "Once in Autumn" while Robert wanted his "Evening" or "Foreword" for inclusion in what was probably Ezra Pound's *Des Imagistes* anthology.[10]

Robert and Elinor shared in the reading of the various poets, and Robert passed along word of Elinor's preferences when they differed from his, as he did also to Harold Monro. That spring, Flint, his wife Dorothy, and their daughter Ianthe, visited the Frosts in Beaconsfield, and come July, Robert had offered to prepare for them "a vegetarian dish of the American Indian called succotash." Robert and Flint critiqued each other's poems, Robert expressing a preference for his "Trees," "Gloom," and "Easter." They even discussed the possibility of collaborating on a prose book "on Meter Cadence and Rhythm."[11]

It was through Flint that Robert was introduced to Ezra Pound. *A Boy's Will* had been accepted by David Nutt and would make its appearance at the beginning of April; *North of Boston* would appear to even more favorable reviews the following year. Elinor is reported to have wept over Pound's treatment of the family and other "indelicacies" contained in his review of *A Boy's Will* for Harriet Monroe at *Poetry*. Robert fumed over what he considered Pound's philanthropic motives: he told Flint that Pound liked his poems "because I have four children to feed and it flatters his vanity to be in a position to sell me to American editors. Perish the thought"; he knew Pound, twelve years his junior, had accepted him as some kind of a poet but one that was raw and "not quite presentable."[12] He worried, not unreasonably, that Pound's condemnation of American editors for not agreeing to publish RF's work earlier and his treatment of him as an expatriate would make his acceptance by the country he still loved even more difficult. Time would show that Robert's instincts were correct in quickly distancing himself from Pound, who was trying his damnedest to edit his poems and to force him to write in vers libre or risk losing his support. Robert and Pound had some gay times together in Bohemian London and in the Soho, but Robert knew he had to travel his own road and refused to submit to his tormentor's rude and dictatorial style. Anger covered his insecurity at this precarious time; using the weapons of humor and indirection, he separated himself from the image Pound had mistakenly painted of him. Back in the London of 1912–1914, however, ruptures between artistic peers and shifting of loyalties from one literary coterie to another were commonplace.[13]

Robert's own inexperience and lack of social sophistication made him anxious and caused him to exaggerate real and perceived slights. But the "review game" he soon found himself engaged in over *A Boy's Will* and *North of Boston* was a game all the poets played with gusto, often reviewing each other's work. Many poets in England competed for civil service pensions or sought a benefactor, like Eddie Marsh, to tide them over in hard times; some, like Lascelles Abercrombie, were forced to print their own poems, or, even if published by a reputable publisher, often received no royalties unless an unrealistic number of copies were sold.

Robert, as we know, never received a cent of royalties from Mrs. Nutt. And, in America, Harriet Monroe (editor of *Poetry*), in her two essays "Frugality and Deprecation" and "The Poet's Bread and Butter," pointed out that, out of fear that "favor would undermine the precarious vitality of the poet" and in order to protect him from the "soiling hand of money-grubbing, . . . the poet is lucky if he gets a mere pittance from editors, insufficient to support him on bread and water in a hermit's cave."[14] Amy Lowell, with vast family wealth at her disposal, was an exception: while in London, she threw lavish dinners with which she was able to entice away some of Pound's followers.

At Pound's urging, and given his own great admiration of the Irish poet and playwright, Robert did accept W. B. Yeats's invitation to attend the weekly "Monday nights" at his home. In his *Autobiography,* John Cournos, Pound's fellow expatriate, recalls Yeats's place over a cobbler's shop, at 18 Woburn Buildings, which "became oases of light for me in the foggy autumnal darkness of that year [1912]. Here was great talk. Yeats himself is the greatest talker I ever met. I myself sat for the most part silent, drinking in this talk with an avid eagerness. My silence was not due to such nonsense as an 'inferiority complex' . . . but to a lack of experience."[15]

Robert attended several evenings with Yeats, in the spring and again in the fall of 1913, upon the family's return from a two-week holiday in Scotland. In a letter to Sidney Cox, in which he compares Alfred Noyes ("Alfie No-yes") to Yeats, Robert praises the "untameable spirit of poetry" that speaks in many of Yeats's poems. Still, Robert adds, Yeats's affectations may have a deleterious effect on his writing, and he comes "perilously near" to believing in fairies. He tells Cox that he sat and listened to Yeats recount "with the strangest accent of wistful half belief" of a leprechaun he had seen kept in a cage by an elderly couple. The old folks took pity on the tiny creature, releasing it to its mourning companion, with whom it went off hand in hand.[16]

No one challenged the wistful poet, and, like Cournos, Robert remained silent and unnoticed during the sessions. Elinor shared Robert's disappointment that the hoped-for friendship with Yeats did not materialize. She confided to Margaret Bartlett: "Yeats has said to a friend, who repeated the remark to Robert, that [*A Boy's Will*] is the best poetry written in America for a long time. If only he would say so publicly."[17]

Because of her early interest in literature—in Irish poetry and fairies, in particular—Lesley dedicated one of her English compositions at Wellesley College to a critique of Yeats and his *Land of Heart's Desire*. Tracing the Irishman's apparent belief in fairies to his either natural or cultivated dreaminess of the poet, Lesley goes on to describe his "Monday evenings" (which she mistakenly places on Wednesdays) when he would entertain writers, generally mystics like himself, men like Rabindranath Tagore and Ezra Pound. "He sits in a throne-like chair in a dark velvet-tapestried room," she writes, "with a tall candle at either hand (candles are all he burns) and gently touches the tips of his fingers and gazes through the ceiling and talks in a dreamy voice of Ireland and fairies and Gaelic and modern poetry. The rest listen in a hushed silence." We can almost hear her father's voice in her critique of the play: "One of Yeats' prettiest little plays is the 'Land of the Heart's Desire' "; the play treats the longing of young people to be different and not to grow old, in that "place apart" where the "fairies dance." The play is "too imaginative," Lesley writes: "the few places when Yeats drops from language suited to fairies to that of common speech it strikes me so funny . . . for things can be imaginative and wierd and unnatural and yet bring in details that everyone recognizes which rather increase than spoil the desired effect." She mentions the same line her father does—"The butter's at your elbow, Father Hart"—as making her laugh.[18]

Robert made other important contacts at the Poetry Bookshop. John Drinkwater read his poems the evening of the Bookshop's opening. Although many were amused by his fashionable delivery—that of a parson, with eyes raised to the ceiling—no one questioned his stature in the revival of poetic drama, which was by then assured.[19] And it was here that Harold Monro brought Robert together with W. W. Gibson, who, in turn, introduced the American poet to the other so-called Georgian poets.

It is likely that Robert was drawn to Wilfrid Gibson, and to his companion Lascelles Abercrombie, for the same reasons he was attracted to the Irish playwrights—Shaw, Yeats, and Synge.[20] Gibson had recently published the first volume of *Fires* (1912). It was this work that caught Robert's attention because of its seeming authenticity as an expression of the dreams, the labors, and the fears of common humanity; some of Gibson's dramatic monologues had earned him the title in England and in America of the poet of contemporary industrial life.

Wilfrid Gibson had joined with Lascelles Abercrombie, John Drinkwater, and Rupert Brooke to produce a quarterly of their own verses they named *New Numbers* and assembled in The Gallows (the home of the Abercrombies in Ryton) in 1913–1914. W. W. Gibson was the simplest and most uncritical personality among the Georgian group that produced *New Numbers*. In London, in 1913, we find Gibson living in an upstairs room of the Poetry Bookshop, where he soon met and married the Bookshop's secretary, Geraldine Townshend, after a fierce and uncharacteristic row with Monro, who viewed the *New Numbers* project as detracting from his *Poetry and Drama*. The newlyweds moved to the Greenway, known as the Old Nailshop, in Dymock, to be near Abercrombie and to find inspiration in a rustic setting. The shy attractiveness of the poet in his earlier period, when RF met him, would later give way to a greater self-confidence, accompanied by a degree of complacency and conservatism, causing both his personality and the artistic merit of his poetry to suffer.

Gibson's friend, Lascelles Abercrombie, was the most intellectual of the *New Numbers* group.[21] After meeting his future wife, Catherine Gwatkin, he had turned more seriously to the writing of poetry. As a freelance reviewer, he was able to move to the country, bolting in 1910 to the Herefordshire village of Much Marcle, close to Ledbury on the Gloucestershire border and close to a married sister. When attempts to publish his dramatic dialogue *Mary and the Bramble* were unsuccessful, he and Catherine arranged for its private printing in Gloucester, a move that confirmed Abercrombie's reputation. The following year, the Abercrombies moved across the border to Ryton, in the parish of Dymock, where his sister had found the attractive cottages called The Gallows, named for a locally celebrated character known as Jock of Dymock who had been hanged for poaching the king's deer.[22]

The interest of these poets in dramatic dialogue and in the theater, their earned reputations as poets, and their congeniality with country living, appealed greatly to Robert, for whom joining with fellow poets was a novel and stimulating experience. He was delighted when Gibson wrote to him in early August 1913, urging him to come by the Bookshop and "bring some poems." In his later description of this event, in a poem entitled "First Meeting," Gibson suggests Robert had presented his poems to him unsolicited, a minor but significant variation. It was Gibson, too, who invited Robert to attend Abercrombie's reading of his poems at the Poetry Bookshop in late October. By Christmas 1913, Robert had come to believe that "Gibson is my best friend. . . . He's just one of the plain folks with none of the marks of the literary poseur about him—none of the wrongheadedness of the professional literary men."[23] But as his friendship with Edward Thomas grew, and with the proximity of his neighbor in Ledington, Robert drastically redefined his relationship with Gibson. Gibson nevertheless remained friendly over the years, and Robert came to recognize the simple generosity of a fellow poet.

By now, in the fall of 1913, Robert was winning a growing circle of admirers in the literary society of London. Besides Gibson and Abercrombie, Robert reached out with seeming ease to such luminaries as Walter de la Mare, Rupert Brooke, Laurence Binyon, Gordon Bottomley, W. H. Davies, Ford Madox Hueffer, W. H.

Hudson, John Freeman, John Masefield, and the newly appointed poet laureate, Robert Bridges. He was able to meet these men as their peer, and although he soon quarreled with Bridges over poetic theory, his acceptance as a poet of mature judgment and friendly disposition was confirmed.

To his dismay, however, Robert was being drawn further and further into the politics of the literary scene. Davies provides us with colorful details of the *tertulias* during this period just before the outbreak of the war. Tuesday lunches were organized by Edward Garnett at Mont Blanc, a favorite restaurant in Soho. The midday meal was attended, off and on, by Joseph Conrad, Edward Thomas, H. M. Tomlinson, Masefield, and Hudson. Afterward, Davies and Thomas would go along to the St. George's Restaurant in St. Martin's Lane, where there would be another gathering for tea, presided over by Thomas. Davies remembered being taken there first by Ralph Hodgson, along with his dog Mooster, a bull terrier. Hodgson was a "furious and loud talker," whose primary topic was prizefighting; Thomas he remembers as overworked and in poor health, but as "one of the most poetical men" he met in London.[24]

It was in this most casual of atmospheres that Hodgson suggested to Robert that he drop by one of the Tuesday afternoon gatherings (in early October 1913) and meet the journalist-critic Edward Thomas. Thus began one of the great literary friendships of British and American letters, carried forward in London, Beaconsfield, Ledington, and at Edward and Helen's home in Steep. As we shall see, it involved the whole of both families in Ledington, where they gathered during the summer of 1914 on the eve of the outbreak of war.

Still terrified of speaking in front of an assembled group, Robert nevertheless found that the shyness of his Derry years was giving way to a greater assertiveness through exposure to the London scene. By Christmas 1913, the Frosts were already planning (once freed from a lease on their house in Beaconsfield) a move to join the "colony" of poets in Gloucester; Robert had begun to tire of the literary gatherings in London, although not of some of the "nice fellows" he had met. Confiding in his stateside friend and colleague from Plymouth days, Gertrude McQuesten, Robert reviewed his situation in England. Portraying *A Boy's Will* as the product of a shy youth secluded in Derry, he astutely observes that shyness "is a thing one can't keep if one wants to. Once I fled from everybody. But I find I am only a little abashed by the crude human in my later days. At least I grow less and less afraid of imaginary people. The new book [*North of Boston*] proves that." He explains that now and then he has to run into London

. . . as on Tuesday, for a meeting of the younger poets. We'll eat in Soho and then talk about what it is necessary not to know to be a poet. There are two ways out of it for the candidate: either he must never have known or he must have forgotten. Then there is a whole line of great poets he must profess not to have read or not to have read with attention. He must say he knows they are bad without having read them. I should like these fellows in or out of motley. Their worst fault is their devotion to method. They are like so many teachers freshly graduated from a normal school. I should have thought to escape such nonsense in the capital of the world. It is not a question with them of how much native poetry there is in you or of how much you get down on paper, but of what method you have declared for. Your method must be their method or they won't accept you as a poet. . . . But they're nice fellows all the same and one wants to see something of them.[25]

After living in Beaconsfield for almost a year, Elinor confessed that she sometimes "wished that we had taken lodgings in the city itself instead of a house so far out, as the life there would have been more exciting for us all, but of course it is much better for the children's health out here. London is a foggy, smoky place." She was therefore pleased when, in preparing to move from Beaconsfield out further into the country to Ledington, Robert agreed to "make a week of it in London before we drink silence and hide ourselves in cloud." Robert had sold the two poems to Harold Monro at *Poetry and Drama* and he and his family were planning to "take it out in room rent in the upper floors" of the Poetry Bookshop. "It sells nothing but poetry," he explained. "The fellow [Monro] who runs it and edits the quarterly I speak of is a poet and all about him are the poets my friends and enemies. Gibson had a room there for a year before he married [Geraldine] the proprietor's secretary. Epstein, the futurist sculptor, the New York Polish Jew, . . . will be across the hall from us. All the poets will be in and out there. It will be something that Lesley of the children will be sure to remember."[26]

Having taken Monro up on his offer of lodgings at the Poetry Bookshop, the Frosts had left Beaconsfield for London (before moving out into the countryside) by the beginning of April 1914. Robert admitted a disinterest in sightseeing: "We mean to do the city for the youngsters as much as I am capable of doing a city or anything else," he wrote his friend Sidney Cox. "There must be a great deal to see in London if one will look for it. There is the Tower and—well there simply must be something else. I must get a guide book." Despite Robert's reluctance to behave like a common tourist, an attitude similar to one he expressed from Kingsbarns (Scotland) the previous August, the other family members seem to have taken advantage of their days in London to see a little of the city's historic landmarks. The only record we have are postcards from Irma, Marjorie, and Lesley. One is of St. Paul's Cathedral, and two are of Westminster Abbey and its choir. On one, Lesley writes: "We are staying in London for a few days. . . . We went to see Westminster one of the days and many interesting things and the graves of kings and queens."[27]

Geraldine Gibson, after reading Robert's letter to Wilfrid, responded to Elinor from the Old Nailshop at Greenway, Gloucestershire: "We have just this moment got your husband's letter saying you are coming here. We are absolutely rejoiced . . . how perfectly splendid!"[28] By the time the Frosts had completed their week's stay in London, they were ready to move into the cottage picked out for them by the Gibsons nearby in Ledington: Little Iddens, a name they already liked the sound of.

5

Scotland

In Memory of Belle Moodie

*A*t the Poetry Bookshop opening in January 1913, in addition to F. S. Flint, Robert struck up an acquaintance with Mary Wilson Gardner, the wife of Ernest Arthur Gardner, an archaeology professor at University College, and their eldest daughter, Phyllis.[1] It was this chance acquaintance that led the Frosts to Scotland in late August, importuned by the Gardners to join them at the holiday resort of Kingsbarns, a small seaport town near St. Andrews. It also led to important friendships with two other families besides the Gardners—the Mairs and Smiths. These literary families meshed easily with the Frosts: their artistic interests and accomplishments combined with a strong commitment to the nurturing of their children's world of the imagination. Through visits, correspondence, and support for the Frost children's in-house magazine, *The Bouquet,* the friendships that developed in Scotland reached far beyond the London literary scene and greatly enriched the experiences of the entire Frost family.

The literary tradition kept alive through education by poetry in the Frost household had been passed down from Robert's mother, Isabelle (Belle) Moodie. Robert's formative years at home in California and Massachusetts, with his mother and sister Jeanie, left an indelible impression on the sensitive youth unrelated to location. The voice of a distant Scotland, filtered through his mother's Swedenborgian faith and love of Scottish literature, resurfaced in his and Elinor's raising of their children. As a consequence, the two trips to Scotland—the first by all six Frost family members to Kingsbarns in late August 1913, and the second to Edinburgh, by Robert and Lesley alone, in September 1914, not long before departing England for America—assumed poetic, even heroic significance for Robert, and struck a similar emotional chord especially in Lesley of the other children. It would be in Edinburgh, where the Frost family stopped over on their return to Beaconsfield from Kingsbarns at the end of August 1913, that Robert would remember his mother, Belle Moodie: "But Scotland was my mother's country (she was born near Edinborough)," he wrote home, "and I felt as if we ought to get a glimpse of it. My mother used to sing a song that said she couldn't. 'Oh I cannot get a blink o'my ain countree.'" And he recalled her telling him about the city: "I used to hear her speak of the Castle and Arthur's Seat, more when I was young than in later years. I had some interest in seeing those places."[2]

Since early childhood in Derry, *my* mother, Lesley, and her sisters and brother, had been exposed to their grandmother's love of Scotland and its literature, and the reading aloud of tales and ballads during the late evening family gatherings. Only as an adult had my mother come to appreciate the strong influence of her father's Scottish mother in shaping their lives:

Isabelle (Belle) Moodie, my grandmother, harked back to the shores of the Orkney Isles, to the moors of Bruce and Wallace, to the Border Wars and sailing ships. Her forebears listened to tales as legendary as those of Homer. The shepherds on her Highlands watched the stars as curiously and reverently as had the Wise Men. The captains of her great seaports sailed away, like Sir Patrick Spens, never to return except in balladry. In later years, yielding to an atavistic tide, I, too, was to sail the coasts of Scotland, through the Hebrides, the Orkneys, through Pentland Firth, and come to understand Odysseus and his Sirens. Islands on a "wine-dark" sea as the "rosy-fingered dawn" appeared, these were his seducers, and mine. I, too, was to plead with my captain to permit me to go ashore, perhaps forever. For hadn't I heard, as a child in England, our friend Wilfrid Gibson read, or rather chant,

> You sing, and my soul is borne
> To the isles of the outer seas
> To the far, wind-scarred, wave-worn
> Outer Hebrides.

Like any true Highlander or Celt, [my grandmother] was a mystic. She "heard voices." She believed in "second sight." She dwelt in the "double lives" of Emanuel Swedenborg, her mentor: the outer and the inner, the actual and the spiritual. The lines he and she faintly drew between fact and fantasy, nature and the nature of man, were all but invisible.[3]

Isabelle Moodie was born in 1844 in Leith, the seaport town of Edinburgh; her father was a sea captain who went down with his ship in a storm at sea shortly after his daughter was born. Belle was raised by her Scotch-Presbyterian grandparents and, at the age of twelve, traveled with her grandmother to Columbus, Ohio, to live with her uncle, a prosperous banker. She was a schoolteacher in Columbus when William Prescott Frost, having graduated from Harvard and assumed the position of Principal of Lewistown Academy in Pennsylvania, called her to join his faculty in the fall of 1872; they were married six months later and moved to San Francisco, where Robert and his sister Jeanie were born.

Belle's sensitive nature conflicted with that of her husband, a hard-living journalist and politician up to the time of his early death by consumption. Her artistic idealism and spiritual sensibilities revealed themselves in her poem "An Artist's Motive" (printed in her husband's newspaper, the *Daily Evening Post,* March 29, 1882) and in her prose piece *The Land of Crystal, or, Christmas Day with the Fairies* (a booklet printed December 10, 1884).

The Land of Crystal takes place in "that realm which lies midway between heaven and earth," where "none but lovers of the little ones can enter." Two fairy sisters, Merrilie and Sombreena, symbolize the good and bad heart. The wayward and stubborn Sombreena is transformed into a tiger, and Prince Agneau-Leon takes upon himself the symbolic task of descending into the regions of darkness to redeem the lost Sombreena from animality, thereby permitting the triumph of good over evil. Sombreena returns chastened and repentant; Merrilie marries the Prince. "The union proved what the prophetic fairies had said. Hand in hand they worked for the good of all, so peace and love flowed in on every side." The symbolic and allegorical story falls into the specialized "metamorphosis" tradition that includes Charles Kingsley's *The Water-Babies.*[4]

Biographers have traced Robert Frost's interest in legendary heroes back to his early childhood and to his sensitive reception of his mother's imaginative storytelling and reading aloud of tales featuring individual bravery in the face of great odds.[5] Belle read to him from Sir Walter Scott's *Tales of a Grandfather,* and the first book he read all the way through before entering high school was probably Jane Porter's *The Scottish Chiefs,* furthering his understanding of the history of his mother's native Scotland. Scott, raised in Edinburgh, was a favorite in the Frost household: his border ballads and tales, his verse romances, and his novels, which developed rural themes that depicted contemporary peasant life, using regional speech and local customs. The *Tales of a Grandfather,* Scott's history of Scotland, written as if told to the author's grandson, "Hugh Littlejohn," retells the heroic exploits of the Scottish patriots William Wallace and Robert the Bruce.

The young Robert Frost would recall how the King of Scotland resided in the province of Fife at Dunfermline (where still stand the ruins of a tower from the King's palace), moving across the Firth of Forth to Edinburgh with the invasion of William the Conqueror; he would remember other kings: Henry II; Richard I (Coeur de Lion), driving the Saracens from Palestine; Margaret of Norway, who died in the Orkney Isles on her way to possess the crown; and Edward I of

England, against whom Wallace and Bruce took up arms. Ill with leprosy, Robert the Bruce asked James Douglas to carry his heart to Jerusalem (the Holy Land) to atone for his sins. Upon his death, his heart was placed in a silver case and hung around Douglas's neck. He never made it to Jerusalem, forced instead to go into battle against the Moors in Spain; after his senseless death, his bones and Bruce's heart were returned to Scotland: the bones to a church at Dunfermline, the heart to Melrose Abbey.

Despite its obvious heroic dimension, much of Robert's early derivative verse— "La Noche Triste," "Caesar's Lost Transport Ships," "A Dream of Julius Caesar," "A Heart in Charge," "The Traitor," and "Greece"—is rooted in concrete historical events. His sources, such as Homer, Virgil, Scott, James Macpherson, and William Prescott, in creating legendary heroes, no less depicted verified acts of valor. Although never collected, Robert's poem "A Heart in Charge" appeared in *A Boy's Will* as "In Equal Sacrifice" and reflects Robert's readings in Scottish history and legend:

> Thus of old the Douglas did:
> He left his land as he was bid
> With the royal heart of Robert the Bruce
> In a golden case with a golden lid,
>
> . . . .
> The heart he wore in a golden chain
> He swung and flung forth into the plain,
> And followed it crying "Heart or death!"
> And fighting over it perished fain.
>
> So may another do of right,
> Give a heart to the hopeless fight,
> The more of right the more he loves;
> So may another redouble might
> For a few swift gleams of the angry brand,
> Scorning greatly not to demand
> In equal sacrifice with his
> The heart he bore to the Holy Land.[6]

A born teacher, Belle allowed her children to stay home from school much of the time. Besides the novels of Scott, George MacDonald, and Porter, she read to her children the poems of Robert Burns and the sea chanties and ballads from her childhood. She tended toward stories with a moral lesson, often involving unusual bravery.

One of her favorite poets, Robert Burns had in his lifetime been hailed by the Edinburgh literati as an artless poet and an instance of the natural genius, a

"Heaven-taught plowman" whose poems were the spontaneous overflow of his native feelings. Burns was, in fact, a well-read man, who broke clear of the decayed English neoclassicism as a deliberate craftsman and turned to two earlier traditions for his models—the Scottish oral tradition of folklore and folk song, and the highly developed Scottish literary tradition. In one of his poems, "Scots, Wha Hae," Robert the Bruce was portrayed addressing his army before the great victory at Bannockburn (1314), at which the English were driven from Scotland. Burns's vigorous affirmation of the radical ideas of liberty, equality, and fraternity, expressed in some three hundred songs, made him the national poet of Scotland. His life and poetry impressed the young Robert Frost, who later drew his eldest daughter's name from Burns's well-known lyric "Ye Bonnie Lesley":

> O saw ye bonnie Lesley
>   As she gaed o'er the border?
> She's gane, Like Alexander,
>   To spread her conquests farther.
>
> To see her is to love her,
>   And love but her for ever;
> For Nature made her what she is,
>   And ne'er made sic anither?
> . . . .
> Return again, Fair Lesley,
>   Return to Caledonie!
> That we may brag we hae a lass
>   There's nane again sae bonnie.
>   (*The Golden Treasury*)

We have enjoyed the Frost children's lively accounts (in "An Important Year") of the Scottish characters on board the SS *Parisian,* their docking in Glasgow, and the family's train ride to London: Carol's "Glasgow Harbour" and "The Cannals," and Lesley's "Three Scotchmen" and "Heather Hills." Observed during the eight-hour train ride from Glasgow to London's Euston Station, the sloping hills, "blazing purple in the sunlight" reminded Lesley of "the people who in the wars with England had crouchingly crept among that heather and over those hills to escape from either the Scottish or English." Believing no heather grows in England, except perhaps near the Scottish border, she will have to wait to have heather in her hands "until we go up through Scotland again."

When Robert and Mary Gardner first met in the Poetry Bookshop, the possibility of traveling to Scotland was not discussed. Robert was pleased only to discover the possibility of friendship between their two families. Phyllis, whose "classical beauty and flaming copper hair" inspired Rupert Brooke to pay her a passing tribute, was twenty-two years old at the time and making her way as an artist.[7] The other two Gardner children, Delphis and Christopher, approximated the ages of Lesley and Carol, and Elinor shared her husband's delight at their meeting:

> Robert has made some pleasant acquaintances among the younger writers in London, and several of them have been out to see us. We have become very well acquainted with the family of one of the professors at London University—Professor Gardner. His wife is author of a Greek grammar and is very kind-hearted, clever and impulsive. There are three children, a daughter, 22 years old, who is an artist, and two younger children, Lesley and Carol's ages. We like them all very much, and they have been very nice to us, but they live on the other side of London, in Surrey, and we cannot see much of them.[8]

The distance between Beaconsfield and the home of the Gardners in Farm Corner, Tadworth, Surrey, on the other side of London, was a problem; still, the two families were soon exchanging visits to each other's homes during the spring and early summer of 1913.

It was from Kingsbarns in Scotland that Mary Gardner wrote the Frosts urging them to come to stay: "We had a fine voyage here, and already I feel much stronger. . . . We hope that you and your family will make this little trip and come to Fife before we return. We could *lend* you this cottage for the last week in August as I want to go jaunting round. Let us know if you are coming north and when."[9]

To please the family, Robert accepted Mary's rather insistent invitation; Lesley and the other Frost children were naturally excited at the prospect of a vacation in Scotland. With instructions from the Gardners, the Frosts traveled from London to Dundee, Scotland, by coaster steamer (of the Dundee, Perth and London Line), making their way by train to Kingsbarns.

As might any tourist visiting the area, Robert points out, in a letter to John Bartlett, that Kingsbarns is a "pretty little village . . . where the king used to store his grain when his capital was Dunfermline Town and his Piraeus at Aberdour." He tells Bartlett to "read again the ballade of Sir Patrick Spens"; on a mission for the king who "sits in Dunfermline town / Drinking the blude-red wine," Sir Patrick meets with disaster at sea on his return from Norway:[10]

>   The ankers brak, and the topmast lap,
>   It was sic a deadly storm:
>   And the waves came owre the broken ship
>   Till a'her sides were torn.
>   . . . .
>   They fetch d a web o' the silken claith,
>   Another o' the twine,

> And they wapp'd them round that gude ship's side,
> But still the sea came in.
> . . . .
> Half-owre, half-owre to Aberdour,
> 'Tis fifty fathoms deep;
> And there lies gude Sir Patrick Spens,
> Wi' the Scots lords at his feet!
> *(Oxford Book of Ballads)*

In Scott's version, the object of the ill-fated expedition is the bringing to Scotland of the Maid of Norway, who dies on her way to marry Edward, Prince of Wales.

In the same letter, Robert also tells Bartlett that "Right foreninst us is the Bell Rock Lighthouse which was the Inchcape Bell of Southey's poem," adding that "The children like it." In Robert Southey's ballad, the Rock, off the Firth of Tay, is dangerous to mariners. When the abbot places a warning bell on it, a piratical character (Sir Ralph the Rover), out of spite, cuts the bell loose from its float, only to be wrecked himself upon the rock as he makes his way home:

> But even in his dying fear
> One dreadful sound could the Rover hear,
> A sound as if with the Inchcape Bell,
> The Devil below was ringing his knell.
> *(Oxford Book of Narrative Verse)*

As he had been in London, Robert was a grudging sightseer, indulging in visits to historical monuments, such as the Bell Rock Lighthouse or the Edinburgh Castle, primarily to please the rest of the family. Conceding that visiting such Scottish sites "wont hurt my New Hampshire impressions as I have always been afraid learning a new language might hurt my English style,"[11] he tries to explain his attitude in a letter to Sidney Cox:

I really do take an interest in the historical places. . . . I didn't fail to notice that I passed the scenes of two battles—Eversham and Worcester—when I was travelling the other day. But I dont know what I would have done if I had been set down in either of them. It thrilled me enough merely to see the names on the stations. I got as much out of seeing Dunfermline town from the train as from straggling around Edinburgh Castle for a day. The best thing in Edinburgh Castle was the Black Watch on parade. Places are more to me in thought than in reality. People are the other way about. (Probably not so—I am just talking.)[12]

Finding themselves "near St. Andrews where John Knox knocked and Golf took its rise," the Frosts did do a little sightseeing, visiting the tower "that has figured in history since the sixth century—St. Regulus' Tower." Robert wrote

Bartlett, "All around us were the ruins of the great cathedral that John Knox preached his followers into setting on fire during the Reformation." He quickly and self-consciously added that he hasn't given him "much of this sort of thing. Sounds very travelly." The best part of the "adventure," from Robert's perspective, was the time in Kingsbarns (where there are few tourists and summer boarders) and "the new friends we made by chance on the beach." In pleasant contrast to his experience in the south of England, where the people "don't know how to meet you man to man," in the north the people "are more like Americans. I wonder whether they made Burns' poems or Burns' poems made them." And the "stone walls (dry stone dykes)" reminded him of the New England that inspired his poem "Mending Wall."[13]

The new friends the Frosts made "by chance on the beach" were friends of the Gardners: Jessy Thomson Philip and David Beveridge Mair and their children: Lucy Philip, Ethel Marjory, Elizabeth Christian, and Philip Beveridge; and Edith Abbot Philip and James Cruickshank Smith and their four daughters: Edith, Amy, Hope, and Anne.

As soon as she got back to Beaconsfield, Lesley wrote her new friend, Amy Smith, describing her adventures in the Scottish capital; Amy's prompt response confirms what must have been Lesley's and the other children's thrill at seeing the Castle and the Black Watch with a band of bagpipes: "I am very glad you liked the castle at Edinburgh, and the soldiers must have been lovely! We often see regiments of soldiers in Edinburgh."[14]

The final leg of the Frosts' journey home, after spending the night in the Waverly Hotel in Dundee, was a trying one for at least one family member. Lesley had not forgotten how seasick she was on the SS *Parisian,* and she suffered a recurrence on the coaster steamer from Dundee back to London, as Amy mentions in her letter: "It was a horrid shame that you were so sick on the voyage. You told me you would be didn't you?"[15]

The boat trip seems to have been more enjoyable for the other three children, who wrote the captain (W. J. Harding) once safely home in Beaconsfield. On September 15, 1913, Captain Harding sent from the Thames, London, a longhand note to each child, using the Carron Company Shipping Department memo paper. His generosity toward the children stands in sharp contrast with the manner of the captain of the SS *Parisian* we heard about from Carol and Lesley in "An Important Year." Here are the captain's messages:

> Dear Carol, I am glad to hear you arrived home safely and that you enjoyed your sea trip down from Scotland. I'm glad your wants were satisfied and that you got on the bridge and saw the Compass. Perhaps, the next time you come to Scotland I shall have the pleasure of renewing the acquaintance of yourself and your dear little

sisters. Yes, the wheel on the lower deck (aft) is used when the steam gear breaks down, or if no steam is in the ship. Best wishes. Your ole shipmate.

Dear Irma, I was pleased to receive your long letter. I'm afraid if Carol was chief and you 2nd and Marjorie 3rd officer, there would be very little work done. I'm afraid I should have great difficulty in navigating the ship safely, as I believe you would all choose your own routes and all want to go to different places at the same time. Get Carol to build his ship. Then I will come as your Captain. Yours faithfully.

Dear Marjorie, I received your welcome letter today. Many thanks. I'm pleased to hear you enjoyed your trip, and that you will always remember me. I hope I may have the pleasure of again renewing our friendship. Who knows? Yours faithfully.

For the Frosts, the trip to Scotland had been a new and exciting adventure, but relations with the Gardners were not entirely cordial. When Robert met Mary Gardner and her daughter Phyllis at the Poetry Bookshop on that fateful evening of January 8, 1913, he was mildly annoyed by Mary's somewhat assertive personality. Whereas Frank Flint's book, *In the Net of the Stars,* had been published three years earlier by the respected publisher Elkin Matthews, Mary Gardner's slim volume of twenty-one poems, *Plain Themes,* although published by a known house, Dent, was clearly subsidized and overwhelmingly illustrated with her daughter's woodcuts. Mary generously praised *A Boy's Will* after she saw a copy, and wrote Robert that she did not "think quite a large dose of success would spoil you."[16]

Robert was convinced that Mary was hoping he would help promote her book, and he was put off by some of her offhand remarks. Furthermore, the holiday in Scotland had added to the Frost family's financial worries, and Robert felt pressured by their overly solicitous hosts: "They have meant to be kind and I count it to their credit that they have embraced the whole family in their attentions," he unburdened to his friend John Bartlett. "But, but! There is a string to it all, I find. . . . The Missus Gardiner is the worst."[17]

Not only was Robert having trouble being tactful about Mary's volume of verse, but tensions had quickly developed between Robert and Mary's husband, Ernest, over wall carvings recently discovered in a cave on the shore of Fife Ness. Robert prided himself on an amateur's knowledge of archaeology, but he was probably sufficiently intimidated by the country's leading classical archaeologist not to convey to him the depth of his reservations over the authenticity of the drawings at Constantine's Cave, where he had been taken for a private showing.[18]

Despite the grumblings, contacts between the two families—although probably not between Robert and Ernest—did, in fact, continue after the vacation at Kingsbarns. During the school holidays over Christmas, Mary offered to care for the two younger Frost children (the other two being away visiting friends in London), so that "you and Mr. Frost could have a sort of little honeymoon together." Mary asked that they let her know "how this strikes you. I think it a lovely idea." The offer appears to have been declined.[19]

After the Frosts returned home there was infrequent communication between the two families. Over the years, at least until Mary's death in 1936, the Gardners, Mairs, and Smiths were in close touch with each other and shared letters and news from the Frosts in America. And it was Mary Gardner who, shortly after she and Robert met at the Poetry Bookshop opening, had written Robert that she wanted him "to meet my friend Mrs. Mair who lives at 14 Campden Hill Gardens, Kensington. You would like her very much."[20] In all likelihood, the Frosts and Mairs did not actually meet until they were all vacationing together in Kingsbarns. Jessy Philip Mair, together with her sister Edith Philip Smith, brought their families to Kingsbarns for the summer holidays, and it seems that they encountered the Frosts for the first time after reaching the seaside resort in late August.

Jessy was married to David Beveridge Mair, a mathematician, and they had four children: Lucy Philip, Ethel Marjory, Elizabeth Christian, and Philip Beveridge. Of Scottish lineage, the children had been born at Banstead (Surrey), not far from the Gardners, and had moved with their parents to London in 1912, and into the house at 14 Campden Hill Gardens early in 1913. During and after World War I, Jessy served with Lord William Beveridge, whom she married upon the death of her husband in 1942.

In his family memoirs, *Shared Enthusiasm: The Story of Lord and Lady Beveridge,* Philip Mair describes his family's keen "interest in poetry and fiction [which] was evident from the group which came together in 1912." He describes the gathering at Kingsbarns near the east tip of Fife: "My mother's eldest sister Edith brought her family. Her husband, James C. Smith, a distinguished English scholar who had just successfully published *An Anthology of Verse,* had with him the American poet Robert Frost who had just settled his family in England."[21] Because of the close association between the three families—Gardners, Mairs, and Smiths, who were joined on this occasion by Margot and Sarah Adamson, daughters of friends of the Smiths—the exact circumstances of the initial contacts with the Frosts are not entirely clear.

While at Kingsbarns, twelve-year-old Lucy Mair (who, according to her brother, was reading by the age of three and showed a "rapid intellectual unfolding," later becoming a professor of applied anthropology), joined Delphis Gardner and Amy Smith as Lesley's special companions. Back in Beaconsfield, the Frosts and the Mairs, who had moved to Campden Hill Gardens earlier in the year, were in close contact. Writing Lesley from Westbank, Innellan, Argyll, a few days before returning to London and school, Lucy asks "the name of your father's book of poems." She writes again almost immediately to say "I hope you haven't told anyone. I wanted to know the name of Mr. Frost's book. Please don't." Besides being sorry her friend was seasick on the coaster steamer, she mentions the bathing at Kingsbarns, and says she will send the photos she took there, including one "of all the Smiths."[22]

Just before Christmas 1913, Lesley and, probably, Carol spent a few days in the Mairs' London home, large and luxuriant when compared with their modest Bungalow. Writing for her English composition class at Wellesley, Lesley would recall the lonely experience in a brief essay entitled "A Train Whistle At Night":

> I was away from home for overnight for the first time in my life, and in the great, wide city of London. Dinner was at half past seven, quite late for me, and they fed me food that I wasn't at all used to. I can especially remember the heavy white dough patties served with the meat and vegetables. By bed time I had a stomachache, a big one. I was put way upstairs on the third floor in a cold, richly furnished but desolate room, with everything so exactly in the right place that I scarcely dared move. When I had climbed into the high, stiff-sheeted bed, I found that a white arc light in a nearby street was staring stonily in at the windows (uncurtained except for soft lace things) and was making the high strangely-patterned walls look unreal and unkind, like marble in a garden of moonlight. Then came the whistle of a train far out over the night of the city—three lonely calls and one long dying cry. That was too much. I curled up under the bed clothes and cried.[23]

But it was with the Smiths that Robert and his children, especially Lesley, formed the strongest bonds during their vacation in Scotland. Robert was drawn to James Cruickshank Smith—who, in 1911, had become chief inspector for training of teachers in Scotland—because of Cruickshank's extraordinary appreciation of the English poets RF greatly admired. Writing home at the time to his former principal, Ernest L. Silver, he hoped to impress him with his new friend:

> I have really made the acquaintance of but one schoolman and of him entirely through my writing. He is a Scot in Edinburgh named J. C. Smith who earns his living I believe as inspector of the five or six so-called teacher's training colleges in Scotland. With all the work he must have to do, he still finds time to edit Shakespeare for the Oxford press and run after everything new in English literature. Like all of them over here he reads in half a dozen languages and like all the educated ones I have met over here he is so utterly unassuming that you might look and not see him. He is in the civil service which may partly explain his comfortable unaggressive assurance. He doesnt have to think of holding his own against anyone. He doesn't have to think of getting on. Oxford too partly explains him. The saying is that a man who has been to the English universities always appears to know less than he knows; a man who has been to the Scotch appears to know more than he knows. I don't mean that Smith's knowledge doesn't show when and where it should. The last time I saw him I don't know how many poems by all sorts of great poets he recited whole. He would say to me "How does that lyric of Shelley's go?

'Life of life they lips enkindle—' You know it. Help me." And when I didn't help him, he would proceed to reconstruct the poem himself.[24]

J. C. Smith was, indeed, accomplished. He had edited a volume of Shakespeare's plays and Spenser's *Faerie Queen* and *Poetical Works* and, according to Robert, knew "by heart all the great poetry in Greek Latin and English."[25]

Robert was especially drawn to this man—admittedly with a secure civil service post—who managed to combine successfully the interests of education, literature, and the responsibilities of a growing family. The only reservation he expressed concerning his new "literary friend" was that he had introduced him "to an entirely new set of people and that looks like the beginning of more running to London." He had to remind himself that he was in England "primarily to write and not to see society."[26] Once again, he found himself torn between showing his family a good time and his own demands as a poet.

Having received from Robert a copy of *A Boy's Will* and the manuscript poems to appear the following year in *North of Boston,* J. C. Smith admired their content as "the work of a sincere, original, and essentially poetic mind." While encouraging the poet—suffering at the moment from a dry period or "cold fit," as Smith called it—not to abandon the Muse, he raised questions about the advantage of writing in verse over prose in, for example, "The Death of the Hired Man," concluding: "You can speak out in verse as you can't in prose." Besides a general appreciation of Frost's early poems and evidence of the strong personal encouragement Smith lent his new friend, we gain in this exchange important insights into individual poems like "Mending Wall" and "Birches," which reflect the Frost family's unremitting nostalgia for New England and the Derry farm.[27]

At one point, Smith mentions that Margot and Sarah Adamson—the young teenagers the Frosts had met on the beach at Kingsbarns—are preparing to present the "new American poet" Robert Frost to the Edinburgh branch of the English Association, of which Smith was president. Sarah "reads beautifully" while he, Smith, will supply "any patter that seems needed."[28] Having mentioned that his brother-in-law (David Mair) is coming from London to Edinburgh, he suggests that Robert come in March *and read us your poems yourself.*" Sufficiently buoyed by Smith's invitation, Robert mentions to his friends in Vancouver that an evening will be given "to a new American poet named Me before an Edinburgh literary society in March."[29] Robert may have attended the session, but there is no record of his having read his own poems at the association's March meeting, leaving the reading to the young Sarah in his stead.

With the outbreak of the war, J. C. Smith urged Robert to come with Lesley, who was also being urged by Amy, "anytime after (say) the middle of September, and come for at least a fortnight. You won't exhaust Edinburgh and the English Poets in that time. The girls are all looking forward in high glee to a visit from Lesley . . . [and] I want to see you again before you go."[30]

In taking up this invitation in late September 1914, Robert and Lesley traveled alone by train, and without a compartment, to Edinburgh. We learn from Amy details of what life in the Smith home on Baird Avenue must have been like in the fall of the year: "The avenue we live in has a row of trees up either side," she wrote Lesley, "and all the leaves are lying in heaps and drifts on the edge of the pavement. The trees are standing up bare and gaunt and the leaves still left on are brown and orange flaked and tipped with different shades of red." The Smiths would have been preparing for Halloween and Christmas. With no pumpkins in England, they would use "large turnips, which really make quite nice lanterns; apples and pears, and all sorts of autumn fruits, and we have a corn-popper, and make popcorn sometimes, though it cannot be so good as real American corn." There were only a few flowers blooming in the garden: "We have only chrysan-themums and a few pansies. The chrysanthemums are lovely—all white, and lemon-colour, and coppery-red, and a sort of light, pinkish brown. We use them a great deal for ornament, and there is a bowl of them in almost every room."[31]

During the two-week visit in the Smiths' home, Robert was sufficiently ill to require a doctor: "Here I am among professors and schools inspectors chiefly," he wrote Haines in Gloucester. "We talk about poetry to a certain extent, but more about the war. . . . I haven't been very well for a few days and am shut in today, a little worse than I have been. Half-heated English houses are the trou-ble." He later conceded that, although under a doctor's care while in Edinburgh, his "visit was not altogether spoiled by the bad luck. I had a better time than I should have thought anyone had reason to give me."[32]

Robert and Lesley had to return home "on a summons." The children were sick and Elinor was tired out, Robert said. In writing to Lesley after their return home, Amy was understanding:

> I am so glad you got safe home and had a good journey considering the hurry you were in and the anxiety you felt about Carol. And I am also very glad indeed that he is better and that he liked the knife. . . . I wish you were still here! I enjoyed having you to sleep with and play with and talk with *so* much, and so did we all, though nobody else slept with you. I am just longing to see you again, but, alas, that may not be for years. However, you'll always write to me, won't you? If you don't, I'll never forgive you.[33]

J. C. Smith was anticipating the Frosts' departure for America. He regretted being unable to get away from other obligations to see the Frost family off: "For nearly a week I have had a premonition that you would sail with the St. Paul on the 13th, and lo! it has come true. And you are doing wisely, I am sure. Whether I really wish that Edith and the children were going with you is more than I can tell. Sometimes I think it is the only safe course, but in other moods I feel that no immediate danger threatens them." He insists that his loan to Robert not be repaid with interest, and he promises not to forget Edward Thomas. "Edith has written, and Anne; and Amy is writing to Lesley. Take all our good wishes. And don't forget us."[34]

Two months later, acknowledging the warm welcome Robert was receiving in the United States, Smith provides strong encouragement: "Your pilgrimage here has not been in vain. . . . Now that you've got your foot on the ladder, go on mounting. It's only the first step that costs. You will find subjects pouring in upon you, and applaud the wisdom that sent you back to where your roots are. Keep on writing—I mean in two senses. . . . And let Lesley keep up her correspondence with Amy; I'll do my best to keep Amy up to the mark. These things all count: they make life worth living for individuals. . . . Also I have a premonition that we shall meet again, either on your side of the water or on mine."[35]

True to Smith's premonition, the two friends did meet again briefly in Edinburgh in the summer of 1928.[36] Lesley continued to receive letters from Amy Smith (as well as an occasional note or drawing from Anne or Edith). She and Amy exchanged photos and memories of their time together on the beach. "It seems such a short time since we were at Kingsbarns," Amy writes, "bathing every day and rushing about barefoot on the sands and rocks, or going for milk in the morning. I did *not* say goodbye to the little pigs at the farm. I forgot all about them! I expect they are big, fat, piggies by now, and kept apart in the common stye."[37] She describes an outing with her mother and several friends to a circus, where she saw "beautiful little Hungarian ponies," monkeys dancing on a tightrope, and queer sea lions raising large balls. Both girls were interested in birds and trees. Responding to a question from Lesley, Amy writes:

I do not know what the bird is—that brightly coloured one—which comes to you to be fed, but I think it may be some kind of finch. We have only two dull tortoises for pets, and we had some pidgeons, but they flew away. . . . Every morning as we go to school, we see a little, slender birch-tree, with a lace-work of tiny branches, and in it there are *always* sitting some little sparrows waiting for the feast of scraps which is thrown out to them.[38]

She asks Lesley to describe for her "what a 'butternut-tree' is like. I have read about it in several books, and to me it sounds fascinating." She had met another American, who said she had never seen one.[39]

Just prior to the Frosts' sailing on the SS *St. Paul* from Liverpool, Amy sent Lesley a farewell letter, with nine numbered items enclosed: "The enclosed things are to be opened one by one as they are numbered, one on each day, and if there are any [left] over open them all on the last day. Salve et Vale! Best love, wishes and goodbyes from Amy." Some of the items are missing, but those we have show a serial story about a gnome who tries to get money from a beaver to cover his failure to produce all the carrots and turnips in the world; another of silly faces drawn for a Red Cross sale at school; and another gives love to each child, and to "dear Marjorie, last but not least." In saying goodbye, Amy describes a sudden snow just as spring is in the air and how "it just drew me back and back into old times and magicness, and all that quaint, happy, half-sad time. Doesn't it you? Dear Lesley, we won't see each other for a long time, but I've got a photograph of yours and I'll remember you—this is getting sentimental!"[40]

6

Gloucestershire

"Elected Friends"

Shortly before Robert's fortieth birthday (March 26, 1914), the family had found a tenant to take over the lease at The Bungalow in Beaconsfield and the Gibsons had reached agreement on a lease at Little Iddens in Ledington. By mid-April, having completed a week of sightseeing in London, the Frosts boarded a train for Gloucester. There were at that time three trains a day from Gloucester to Dymock that connected with trains from London-Paddington. The Abercrombies and the Gibsons met the train at the Dymock railroad station with two large carriages, in all likelihood two of the Beauchamp Arms traps, which could be called upon to meet the train from Gloucester.[1] Making their way across the river Leadon, past Greenway Cross and the Gibsons' Nailshop through the scattering of houses at Ryton to The Gallows, and from there on to Little Iddens, the Frosts must have been impressed and pleased by both the warmth of the welcome and the beauty of the landscape.

The poet's newfound English friends—W. W. Gibson, Lascelles Abercrombie, John W. Haines, Edward Thomas, and Eleanor Farjeon—have celebrated in prose and verse the rural idyll of the Leadon river valley and its villages, tiny hamlets, and cottages, today much as it was then. The river Leadon flows south through Ledbury to join the Severn at Gloucester. The countryside is gently contoured, mixed farming land, bordered on the southwest by the Forest of Dean and on the northeast by the steep outcrop of the Malvern Hills. The soil is a fertile loam, deep red in color, and the small irregular fields and orchards are interrupted by scattered woodland, spinneys, and thick hedgerows. Everything seems on a small scale: fields, streams, villages, roads, even the stations of the now-uprooted single track railway. There is the impression of remoteness, prettiness, and easy fertility, with daffodils blooming wild in the springtime. It is the epitome of the cultivated English landscape, reminding one of "The Daffodil Fields" of the poet laureate John Masefield, who was born at Ledbury only two or three miles away in Herefordshire.[2]

Lascelles Abercrombie's wife, Catherine, would recall the "rich red loam, small hills covered with firs and birch, and acres of orchards," there in the midst of the cider-making country: "The sight of the blossoming of the apple and cherry trees in spring was unforgettable, with miles and miles of daffodils pouring over the ground. In medieval times there used to be a flourishing industry of making a dye from the daffodil flower to dye cloth and hessian. They were grown as a crop and have spread and flourished ever since." She would quote her husband:

> But here's the happiest light can lie on the ground,
> Grass sloping under trees
> Alive with yellow shine of daffodils.
> If quicksilver were gold
> And troubled pools of it shaking in the sun,
> It were not such a fancy of bickering gleam
> As Ryton daffodils when the air but stirs.[3]

Shortly after their arrival, Robert tried to explain the new location to his friend Sidney Cox:

> We are actually in Gloucestershire but near the line and our postoffice is at Ledbury in Herefordshire. This is a great change from Beaconsfield which was merely suburban. We are now in the country, the cider country. . . . We can go almost anywhere we wish on wavering footpaths through the fields. The fields are so small and the trees so numerous along the hedges that, as my friend Thomas says in the loveliest book on spring in England [*In Pursuit of Spring*, 1914], you may think from a little distance that the country was solid woods.[4]

Elinor added her own appreciation of their surroundings in a letter to her sister Leona:

> I wish I could make you feel what a lovely country this is. When we first came, the meadows were covered with yellow daffodils and the cuckoo had just begun to sing. For nearly two months it sang all day long, but it has already stopped singing. The pastures here are so rich that they are just as green as the mowing and wheat fields, and they are separated by dark geen hedges and bordered by huge elms. Great flocks of sheep and herds of cows are everywhere. From a hill about four miles away, one can see the Severn river winding along, and the mountains of Wales in the distance.[5]

But it was Edward Thomas, in his beautiful essay, "This England," who captured the most poetic vision of the land he and Robert traversed together those fateful months in 1914. Edward was in Ryton/Dymock for the third time, in August, during the gathering of the wheat harvest into the ricks: "The sun shone, always warm, from skies sometimes cloudless, sometimes inscribed with a fine white scatter miles high, sometimes displaying the full pomp of white moving mountains, sometimes almost entirely shrouded in dull sulphurous threats, but vain ones." Remembrance of his friend Robert gives form and meaning to the landscape: "Three meadows away lived a friend, and once or twice or three times a day I used to cross the meadows, the gate, and the two stiles. . . . The path led across the middle of the meadow, through a gate, and alongside one of the hedges of the next, which sloped down rather steeply to the remnant of a brook, and was grazed by half a dozen cows." Edward would stroll past hedgerow elms, stopping to talk to whoever was about, over to the "little house of whitened bricks and black timbers, . . . a vegetable garden in front with a weeping ash and a bay-tree, a walnut in a yard of cobbles and grass behind, a yew on the roadside, an orchard on the other."[6]

Little Iddens, the black-and-white timbered cottage that would house the six Frosts from April through September 1914, was "very old," Elinor wrote her sister: "about 350 years old, and all the floors downstairs are brick tiled and the beams show above." Although she did not complain about being cramped, she must have found the five-room cottage far more primitive than The Bungalow in Beaconsfield.[7]

A squarish, two-story, half-timbered structure, Little Iddens has, unlike its more ostentatious neighboring houses—The Gallows and The Greenway—survived virtually intact, preserved in part because of its humble condition, not suited to grander country living or restoration, and partly because it is located on a larger property owned by the Churchill family. The exterior walls were whitewashed brick, with the blackened and crumbling timbers left showing. The buckling effect added to the cottage's quaint air and "picturesque decrepitude."

When the Frost family occupied Little Iddens, there was a tiny kitchen with pantry in the downstairs, with an earthen floor and an old-fashioned wood stove and baking oven. Flanking the kitchen was a combination living-dining room separated from another living area by a hallway running front to back, each end with a door leading to the outside. The hallway provided cross drafts in summer, but, although there was a fireplace in each of the two main rooms downstairs, with their undulating brick floors, the cottage would have been virtually impossible to heat in winter. A part of the ground floor was taken up with a shed that made the cottage seem larger from the outside than it was. To get furniture upstairs, past the steep, narrow stairway, the occupant would have to remove part of an upstairs wall in order to gain access to the two bedrooms and sleeping alcove on the second floor. The hinged windows, all diminutive, carried leaded-glass panes. Ceilings throughout were low. There was no indoor plumbing, as there had been in Beaconsfield; the water pump in the front yard is still there, as is the yew tree crowded up against the shed that shields the cottage from the road.

But the Frosts, and Robert in particular, had sought out Nature in the wild rather than cultivated, and with spring at hand and summer not far behind, the surrounding terrain was of greater appeal than the interior of Little Iddens. Having moved the family's few possessions into the cottage, Robert soon gravitated toward those persons he believed understood their environment through direct, unromanticized observation.

When John W. Haines, a Gloucester solicitor, botanizer, and friend of poets, presented himself one day near Little Iddens, Robert soon discovered that he had already read in manuscript a copy of *A Boy's Will* lent to him by Lascelles Abercrombie.[8] However, his reason for being that day "in one of the flowery country lanes north of Dymock," was that he had been botanizing, and he was carrying his vasculum (or canister for tall flowers, as RF called it). Years later, he recalled that Robert's eyes "froze onto that tin, whilst he explained that he also was a botanist, as indeed I had known from his poetry. With this link between us, . . . we met and wandered over May Hill, the Leadon Valley, and the ridges of the Cotswolds, hunting flowers together, and talking ceaselessly of poets and of poetry."[9]

Both men retained a vivid recollection of "the night when to illustrate our talk about the internationality of ferns," Haines boosted Robert "up a small cliff to see by matchlight a spleenwort he knew of there."[10] Back in Franconia, Robert mailed Haines a specimen of the Walking Fern, describing it for Haines as "a little thing that spans its way along by rooting at the tips" that he has adopted as "his emblem."[11] They recalled nostalgically climbing May Hill

> with its dish-cover shape and clump of firs on top and the widest view in the West Midland for all its mere thousand feet, the bread and cheese [they] used to eat in the tiny pub at its foot, the walk in the Leadon Valley by the Ketford Mill . . . and the unusual flowers of that valley, the Ladies Tresses, the Little Teasel, the Spreading Campanula, loveliest of harebells, and the queer things that grew in the salt springs that burst out of the Leadon.

During these walks, Haines was astounded by the ease with which Robert and his children "jerked stones across to the further bank."[12]

From early July 1914 and their first chance encounter near Little Iddens,

Robert felt comfortable with his botanizing friend: "I don't believe I had one uneasy moment with you the other day," he wrote Jack Haines in Gloucester. "I should think you were the kind of person I could ask over here to sprawl—not call. I object to callers more and more in my old age. In my wife's present state of health I have to do some of the meals (so to call them), but you won't mind that will you? And you will overlook some other things if we can laze and talk for a day. . . . When are you going to ask me to Gloucester to meet your wife?"[13] Jack and his wife, Dorothy, would become the link, in correspondence and in person, between all the poets and their families; their son, Robin, would help maintain those important contacts over the years.

The American poet, during his and his family's brief stay in the Ryton/Dymock area, would leave an indelible impression on his English friends, recalled in later years.

Jack Haines would remember Robert as "a very fine looking man indeed," with a splendid physique, especially broad shoulders, and extremely penetrating jade blue eyes. Cheerful, with a usually kindly sense of humor that pervaded all his talk, he "liked occasional long silences and especially late at night enjoyed giving long, slow soliloquies on psychological and philosophical subjects."[14] Edward Thomas's wife, Helen, spoke of Robert's "clear blue" eyes and "rugged and lined" face, his rustic, earth-stained clothing, and his "slight American accent."[15] But Eleanor Farjeon's recollection is, I believe, more sensitive to the complexity of her subject:

> I think Robert had always taken life as it came where he found it. It had never succeeded in binding him to a routine job. . . . Whatever he did he made worth doing by the reality he carried within him, in his brains and in his hands. I remember his figure as middle-sized and compact, his manner friendly and undemonstrative; he looked at you directly, his talk was shrewd and speculative, withholding nothing and derived from nobody but himself. His New England speech came readily and leisurely, and of all the writers of worth whom I had met he spoke with the least sophistication. He was unhurried in all he said and did, an attitude reflected in his answer to my question "Is there time for it?": "There's all the time there is."[16]

Like many others, Lascelles Abercrombie's wife, Catherine, would remember Robert Frost the conversationalist: "He had the most marvellous way of talking—he could talk and talk and talk, and people would sit absorbed because everything he said seemed to be extremely valuable. . . . And you couldn't have had a nicer man, or more pleasant, gentle, humane man than Robert Frost."[17]

Besides the Gibsons and the Abercrombies, whom the Frosts had met in London, Edward Thomas and his family—Helen and their three children, Merfyn, Bronwen, and Myfanwy—soon made their way to Little Iddens. And Eleanor Farjeon would join them later in the summer.

For Robert, having shed much of his shyness and finding himself for the first time confident and at ease among equals, the days and long evenings that spring and summer of 1914 were absorbed in seemingly endless hours of walking and talking—about Nature and the nature of poetry. Elinor, who shared her husband's excitement at the proximity of so many writers and their families, wrote her sister Leona:

> Wilfrid Gibson and his wife live about a mile from us and Abercrombie and his wife and two children are three miles away. We see them all often. We have had quite a little company since we came, and some friends from near London have been down and taken lodgings near us. Edward Thomas, who is a very well known critic and prose writer has been here with his two children and he is going to bring the whole family to lodge near us in August. Rob and I think everything of him. He is quite the most admirable and lovable man we have ever known.

At the same time, Elinor, unlike Robert, was feeling the strain from the recent move from Beaconsfield and the adjustment to the sheer number of callers: "I have been feeling quite worn out," she confided to Leona. "The household and teaching and the excitement of meeting so many people constantly, has been almost too much for me. Three weeks ago I felt that I was on the edge of complete nervous prostration, but I pulled out of it and am feeling considerably better now."[18]

Robert had met Edward Thomas the previous October, and he was instantly taken by the thirty-five-year-old writer.[19] Although Edward's parents were Londoners, and Edward was born there in 1878, the family was from Wales, with a trace of Spanish blood. One of six sons of a civil servant, Edward, from childhood, preferred the study of nature to attending school. A frequent visitor in the home of the critic James Ashcroft Noble, who encouraged him as a writer, Edward soon fell in love with Noble's daughter Helen, whom he married in June 1899. A year later, having graduated from Oxford, he chose to become a writer.

With the birth of their son, Merfyn, in January 1900, and their first daughter, Bronwen, in October 1902, life for the young Thomas couple was full of hardship. They determined to live in the country, which they both loved, but Edward made frequent trips to London to find work as a literary reviewer, and he took long hikes on foot and by bicycle in search of material for his books on nature. By 1906, after frequent moves, the family was settled in Steep, in the district around Petersfield (Hampshire), and close to the Bedales School. Helen supplemented their meager income by teaching in the kindergarten and accepting school boarders during the vacations. A second daughter, Myfanwy, was born in August 1910.

By 1913, when he met Robert, Edward Thomas was a moderately successful reviewer, biographer, and writer of books on the English countryside. Twelve books were in print, including biographies of Richard Jefferies, George Borrow, Maurice Maeterlinck, and Swinburne, as well as several volumes based on his direct observations, such as *The Heart of England* and *The South Country.* Even before they met, Edward had made a number of literary friends. He had helped W. H. Davies publish his *Autobiography of a Super-Tramp;* he was a close companion of Walter de la Mare; and he had only recently met Eleanor Farjeon, who became a devoted friend and family intimate. At the time Ralph Hodgson introduced him to Robert, in October 1913, Edward was doing the fieldwork for *In Pursuit of Spring,* had begun *Keats* and *Four-and-Twenty Blackbirds* (a collection of proverbs), and was planning his autobiography, *The Childhood of Edward Thomas.* He continued his restless roaming of the countryside in lonely solitude, spending long periods in Wales, or visiting friends like Clifford Bax and Vivian Locke Ellis. He suffered from debilitating bouts of nervous exhaustion and depression; his outbursts of irritability increased the strain on his marriage, adding to these periods of despair and self-loathing.

Others have written about the importance, in both personal and literary terms, of the intense friendship that formed between Robert Frost and Edward Thomas.[20] As I discovered, their relations surface as a compelling leitmotiv through the lives of the Frosts and their friends in poetry, throughout 1914, in the years until Edward's death in 1917, and in the ache of memory.

There were significant parallels in their lives and, as Robert pointed out, what they had in common they had before they were born. Both men had fallen in love at a young age and consummated their marriages secretly before taking formal vows. Both their wives willingly and uncomplainingly accepted their husbands' choice of a literary career and its inherent deprivations, which would last for both men into middle age. And both men were passionate in their preferences. At the time of their meeting, however, there were noticeable differences—differences that permitted Robert to help bring out the very best and loveliest in his friend. Elinor, frailer and more subdued than Helen, had learned to handle her husband's fluctuating moods and periods of self-doubt, and Robert's single-mindedness of purpose and natural gregariousness contrasted with Edward's deep melancholia and indecision, exacerbated by his being dragged down by the often unrewarded work as a commissioned writer of prose. As Catherine Abercrombie pointed out, "It was only when Robert encouraged [Thomas] to turn to writing poetry that he became happy in the delight of his new-found powers."[21] R. George Thomas, editor and biographer of Edward Thomas, accurately summarizes the importance for poetry of their meeting:

Nothing can take away from Robert Frost the credit for pushing Edward Thomas into the writing of verse. In the spring of 1914 Frost pointed out to Thomas that much of the prose in his travel book *In Pursuit of Spring* (1914) was essentially the raw material of poetry. Thomas stated unequivocally in a letter that Frost was the "onlie begetter" of his verse and Frost wrote privately in 1921 that "there's a story going round that might lead you to exaggerate our debt to each other. . . . I made him see that he owed it to himself and the poetry to have it out by himself in poetic form where it must suffer itself to be admired. . . . The accent is absolutely his own. You can hear it everywhere in his prose, where if he had left it, however, it would have been lost." This is a true record that matches everything we can know from those who saw the rapidly ripening friendship between the two writers between October 1913 when they first met and February 1915 when they last met at Steep before Frost sailed for America (with Merfyn, Edward's son). By this date Thomas had written his first thirty-three poems in three months. It was like the bursting of a long pent-up dam.[22]

But I get ahead of myself. When the two men met, Edward was living apart from his family, struggling with his seeming inability to return Helen's love in its full radiance. His sense of inadequacy—and a deeply felt desire to express honestly his peculiar love, but love nonetheless—resulted in the powerfully compressed verses in "No one so much as you":

> I at the most accept
> Your love, regretting
> That is all: I have kept
> A helpless fretting
> That I could not return
> All that you gave
> And could not ever burn
> With the love you have,
>
> Till sometimes it did seem
> Better it were
> Never to see you more
> Than linger here
> With only gratitude
> Instead of love—
> A pine in solitude
> Cradling a dove.[23]

Robert viewed Helen and Edward Thomas as opposites, she "the vigorous type, always effusive about everything," he "quiet and modest and undemonstrative; but like still water there was nothing shallow about him." He thought Edward couldn't abide Helen's "taking on over him all the time."[24] Under Robert's empathetic but firm guidance, his friend for the time being put aside his torturing self-doubts and moved back with his wife and three children.

Among the poems that flowed from the reconciled husband and father were his "Household Poems." The first, for his daughter Bronwen:

> If I should ever by chance grow rich
> I'll buy Codham, Cockridden, and Childerditch,
> Roses, Pyrgo, and Lapwater,
> And let them all to my elder daughter . . .

The second, for his son, Merfyn:

> If I were to own this countryside
> As far as a man in a day could ride,
> And the Tyes were mine for giving or letting,—
> . . . I would give them all to my son . . .

The third, for little Myfanwy:

> What shall I give my daughter the younger
> More than will keep her from cold and hunger?
> I shall not give her anything . . .
> But leave her Steep and her own world . . .

In another poem, "Snow," we are told that the child "crying for the bird of the snow" is also Myfanwy. The last of the "Household Poems" is for Helen, whom Edward longed to please:

> And you, Helen, what should I give you?
> So many things I would give you
> Had I an infinite great store
> Offered me and I stood before
> To choose. I would give you youth,
> All kinds of loveliness and truth,
> A clear eye as good as mine,
> Lands, waters, flowers, wine,
> As many children as your heart
> Might wish for, a far better art
> Than mine can be, all you have lost
> Upon the travelling waters tossed,
> Or given to me. If I could choose
> Freely in that great treasure-house
> Anything from any shelf,

> I would give you back yourself,
> And power to discriminate
> What you want and want it not too late,
> Many fair days free from care
> And heart to enjoy both foul and fair,
> And myself, too, if I could find
> Where it lay hidden and it proved kind.[25]

Edward was not at all sure he could find where it lay hidden or that it would prove kind. Closer now to his family, he composed "When we two walked," about a walk with his wife in Lent: "And we that were wise live free / To recall our happiness then."[26] Eleanor Farjeon would declare, "In those days of the king-fisher, before the breaking of the storm, Edward had more calm and happy spells with Helen and the children than he had had for a long time."[27]

Edward Thomas had visited the Frosts at The Bungalow in Beaconsfield in late March, in April, and again for a few days in June, 1914, shortly after the Frosts moved into Little Iddens. As the bond of affection grew, they made plans to bring the two families together in August. Edward and Merfyn bicycled from Steep to Little Iddens, where they were joined on August 4 by Helen, accompanied by Bronwen and Myfanwy, as well as a Russian boy from the Bedales School named Peter Mrosovsky, who was spending the holidays with the Thomases. The Thomases and their guest settled at Oldfields, a farmhouse that stood among large orchards of choice dessert plums no more than a quarter of a mile across the fields from the Frosts at Little Iddens.

Recognized as an important critic of the Georgian poets, Edward Thomas was welcomed by the four poets who were hard at work at The Gallows putting together *New Numbers,* a short-lived spin-off from Marsh's *Georgian Poetry.* Catherine and Lascelles Abercrombie had been successful in printing two of Lascelles's longer poems, "Mary and the Bramble" and "The Sale of St. Thomas," and selling them by post. Their experience joined with an earlier scheme of Gibson's to bring out a series of little books of verse similar to "The Shilling Garland" and calling it the "New Shilling Garland." Rupert Brooke and John Drinkwater were invited to collaborate in the magazine, which they renamed *New Numbers,* and agreed to publish four times a year (at 2*s.* 6*d.* a number) by subscription.

Harold Monro at the Poetry Bookshop was furious at these developments, accusing Gibson of marrying his secretary, Geraldine Townshend, and going off into the countryside with the express intention to publish what he viewed as a competing publication with *Poetry and Drama.*

Once undertaken, however, the quarterly was produced with surprising harmony and provided a communal focus for the poets' activities. Because most of the work—of formatting, publishing, and distributing—devolved to Catherine Abercrombie, and the contributors were often slow to submit their manuscripts, the first issue, delayed several times, wasn't printed until February 1914; the second appeared in April, the month the Frosts arrived. Robert had not been invited to contribute to *Georgian Poetry* I or II, and no effort was made to include him in *New Numbers*. As the war approached during those slow summer months, *New Numbers* 3 was being assembled; the issue wasn't ready for distribution until October, by which time the start of the war had made its contents seem frivolous. The fourth and final number, containing Brooke's impassioned *1914* sonnets, was not fully assembled until February 1915.

In late June and again in July, returning from his Pacific travels, Rupert Brooke paid two flying visits to the home of W. W. Gibson at The Old Nailshop at Greenway, where he took a belated part in assembling the quarterly and harvested images of the English countryside for his journey to the Dardenelles and his final resting place in the Aegean Sea on the Island of Skyros. Unlike the others, he was preoccupied with the imminence of war and what it would mean.

For the moment, however, the small community of poets gathered at Ryton/ Dymock in the Gloucester countryside savored its last pleasures, as Gibson would recall years later in "The Golden Room":

> Do you remember the still summer evening
> When, in our cosy, cream-washed living room
> Of the Old Nailshop, we all talked and laughed—
> Our neighbours from The Gallows, Catherine
> And Lascelles Abercrombie; Rupert Brooke;
> Elinor and Robert Frost, living awhile
> At Little Iddens, who'd brought with them
> Helen and Edward Thomas? In the lamplight
> We talked and laughed, but for the most part listened
> While Robert Frost kept on and on and on
> In his slow New England fashion for our delight,
> Holding us with shrewed turns and racy quips
> And the rare twinkle of his grave blue eyes?
>
> We sat there in the lamplight, while the day
> Died from rose-latticed casements, and the plovers
> Called over the low meadows, till the owls
> Answered them from the elms, we sat and talked—
> Now a quick flash from Abercrombie, now
> A murmured dry half-heard aside from Thomas,
> Now a clear laughing word from Brooke; and then
> Again Frost's rich and ripe philosophy

That had the body and tang of good draught cider
And poured as clear a stream.
>'Twas in July
Of nineteen-fourteen that we sat and talked;
Then August brought the war and scattered us.[28]

"It has been a strange life over here more on account of the people I have seen than the places," Robert confided to Ernest Silver at the time.[29] By way of illustration, he mentioned the Welch poet W. H. Davies, who showed up that spring and summer in Ledington, where he stayed with the Gibsons at The Old Nailshop. Robert and Edward Thomas looked askance at both Davies and Gibson, whom they often went the mile or so on foot to visit at The Greenway. "But sometimes Mrs. Gibson would not invite them in," Helen Thomas remembered, "as her husband was in the throes of some long poem and must not be disturbed. This evoked in Edward and Robert an attitude of faintly contemptuous ridicule. Behind this lay a little honest jealousy, for Gibson was at this time a very successful poet whose work was eagerly accepted by the American magazines and highly paid. . . . On the whole however the relationship between the poets was friendly enough," as we have seen it commemorated in "The Golden Room."[30]

Helen Thomas shared her husband's disdainful view of Wilfrid Gibson, whom she characterized as "very small and mean" in a letter to Robert written shortly before Edward's death.[31] The fact that Wilfrid had by then been rejected for military service and was enjoying a lucrative tour in the states may have colored her assessment. Robert, too, was undoubtedly influenced by Edward's critical opinion of Gibson as poet. As early as 1906, Edward wrote that "Wilfrid Wilson Gibson long ago swamped his small delightful gift by his abundance. He is essentially a minor poet in the bad sense, for he is continually treating subjects poetically, writing about things instead of creating them."[32] Of his later verse narratives, which had attracted Robert initially when they met in London, Edward opined that Gibson "has merely been embellishing what would have been far more effective as pieces of rough prose. . . . The verse has added nothing except unreality, not even brevity." That August, while visiting Robert in Ledington, Edward complained to Gordon Bottomley that he had seen too much of Gibson and too little of Abercrombie, whom he seems to have liked. By October, Robert was voicing his own criticism of Gibson, after receiving a copy of Gibson's latest book, *Borderlands:* "You know what I think of Gibson in this phase. He is rather below the form of *Fires.*"[33]

The poet W. H. Davies had lost a leg under a freight train in America during the six years he wandered as a common tramp; he survived to publish, with assists from established writers like George Bernard Shaw and Joseph Conrad, his *Auto-biography of a Super-Tramp*. His poems made their way into the Victorian anthologies, earning him a pension from the British Government and the adulation of the literary elite. When Robert met him in London, Davies was making the rounds of the literary gathering places. He added a colorful, if rowdy, touch to the gatherings, during which, according to Robert, Davies liked to boast of being the "heir apparent to the Laureateship" after Bridges.

When Davies showed up in the country, both the Frosts and the Gibsons were put off by his lewd behavior and by his inflated ego: "But his conceit is enough to make you misjudge him—simply asinine," Robert complained to Sidney Cox. "We have had a good deal of him at the house for the last week and the things he has said for us to remember him by! He entirely disgusted the Gibsons with whom he was visiting. His is the kind of egotism another man's egotism can't put up with."[34]

Davies had won a reputation as a nature poet, and considered himself an expert on birds: "He set about encouraging Lesley to write about nature," Robert wrote. "It would be good practice for a child. . . . Lesley is old enough to have to struggle to keep a straight face in such circumstances. There now, he said, see that little bird, that little green one, I wonder what kind he is. Says Lesley It's a sparrow and it isn't green, is it? And Davies stumped into the house." This incident provoked in Lesley's father an outburst of paternal pride: "Lesley will hardly be one of the children much longer. She is as tall as her mother and reads a decent paragraph of Caesar off without looking up more than a couple of words. Sometimes too she does a paragraph of English writing I admire."[35] His friend from Edinburgh would have applauded Robert's assessment of his eldest daughter's literary talents.

And so there were get-togethers in each other's cottages—sometimes at The Gallows, sometimes at The Old Nailshop, sometimes at Little Iddens—during those months of late spring and summer 1914. Catherine would remember those carefree days at The Gallows, where she

> had a permanent gipsy-tent under the 'seven sisters' as our elms were called, and sometimes I would have an iron pot over a fire with a duck and green peas stewing in it, and Lascelles, John Drinkwater, and Wilfrid Gibson would sit round and read their latest poems to each other, as I lay on a stoop of hay and listened, and watched the stars wander through the elms, and thought I had really found the why and the wherefore of life. The Great Wars had not started then and one's mind could peacefully rest on loveliness and hopefulness as never again after 1914.[36]

Jack Haines, Eleanor Farjeon, and Helen Thomas would record their impressions of the gatherings at Little Iddens. They pictured Robert and Edward Thomas sitting under the trees in the Little Iddens orchard and Robert reading poems that would be published back in America (in *Mountain Interval*): "Birches," "Putting in the Seed," "Hyla Brook," "The Exposed Nest," and "The Sound of Trees," the latter written for Lascelles Abercrombie, thinking of the clump of tall elms close to The Gallows "but with an ear for trees known to him as a child in America."[37]

Then would come the long evenings listening to Robert speak: "To listen to Robert Frost on poetry, his own and that of others, was a perpetual joy to me," Haines wrote,

> Then came the long evening, especially when seated after a long walk, in the quiet of the cottage, he would sit up to the small hours of the morning pouring forth his views in a steady stream of unforgettable eloquence; for, just as his verse, as was his boast, had in it all the conversational tones of natural speech, so had his actual speech the unmistakable ring of poetry and the knowledge of, and the power to create the beauty that can be wrought from words was at the core of his spiritual being, so that he could never either write or talk seriously save in the tones and cadences of a poet.[38]

Imagine how the Frost children must have responded to their parents and other poets' talks-walking through those slow, lazy months of summer! Participating in the literary adventure of their elders, the children moved ahead with their writing and drawing projects—having completed for Mama and Papa while in England their collective "An Important Year," Irma's "Many Storys," Carol's "Our Old Farm," and Lesley's "On the Road to Fleuraclea." Their efforts to assemble and "publish" *The Bouquet,* the little magazine started at The Bungalow in Beaconsfield, must have seemed as entertaining as they were appreciated. There were also the family picnics at one house or the other, in the woods, or down on the lovely, tree-shaded banks of the river Leadon (where the Haineses would watch RF and the children skip stones across the water).

The children were warmly received by Jack and Dorothy Haines in their home in Gloucester during the summer and fall 1914. The Haineses found Elinor and the children

> quite charming and very easy to get on with. They were most interested in everything we told them. Lesley at 15 was nearly grown up and well educated and very handsome. I fancy she read a great deal. The youngest girl (Marjorie) was very quiet and shy. Irma and Carol were most delightful children, very talkative and lively. Irma looked fragile but was lively enough and was the one who asked the most questions about everything. She was the most American of the four, I thought, but Carol might have been an English boy except for his ability to "jerk" stones across the little River Leadon, at which he licked me hollow, as at least one of the

girls; and R.F. himself was prodigious at it. . . . I did not find the family at all given to sickness.[39]

The Frosts were strapped for money and did little "running around"; but, as Haines recalled, now and again they came up to Gloucester to see the beautiful Norman Cathedral and other sights: "Once the whole family came over for a day to visit the Barton Fair at the end of September [1914], and Elinor and the children had tea with us at St. Helens, and Robert too, I think. Tea was not a meal they were used to at our early hour and they were a bit puzzled over its being celebrated as a somewhat heavy meal."[40]

In her memoirs, *The Last Four Years,* Eleanor Farjeon describes in sentimentally exuberant detail the goings-on of that idyllic interlude before the war broke. Her grandfather was the American actor Joe Jefferson, and Robert had seen him perform when he was a little boy of eight. She had gotten to know the Thomases the previous year, and she was invited to join the covey of poets at Ledington during the August holidays. The Thomases found her rooms at Glyn Iddens, home of the Farmers, which stood on a lane between the Chandlers' farm, Oldfields, rented by the Thomases, and Little Iddens, "the simple cottage higher up which was occupied by the Frosts." Mrs. Farmer "had stepped out of a chapter by George Eliot, her husband out of another by Thomas Hardy," Eleanor wrote, and the house and its mistress exuded "the dingy character one might meet in a mid-Victorian novel."[41] The fruit was of first quality, and there was an unlimited supply of rough home-brewed cider in the cellar.

Helen Thomas would bring her youngest child, Baba (Myfanwy), up to the Frosts, Eleanor Farjeon remembers, "where the air was serenest, and over an alfresco tea Robert and Edward pursued what seemed to be an endless duologue on the nature of poetry." The duet became a trio when Eleanor joined Robert and Edward in a stroll along the lanes, Robert talking about the "cadence" of the human voice, his theory illustrated by a farmer pitching corn or manure across the hedges, whose shouts were understandable without being able to hear words. Or they would join the others and go on a "sumptuous picnic in the woods" with the Gibsons and the Abercrombies.[42] "My chief picture of the picnic," Eleanor recalled, was of the "contrast between them, Abercrombie sprawling at ease and talking freely as he ate, and Gibson, shy and reserved, acting the host as circumspectly as if sitting at a damask tablecloth."

Eleanor Farjeon, who was residing near the Frosts at Glyn Iddens, provides us with an amusing account of a dinner prepared by her host, Mrs. Farmer, to which the Frosts, the Thomases, the Gibsons and the Abercrombies were all invited: "The table was loaded with huge shapes of food, a ham, a great joint of beef, a raised pie and birds, among dishes of butter and pickles and salads, and sauce-boats of dressing, and slabs of home-made bread. If ever a sideboard groaned that sideboard did, with fruit-tarts and trifles and cheesecakes, and at least two flagons of my favourite rough cider." The dinner proceeded with great gaiety to its inebriated conclusion: "Two brace of poets staggered out into the moonlight and went hilariously homeward like two sets of Siamese Twins. I have boasted ever since of the night when I drank all the poets of Gloucestershire under the table."[43]

Like the others, Eleanor Farjeon was sensitive to the meager existence of the Frost family, their financial difficulties having followed them from Beaconsfield. While the laborer's cottage was humble, "it sufficed to accomodate Robert and Elinor and their four children. They were poor, and indifferent to the conditions of poverty." She noted, as had Ernest Silver in Plymouth, that "the Frosts did not live by the clock, their clock conformed to the Frosts. . . . Meals (bedtimes too, I believe) were when you felt like them." Eleanor's memoir describes in rich detail their haphazard family life:

Irregular hours for children meant an extension of experience for them; it was more important for a child to go for a walk in the dark than to have an unbroken night's rest. By day, walks and talks were not shortened for the sake of things less interesting. When the children were hungry enough to be more interested in eating than in what they were doing, they came indoors and helped themselves to food that was left available in the small pink-washed living-room: bread, fruit, cold rice in a bowl. I wonder if memory misleads me here; this is the general impression left on me after forty years. Elinor Frost, fragile and weariable, was not the naturally joyful housewife that Helen was, the home-maker who bustled from job to job on a breath of laughter, whose hearth glowed from her own warm centre; the centre of the Frosts was out-of-doors, and household standards mattered little. If they had, Elinor struck me as too delicate to cope with them, indeed, none of the family seemed especially robust; but though they were pale-complexioned, they were lively and active, and too resourceful to be at a loose end. My dear Thomas children seemed lethargic by comparison, less easily interested and sooner bored. Time hung most heavily on the Russian boy's [Peter's] unenergetic hands, and his more adult outlook (as Edward had suggested in a letter) affected Merfyn. I could not imagine either of them betaking themselves, like Carol Frost, to pick Mrs. Farmer's fruit with tireless care from morning to night, for sheer love of doing it. Small wonder he was Mrs. Farmer's favourite. She entrusted to him her finest Pearmains and Jefferson Gages for the city markets, and gave him good snacks in her kitchen, so that he need not go home for his handful of cold rice. In his absorption Carol seemed to be the very embodiment of Robert's apple-picking poem ["After Apple-Picking"]. He came second to Lesley, a tall girl of noble promise, her mother's chief stand-by in the domestic chores. The two younger girls [Irma and Marjorie] were generally occupied with something. Life, materially meagre, satisfied these children. The American strain inherited from my mother put me quickly at ease with them, and much of my day was spent in sharing their explorations, in the games we devised among us, the fruit-harvesting, and the picnic meals at one house or the other.[44]

On one occasion, in Eleanor Farjeon's account, Robert oversaw a communal undertaking in digging up the Little Iddens potato patch. "Even Carol deserted his pears and plums for awhile, and dug his potato-hill as indefatigably as he had gathered nectarines." That "blazing afternoon turning to twilight in the potato-field, with the welcome drinks [of tea], the bodily toil and ease of spirit, and Edward playing labourer to Robert's boss" left an indelible impression on Eleanor. "The pleasure sprang from Edward's relaxation in Robert's company. The humour of the two friends was in perfect accord."[45]

The accord between these two friends permeated the activities of all the poets and their families that summer. For Edward, as he wrote Robert in America, he would remember those happy days in and around Little Iddens: "But Ledington, my dear Robert, in April, in June, in August."[46] And he would commemorate their "easy hours" together, when rumors of the war were still remote, in his lovely poem "The Sun Used to Shine":

> The sun used to shine while we two walked
> Slowly together, paused and started
> Again, and sometimes mused, sometimes talked
> As either pleased, and cheerfully parted
>
> Each night. We never disagreed
> Which gate to rest on. The to be
> And the late past we gave small heed.
> We turned from men or poetry
> To rumours of the war remote
> Only till both stood disinclined
> For aught but the yellow flavorous coat
> Of an apple wasps had undermined;
>
> Or a sentry of dark betonies,
> The stateliest of small flowers on earth,
> At the forest verge; or crocuses
> Pale purple as if they had their birth
>
> In sunless Hades fields. The war
> Came back to mind with the moonrise
> Which soldiers in the east afar
> Beheld then. Nevertheless, our eyes
>
> Could as well imagine the Crusades
> Or Caesar's battles. Everything

To faintness like those rumours fades—
Like the brook's water glittering

Under the moonlight—like those walks
Now—like us two that took them, and
The fallen apples, all the talks
And silences—like memory's sand

When the tide covers it late or soon,
And other men through other flowers
In those fields under the same moon
Go talking and have easy hours.[47]

The tensions that would develop between Helen Thomas and Robert were not yet apparent; but Helen later observed that Edward was closer to Robert than she was. Stricken by grief when her husband was killed in the war, she found relief in the writing of her memoirs, *As It Was* (1926) and *World without End* (1931), in which she describes the happy, intimate moments of her troubled marriage. Robert and Elinor both found embarrassing such revelations about Edward, a private and somewhat puritanical man, whose memory they hoped to preserve and protect.[48]

By the time Helen Thomas wrote her memoirs, as she readily conceded, Elinor and the children were only a vague memory; she was commenting on the family activities at a time when the Frosts were enjoying a summer holiday—virtually camping out and keeping irregular hours. "Elinor Frost," Helen wrote somewhat condescendingly in 1926, "had a rather nebulous personality and had none of the physical strength or activity of her husband. Housekeeping to her was a very haphazard affair and I remember that when dinner time approached in the middle of the day, she would take a bucket of potatoes into the field and sit on the grass to peel them—without water to my astonishment—and that, as far as I could see, was often the only preparation for a meal." She would recognize, however, how congenial her husband and Robert were to each other. "They were always together," she remembered, "and when not exploring the country, they sat in the shade of a tree smoking and talking endlessly of literature and poetry in particular. When it was wet we all assembled in the Frosts' cottage; and as there were only two chairs in the living room we sat on the floor with our backs against the wall, talking or singing folk songs in which of course the children joined."[49] There were word games, charades, readings of prose and verse, cards, and the inevitable singing of catches and ballads at which Thomas excelled with his light baritone voice. Cider and country food helped things along.[50]

My mother would recall that same voice in her college eulogy to Edward

Thomas she entitled "How Sleep the Brave" after William Collins's poem, with
its reference to fairies:

> By fairy hands their knell is rung;
> By forms unseen their dirge is sung;
> There Honour comes, a pilgrim grey,
> To bless the turf that wraps their clay . . .

Lesley had been first struck by Edward's

> keenly intellectual and melancholy face and the deep, sad, blue eyes, the blue one
> sees so much among his native hills of Wales. He had a wonderful passionate voice
> and would sing his Welsh songs all evening sitting before the open fire and gazing
> into the hollows of red coals. He was unassuming, though at times he had a quiet
> resistless anger that fairly took one's breath away while perhaps he never said a
> word. He loved nature, and loneliness, and there was scarcely a road from Cornwall
> to Northumberland, whether it ended in a dooryard or was one of the Roman roads,
> that he had not set foot upon. He dreaded all contact with pain and suffering that
> could in no way be helped and he was very patient and very sensitive to every
> kindness.[51]

Lesley and the other children helped bring RF and Edward, and their mutual
love of poetry, into their magazine, *The Bouquet,* by expanding the contributors to
the Thomases and other friends of the family. *The Bouquet,* as we shall see, both
enhanced and reflected the changing mood of its participants, from the summer
idyll at Ryton/Dymock and Ledington, to The Gallows and the onset of war, and
back to Franconia and the resumption of life on a New England farm.

7

The Children as Journalists
The Bouquet *and Other Writings*

*F*riends in England remarked on the resourcefulness of the Frost children despite seeming deprivations and the normal problems of adjustment that accompany travels far from home. Undaunted by the often difficult physical circumstances of their stay in The Bungalow and Little Iddens, and nurtured by their parents in their role as teachers, Lesley and her sisters and brother continued to find writing projects that built on the early journals kept while in Derry. Besides Irma's "Many Storys" (Christmas 1912), Carol's "Our Old Farm" (Christmas 1913), Lesley's "On the Road to Fleuraclea" (Christmas 1913), and the collective effort of "An Important Year," there may have been individual "working" composition books, other than Lesley's two working notebooks from this period, that are lost. Looking only at the collection of writings by the four Frost children available to us, the output is impressive.

The crowning achievement, however, was *The Bouquet,* an in-house magazine to which the four Frost children and chosen friends (and several parents) contributed. Lesley had initiated the project in the summerhouse in Beaconsfield, to be continued at Little Iddens and briefly in Franconia; it was she who would type and assemble the little magazine, a single copy of which was to be issued monthly, with stories, poems, essays, and illustrations by the invited contributors. The finished copy would then be circulated to the "subscribing" families, which included the Thomases, Gardners, Mairs, and Smiths. Producing *The Bouquet* was an ambitious undertaking—more so than Louisa May Alcott's *Pickwick Portfolio.* It would bridge the Frost family's stay in Beaconsfield and Ryton/Dymock, in England, and Franconia, New Hampshire, in America, and it would bring together in a common enterprise the different literary families who had befriended the American poet.

The journalistic efforts of these young people reflect their (and their parents') joyous and adventuresome response to their somewhat isolated existence; they reflect, as well, the at-home education by poetry that would become an important part of the Frost family's heritage. The children had been exposed since an early age to the sound of literature emanating from the lips of their loving parents, an exposure that would add to the depth and originality of both generations of writers. The personalities that emerge from the pages of the notebooks and the little magazine, uncomplicated and devoid of cynicism, yet rich in emotional texture and artistic development, give no hint of the troubles that would beset these children as adults. Unless we are prepared retroactively to interpret their intuitiveness and natural wonder as a lack of preparedness for life's hard knocks— a fair enough interpretation in retrospect—we can only marvel at the display of talent and inventiveness of the Frost children and their friends, and experience with them the spontaneous delight in their surroundings. Despite future tragedies in the Frost family, the invitation contained in such poems as "The Pasture," "A Prayer in Spring," and "Carpe Diem," still stands.

No less important, in assessing these journalistic accomplishments is the mutual enrichment derived from their writings by the children, on the one hand, and Robert Frost (as both father and poet) and Edward Thomas (as friend and incipient poet), on the other.

Edward Thomas's lifelong interest in folktales and narratives written for children is evident in his *Celtic Stories* (1911), *Norse Tales* (1912), and *Four-and-Twenty Blackbirds* (1915). His poem "Lob," for example, is about a clown or mischievous Puck-like fairy, and he shared with Walter de la Mare (and, later, with his friend Robert Frost) an interest in appealing directly to young readers.[1]

The Thomases' youngest daughter, Myfanwy, remembers how her brother Merfyn "as a very small boy loved to sit on Edward's knee and be told stories or read aloud to, and often his father would read him poems and ballads with words and meaning that Merfyn couldn't understand, but he sat quiet and absorbed, watching his father's face." She recalls sitting astride her father's foot, with him holding her hands "and waving his leg up and down, higher and higher. . . . It was a particular pleasure to be on my father's knee," she wrote, "wrapped in a blanket after being bathed, while he sang in Welsh, or my favourite 'Oh father, father, come build me a boat,' or the sea shanties he had learned from Marston, one of the crew from Shackleton's Polar expedition."[2] De la Mare, like the others, reminds us, in his introduction to Edward's *Collected Poems* (1921), how Edward's "voice was low and gentle, but musical, with a curious sweetness and hollowness when he sang his old Welsh songs to his children."[3]

Now and then a poem of Robert Frost or Edward Thomas was included in *The*

Bouquet. In the notebook he carried in his pocket while in England, Robert had jotted: "Hollis said I could have all the brushwood I wanted to brush my peas,"[4] and an early version of his poem, "Pea Brush," was placed anonymously in the July 1914 issue:

Pea-sticks

I walked down alone Sunday after church
To the place where John has been cutting trees
To see for myself about the birch
He said I could have to bush my peas.

The clearing burned with the sunny day.
I dimmed my eyes and set my cap,
And forgetting I hadn't come to stay,
Drank the smell of the heated sap

With which the trunks of trees were wet.
I must go as soon as I have the time
And take what boughs I am going to set:
These things my garden peas will climb

Weren't helping anything growing wild:
There were trilliums bent down under some.
They had budded before the boughs were piled
So that those that were coming up had to come.

An early version of a second poem, "Locked Out," was included in the September 1914 issue of *The Bouquet:*

Locked Out

Always when we lock up at night
We lock the garden flowers outside
Cut off from even window light.
To think! - the night the door was tried
And brushed with buttons upon sleeves,
The flowers were out there with the thieves
Yet nobody molested them.
We did find one nasturtium
Upon the steps with bitten stem.
I always blamed myself for that:
I always thought it must have been
Some flower I played with as I sat
At dusk to watch the moon down early.

"Pea-sticks" (as "Pea Brush") and "Locked Out" (as "Locked Out, As told to a child") would appear in *Mountain Interval* (1916). Although both poems were contributed to *The Bouquet* anonymously, they were later signed by the poet as his.

Edward Thomas did not begin writing poetry until late November or early December 1914, so that the inclusion of his poems in *The Bouquet* represents a significant first step as a published poet. The three poems he contributed to *The Bouquet*—"The Combe," "Nettles" (later changed to "Tall Nettles"), and "October"—would eventually be collected with only slight variations. Edward had not yet adopted the pseudonym, Edward Eastaway, and he did not hide his identity in the children's magazine; "The Combe" was placed over his initials, *E. T.,* in the April [1915] issue, and "Nettles" over his name, *Edward Thomas,* in the June 1916 issue. The third poem, "October," accompanied a letter from Edward to Lesley (dated December 30, 1914), but the issue of *The Bouquet* in which it may have appeared is missing.[5]

Lesley had sent Edward Thomas a picture (drawn or painted by her) of The Gallows, which he told her in the letter he had hung over his table at Steep where he was working. The picture was part of a Christmas 1914 parcel from the Frosts. In his reply, Edward expressed the wish to join the Frosts at Ryton, but wrote that he would be tied up until mid-January; he planned to ride over on his bicycle when the weather permitted, so that he could do it in two days: "We wish you all a happy New Year in Gloucestershire and New Hampshire and wherever else you go," he wrote, "and I hope to share some of it with you." In a PS, he asked, "Would you care to put these anonymous lines in your next magazine? I never told you how much I liked your contribution in the last one I saw, and especially the sentence about the long grass by the fence, and how it looks as if it were asking you to return the compliment." (The reference, perhaps to a story in the September 1914 issue of *The Bouquet,* is unclear.)

Adult for her years, Lesley felt comfortable with Edward Thomas. He presented her with a 1912 edition of A. E. Housman's *A Shropshire Lad* (Grant Richards, publisher), inscribed "Lesley Frost from Edward Thomas," that I treasure among my papers. Lesley and Edward corresponded after the Frosts returned to America, and, as noted earlier, one of Lesley's college compositions eulogizes the English poet for his bravery and deeply poetic nature.

Lesley's black-covered working notebook, untitled and undated, contains several early drafts of what she later placed in *The Bouquet.* Her father has written on the notebook that internal evidence places it at Little Iddens, 1914. I would agree. Of particular interest is a two-page entry entitled "What a Swallow Is," that became "What a Swallow Must Be" in the July 1914 issue of *The Bouquet:*

I think somebody's bow and arrow must have flown away together. I never look at a swallow but what I think so. Some little child with a very tiny bow, like those I used to make for Marjorie out of the limbs of my large bow. I really think it must have been Marjorie who made the first swallow. She was probably down in the meadow below our farm, and laid the arrow on the bow so that it stuck, and they both flew off across the brook leaving her empty handed. Funny she never mentioned it! Anyway I advise you to try catching your arrow on the bow that way next time you have one. But do it when you are alone as Marjorie seems to have. Only *you* tell what the consequences are.

From this brief, but imaginative tale, its opening simile—"I think somebody's bow and arrow must have flown away together"—was one Lesley was proud and pleased to give to Edward Thomas when he asked for and later included it in his poem "Haymaking":

> While over them shrill shrieked in his fierce glee
> The swift with wings and tail as sharp and narrow
> As if the bow had flown off with the arrow.

Elizabeth Sergeant, in her Frost biography, while she seems to have been unaware of the notebook entry, nevertheless correctly attributes the source of the simile to Lesley, noting that Robert told her that Edward "asked if he might use this fine simile in a poem."[6]

Each issue of *The Bouquet,* besides featuring a mix of contributors, was designed for balance between original prose and verse pieces, on the one hand, and, on the other, visual elements that included a profusion of illustrations, puzzles or riddles, and advertisements.

The contents of the six surviving issues of *The Bouquet,* taken together with the other composition notebooks, present an extraordinary variety to the reader in terms of literary techniques and forms, journalistic devices, and the range of imaginative and real elements. Given the ages of the children who contributed to the magazine, there is little to comment on with regard to the relative success or failure of their compositions as literature; we must express amazement, however, at the maturity of their various writing projects. And, as we have seen, the children's efforts tell us a great deal about the family dynamics and the shared poetic experience of its members. The ongoing and almost constant exposure to each other's ideas, opinions, and artistic tastes—at a time when RF was in close contact with other poets—enriches the pages of the Frost children's journals and magazine while it helps us better to understand their father's poetic output during this critical period.

The body of compositions and artwork gathered by the Frost children and their friends while in England are remarkable, then, for the reflection in them of a sensitive and rich power of observation and imagination. Like their parents, the children were experimenting with various techniques for artistic effect; they were seeking to convey a range of emotional responses, sometimes exaggerated, but not to the point of destroying credibility. Psychological realism is evident in the treatment (often on a moral plane) of anger, fear, revenge, joy, laziness, curiosity. The fluctuating moods and feelings, and the tricks they play on the brain, are used knowingly by these young writers for suspense and excitement, for surprise and wonder.

There is a similar range of subject matter. The poems and stories display an intellectual curiosity about religion, astronomy, legend, history, and myth. They portray the idyllic countryside, rich in flora and fauna, on the one hand—ferns, flowers, birds, trees, rivers, and springs—and, on the other, a sense of the reality of their surroundings, whether in the rolling hills and fields of rural England or in the mountains of New Hampshire: mud, torn clothes, fright, being cold and wet, quarrels and teasing between siblings, the lack of money, and the onset of war.

As the mastermind of *The Bouquet,* Lesley came to her task with "a literary yardstick."[7] She had learned through her early composition writing at Derry, under her parents' guidance, "to put the thing seen, heard, or felt on paper in words that made our parents sit up and take notice." Well in advance of her sisters and brother, she had learned to compare, "to bring on metaphor," to differentiate character with "tones of voice," and to release the "imagination thing." Because the education by poetry—the reading, transcribing, and memorization of poems "that taught courage, honor, generosity, pity, discipline, beauty, love, and hatred of evil"—continued in England, the compositions the children prepared for their parents and for publication in *The Bouquet,* while grounded in direct observation, were in a real sense derivative. Lesley more than her siblings successfully wove observed details of the surrounding flora, fauna, and even the stars, together with the human nature no less observed, into stories and poems with often telling artifice and flair.

In five of the six issues that were preserved, it is also apparent that Lesley, as the "managing editor" of the enterprise and typist of the single copy, helped her sisters and brother in putting the final touches on their otherwise original compositions. Under her close scrutiny, all the contributors to the magazine were expected to achieve some degree of literary effect—with humor, telling psychological detail, or flights of pure fantasy.

Typing phonetically by the age of four, Lesley transcribed, on the family Blickensderfer brought from America, the manuscripts for her father's first two volumes, *A Boy's Will* and *North of Boston.* While at The Bungalow, she and the children used the summer- or greenhouse in the backyard for many of their games and writing projects. Before leaving Beaconsfield for London and then on to Little Iddens in Gloucestershire, they converted the greenhouse into the publishing house for *The Bouquet.*

In the September 1914 issue of the little magazine, Irma has provided us with a drawing of the summerhouse with an inscription, "this is where *The Bouquet* was published." It was here that Lesley began typing and assembling the magazine, with contributions from the four Frost children, two of the three Thomas children, Amy Smith, and two or three others. Lesley believed there were "14 or so" issues of *The Bouquet* in circulation, but only six are still in existence.[8] Because some of the "subscribers"—such as the Gardners and Mairs—may also have had selections in issues lost to us, the survey of name contributors must remain tentative.

Lesley had made friends with the Gardner, Mair, and Smith families in August 1913, and the idea for a magazine may have come from them rather than from Lesley's parents. The Frost children knew of the assembling of *New Numbers* at The Gallows—by the four Georgian poets Abercrombie, Drinkwater, Brooke, and Gibson—but there is nothing to suggest that the poets' in-house production prompted their own undertaking.

Lesley, you will recall, was familiar with Dickens and Alcott, and had been a regular reader of *The Youth's Companion* and *St. Nicholas,* illustrated magazines for young readers. Creating *The Bouquet* was a logical continuation and progression from the journals the Frost children kept in Derry and Plymouth; Lesley's organization of "An Important Year" and her own Christmas 1913 "On the Road to Fleuraclea," as well as Irma's "Many Storys" and Carol's "Our Old Farm," certainly opened the way to the more sophisticated and ambitious journalistic effort. Besides, as will become apparent, friends of Lesley's with whom she corresponded were engaged in similar literary activities.

From the letters that went back and forth between the young people and between their parents—while in England, and for a short time after settling back in Franconia, New Hampshire—we can reconstruct the manner in which *The Bouquet* was conceived and was subsequently expanded to include contributors from outside the Frost family.

The first surviving issue of *The Bouquet,* for June 1914, was begun at Beaconsfield, and it is improbable that any earlier issue was prepared there before the family moved further out into the country. Amy Smith, whom Lesley had known since the vacation at Kingsbarns, would become a frequent contributor; her letter thanking Lesley for inviting her to "join" the magazine, the name of which she still did not know, was dated June 23. Lesley seems also to have invited Edward Thomas's fourteen-year-old son, Merfyn, his nine-year-old sister, Bronwen, and their cousin Margaret Valon to join as contributors.

Margaret Noble Valon was the daughter of Helen Noble Thomas's younger sister, and, at the time, was attending a school in Chiswick (London). Edward and Helen Thomas decided to put their daughter Bronwen in the same school with her cousin Margaret for a term in the fall of 1914, in the hope that the gymnastics offered there might provide treatment for flat feet and a stoop that she had developed.[9]

Writing Lesley from Steep sometime in late spring, Merfyn Thomas was anticipating his family's holiday at Oldfields, just across from Little Iddens. "This sum I have sent you is to prove that if you take 45 from 45, 45 is left. Do send the magazine here for me to see when it is ready. We will have some fun when I come to stay with you. The term ends on the 28th of July I think. Daddy and I are going to ride on our bykes to Leadington. It will take three days." In his next letter, also undated, he apologizes for not returning the magazine earlier, "but I did not have time to read it. I think it is a great succese. . . . I enclosed the magazine [in all likelihood the June issue] and a story of a bicycle ride . . . for the July number." He hoped the weather—it was pouring rain at the time—would improve by August.

In a letter addressed to both Irma and Lesley from Chiswick, Bronwen thanked them "so much for sending the magazine [probably the June 1914 issue] and I also like the name of it. I expect you will have to put my story into the magazine in pieces, because it is rather long. You will find a picture in the middle of Margaret's story, and it belongs to the story. Thank you ever so much for your letters and post-cards." Margaret Valon's contribution, "Saved by an Indian" (with an illustration of Jim Bulling on his pony Prince), and Bronwen's piece "An Autobiography of a Wolf" (with a drawing copied from Rossetti), were included in their entirety, along with Merfyn's "A Bicycle Ride," in the July 1914 issue, which ran 53 pages (the longest of those surviving). Myfanwy, the youngest of the Thomas children, was too young to contribute.

It is apparent from these letters that the June 1914 issue of *The Bouquet* was, in fact, the first the Frost children assembled. Lesley indicated that the little magazine appeared monthly; therefore, we may surmise that the issues for August, October, November, and December 1914 are missing, as well as some from 1915 and 1916, after the Frosts returned to America and settled in Franconia, New Hampshire. We have, then, the issues for June, July, and September 1914; [January] and April 1915; and June 1916.[10]

The loss of the other issues is not surprising. A single copy was circulated among the "subscribers," such as Lesley's friends, the Smiths, Mairs, Gardners, and Thomases; more than one issue may have been sent at any one time or the "subscriber" may have accumulated more than one issue before passing them on. There are letters to suggest that, on at least one occasion, the Thomases and the

Smiths were slow in returning the issues Lesley had provided them. Similarly, what seems to be an issue of another in-house magazine, *The Rein* (No. 6, the so-called War number), produced by Lesley's friend Delphis Gardner and circulated to the Frosts and others, was never returned to Delphis, and today resides in the University of Virginia Library along with the six issues of *The Bouquet.*

As we know, while in England, Lesley, who turned fifteen on April 28, 1914, had already caught the eye of J. C. Smith, of Jack Haines, and of Eleanor Farjeon, as a young woman with great promise. And her father had openly praised her readings in Virgil and Caesar, as well as her compositions. From her Reynolds Road, Beaconsfield, red-covered notebook, 1912–1913, Lesley sent a copy of her story "The Valley of Mist" to the Smiths in Edinburgh. Writing to Robert in late January 1914, J. C. Smith commented on Lesley's story:

> You are not only a poet yourself but (unless I am mistaken) the father of one. I read Lesley's last affusion (as Wordsworth would call it) with the greatest interest. Scientifically, I'm afraid her theory wouldn't hold water; but her description succeeded in conveying with remarkable vividness the *feeling* of a water-logged valley—vegetation, everything soaked, . . . Yes, quite remarkable. Keep your eye on Lesley. . . . I am writing this on my knee as you may guess—with Edie deep in Paradise Lost, and Hope in Punch, and Amy upstairs embibing herself in oranges. My wife is at Newport with Anne. She (my wife) hasn't been well since Christmas.[11]

In another letter, sent to Franconia, his Scottish friend urged Robert to write what the public wants only in prose, but not in verse. In closing, he sent best wishes "to Mrs. Frost and the children. Tell Lesley to keep on writing—we look forward to her letters. Lesley wil be an ornament to American Literature one of these days. And perhaps I'll be there to see." Lesley's father had echoed these sentiments in writing Sidney Cox from England the previous year.[12] Eleanor Farjeon and Jack Haines had similarly observed Lesley's unusual maturity.

As had her father, Amy Smith became actively involved in the Frost family's literary activities. In their letters, begun shortly after the Frosts returned to Beaconsfield from Kingsbarns in late August 1913, she and Lesley exchanged poems and stories freely and shared opinions about their readings in English literature. Amy commended to her friend *Hamlet* and *The Land of Heart's Desire,* probably unaware that Yeats's play was frequently read aloud in the Frost household. In recommending to Amy that she read Henryk Sienkiewicz's *The Deluge* and *With Fire and Sword,* Lesley probably realized that the Polish trilogy was a favorite of her father's (dating back to 1894).

Characteristically, in her replies to Lesley's long letters, Amy sought literary effect, typically when describing a landscape or weather pattern:

We have been bathing a great deal lately. Today the sky was simply exquisitely blue, and the sea as calm and clear as a mirror, reflecting the drifting clouds and the blue sky. When you were in the water it looked like dull green glass, through which you could see the brown gleam of the sand, but from the shore the sea looked bright and blue, with little crisp sparkles of gold where the waves broke in the sunlight. Last night coming home from the farm the sky was very beautiful, all crimson and purple, fading into deep rose, and violet and gold, and salmon, and pale lemon colour fading into green. Just below I saw a boat coming into harbour and the setting sun glowed on the sails. It was lovely![13]

In one letter (dated 30 December), Amy praised two of Lesley's poems, "On the Road to Fleuraclea" and "The Far-Off Whistle."[14] Between November 5 and December 24, Lesley had assembled these and other poems and stories into a "book," "On the Road to Fleuraclea," which she dedicated to Papa for Christmas 1913. Amy took the opportunity to express her appreciation of Lesley's letters: "I wish I wrote as nice letters as you do!" She enclosed one of her own poems, "The Flint Arrow-Head," as well as a photo of her father, and promised to forward a story she was writing when it was finished. Her poem appeared in the July 1914 issue of *The Bouquet.*

Amy joins her father in commenting on Lesley's fanciful story "The Valley of Mist": "It was very kind of you to send it," she writes,

and I like and admire it greatly. Some parts are *very* delightful and interesting. I like especially the parts where you describe the sodden, yellow, water-logged trees and the strange flower that grew on the watery cliff. You will find my stories not at all like that, I am afraid. I am not so observant of the natural growth around us, and I have to make up the rest with imagination, which does a great deal of service. I will send you some of my stories soon, but they will not be type-written. How can you have the patience to type all those stories? It seems to take me such a long time![15]

Amy includes a description of a dream in which Lesley takes part:

I had a queer dream the other night. I dreamt that there was a great park composed entirely of grey, gravel paths, cold, bare, black flowerbeds, and chilly trees. In the middle of this was a perfectly round pond, with a rim of stone, and dark, icy water. In this pond our family and your family disported themselves, all in full dress with big, heavy coats on. I mean, all of us except you, for you stood on the edge, and asked me most puzzling questions. I remember that you and I talked together exactly as if we had met after a long time, and as if we had written to each other all the time, as we have really done. Afterwards we went to a bathing shed, and ate cold potatoes. It was rather ridiculous, wasn't it?[16]

Lesley and Amy gave themselves noms de plume, chosen from among the historical and literary figures that peopled their extensive reading, which they used occasionally in their imaginative letter writing. Amy's choice, Flora Macdonald, was a Jocobite heroine from the island of South Uist (Hebrides). In June 1746, Prince Charles Edward took refuge, after the battle of Culloden, in the Hebrides where Flora was living. Having helped the prince to escape (in a disguise as an Irish spinning maid, Betty Burke), she came under suspicion, was arrested, and briefly held in the Tower. Once left at liberty, Flora met and married Allen Macdonald, with whom she emigrated to America in 1773. Allen served the British government in the War of Independence, and was taken prisoner; Flora returned home in 1779.

From Beaconsfield, Lesley reported to Amy having met the great granddaughter of Flora Macdonald while in Edinburgh: "I only wish I could have been there to see her!" Amy replied.[17] Lesley had chosen "Hamish" as a pen name; perhaps one of her letters to Amy, unfortunately lost, might have helped explain the significance of her choice.

Here is an example of Amy's gibberish and tease:

> Now, Hamish, I *am* dense, so *don't* attempt to deny it! I mean I am not dense, 'not by no means,' so don't you try to say I am, Hamish, my boy. (How are the rheumatics just now?) Do you know, I was walking through the wood only tomorrow and as I went slowly along on my nose I looked up into the *very* trrree where you—I mean *I*—saw that pike. (I *did* see it first, so *don't* you say I didn't!) And fastened by the tail to a twig with a safety-pin I saw a hare licking its eyeballs and scratching its toe-nails with its whiskers! Now, there was nothing queer in *that,* but as I hopped gently on upon my knuckles I saw a fly sitting on a leaf and *that fly flapped its wings*!!! *Now,* Mr. Hamish Z. Snazle, ain't you glad you married me?
>
> Well, I must really stop now. . . . Your ownest own Jemima[18]

Amy enclosed another poem, "October Weather," telling Lesley that she "can put it into the Bouquet if you think it is good enough. *Please* send me some of your poetry. I love reading yours, and decidedly not Margot's. Give my love to all, please, and heaps to yourself. Yours truly Amy, (or Flora, Or Jemima Dowsabella Blowsalinda Frittilea Hudger Prowl Stinkler Snazle!)"

Obviously impressed with Amy's writing talent, in June 1914, Lesley had invited her friend to contribute to *The Bouquet.* "Thank you very much for asking me to join your Magazine," Amy replied. "I should love to, if you think I am good enough; and by all means put in the poems if they will do! I am sending two with this and I shall send some more things if all goes well. I have joined another Magazine of which I am the Art Editor, but it couldn't be as nice as yours— especially as *I* have to do all the illustrations, for no one else can be made to draw! Also it is not type-written, which is a great drawback." In a PS, Amy asked

Lesley for the name of the magazine. She enclosed two poems, "The Passing of Elaine," and "Ode to Late October."[19]

Edith, the Smiths' eldest daughter, wrote Lesley in late July, returning several copies of *The Bouquet:* "We have all enjoyed seeing the copies of the 'Bouquet' that you sent us very much. It is so attractively got up and is delightful to read, too. Did you invent 'The Usual Story Reversed' [found in the July 1914 issue] all yourself, or has it any foundation in truth? I enjoyed it most of all, I think ... with all good wishes for your success, I must beg to subscribe myself, Your interested reader, Edith Philip Smith."[20]

The Frosts returned to America in mid-February 1915, taking with them Edward Thomas's son, Merfyn. After surviving several days in captivity on Ellis Island—in a hair-raising episode described in a later chapter—the fifteen-year-old reached East Alstead, New Hampshire, where he was delivered to Russell Scott, a family friend and ex-master at the Bedales School in Steep. From East Alstead, Merfyn continued to correspond with Lesley and Irma nearby in Franconia. His letters often mentioned *The Bouquet* and his own contributions to the magazine. He offered a written piece in cipher: "If any one can read it before the second magazine is published," he told Lesley, "they will recieved [sic] 25 cents as a reward. The cypher is very easy to find out. The drawing is a drawing of our house here." While he would continue to "send some drawings or something for the magazine," his friend Herman Chase, with whom he took lessons in East Alstead, would not be writing anything "for the magazine and he can't draw."[21]

Lesley added still other contributors to *The Bouquet.* Once settled in Franconia, she quickly invited Beulah Huckins, a school friend in Plymouth with whom the Frost children had corresponded while in England, to join the magazine. Writing to Lesley in late March, Beulah asked: "For that paper you spoke about, do you send stories or what? Please write me all about it and I think I will try and send you something for it." Two entries by Beulah, "Tommy Goes to a Circus" and "What Happened to Helen and Doris," appeared in the next issue (c. May–June 1915) of *The Bouquet.*[22]

The Mairs and the Gardners were among those to whom *The Bouquet* was circulated, even after the Frost family returned to America. In Franconia, Lesley received a letter from her friend Delphis Gardner, describing her efforts to produce her own magazine, and acknowledging *The Bouquet.* She told Lesley that she was working on a war number of a magazine called *The Rein,* which she would send to her separately: "I am afraid the contributions to the *Rein* are not quite those you are used to, but they were the only ones that could be poked up to write for it in War-time. (signed) the Editor."[23]

In the diaries of Ernest A. Gardner, recorded in the University College Library,

London, there are papers describing Professor Gardner's daughter, Delphis, as the "head" of a "society" entitled The Sausages; her sister, Phyllis, and brother, Christopher, are listed as "good members." Apparently, the Sausages was organized to write stories, some of which are listed: one is about a castle, with its princess and king of "Horseland"; another is entitled simply "A Silly Story." There are no dates attached to these literary efforts, but they suggest that Delphis did not contribute to *The Bouquet* in part, at least, because of her involvement in other literary activities. In fact, the Gardner children may have provided a direct impetus for the Frost children's publication, along with Amy Smith, who, as we have seen, was Art Editor of another magazine.

The subjects for the children's contributions to *The Bouquet* often suggest life on a New Hampshire farm playing school or playing house or just having outdoor adventures on the farm. Marjorie writes about "How the Fire Was Lit One Morning," and the pains of keeping the fire from smoking and going out; to get the fire to stay lit, first Carol, then Lesley, takes over the operation. Carol describes, in his "What You Can do with Acorns, Chestnuts, & Horse-chestnuts," those times he and Marjorie climbed the fence or the tree above the "long straddle" to reach the nuts for a "nice appetizing meal," or for use as acorn-shell dishes and leafy food in their play house. Carol also writes about the "Domeneques our Hens," and Marjorie includes a piece about an old broken-down house she made of barrel staves. Irma writes about "The New Pig" who was chased by a mother pig and her eleven little pigs into a turnip patch, where the farmer had to come to rescue him.

Other stories and poems would address, and perhaps help conquer, the children's fears, just as they had in the Derry journals. Marjorie describes, with breathless wonder, "What Happened by the Spring," where she spent the night shivering out of fear of what turned out the next morning to be only a cow; or, in "I Found a New Mountain," she walks all night in the woods, eating doughnuts and cake, only to find a little hill, which she names Frost Mountain. And Irma tries to convince the reader of the existence of black bears on and around Mount Lafayette in New Hampshire. In "An Adventure in the White Mountains," she and her sisters and a few friends are on a picnic and eating bunchberries—"you don't have bunch berries in England," she explains—when a dog's barking convinces them there is a bear. Terrified, they run home. "I asked Lesley how a bear would kill us if he got hold of us. She said he would very likely hug us to death. This sounded funny and I think I laughed." In a second story, "The Best Picnic We Have Ever Had," Irma claims a real bear appeared. "We were all so paralyzed we couldn't move. We just stood staring." When the four Frost children ran home and told their parents, "they wouldn't believe us for a long time until a man in the neighborhood killed a bear and we all said the bear he killed was the bear we saw." In a letter to Jack Haines, Irma's father remarks, "I don't see the black bears the children see."[24]

Irma likes to show the evil effects of uncontrolled anger. In "A Very Hard Name," a clerk who is mean to a six-year-old child (who can't pronounce *hydrogen dioxide)* "not long afterwards got sick and the doctor said it was from anger." In "Farmer Shrady's Goats," a farmer gets "angry as a hatter" and makes himself sick and exhausted trying to catch the goats that got loose; eventually they return on their own.

By contrast to the children's "true" stories, based imaginatively on the outdoor life they had experienced, most issues of *The Bouquet* include fantastic tales, often with an instructive denouement. Lesley's ambitious morality tale, "From Beginning to End," describes a man's journey through life: in a beautiful glade, he meets an old man who tells him there is a "place, and that not far away, where the young should not go." Curiosity leads the young man on a long and arduous search; when he arrives, he has found death, learning from the experience that he "would have got here anyway sometime and in searching for it I didn't enjoy myself coming." Suggestively, Lesley weaves in the opening lines from Longfellow's "Evangeline"—"This is the forest primeval, the murmuring pines and the hemlocks . . ."—and those from Christina Georgina Rossetti's "Uphill" that ask,

> Does the road wind uphill all the way?
> Yes, to the very end.
> Will the days journey take the whole long day?
> From morn to night, my friend.

Most contributions, such as this one, even when purely imaginative, include details of nature and an awareness of the psychological verities. The contributions by Bronwen Thomas, Margaret Valon, Amy Smith, and Beulah Huckins are for the most part derivative and tend more toward the purely imaginative. Animated animals and Indians seem to have been favorite subjects.

We are not surprised when, as the German hostilities intruded upon the peaceful summer of the poets and their families at Ryton/Dymock in August 1914, the subject of war appeared on the pages of *The Bouquet*. Merfyn Thomas, who was fascinated by the machinery of war (and enlisted at age seventeen), submitted the first installment of "A Serial Story. The Adventures of a Despatch Rider," which takes place in the trenches in France; he also included drawings of "An English Cruiser about to ram a German Submarine" and "A French Gun in Action." From Franconia, Marjorie, remembering the sighting of the doomed liner as they sailed

on the SS *St. Paul* for home, wrote about the saving of lives on the SS *Lusitania.*
And Lesley included a three-page war ballad entitled "Wilhelm's Death," eulo-
gizing the Belgian farmer who rose up against the Kaiser after he had burned his
farm and pursued him underground:

> The farmer's rage returns at this.
>> He will not now beware.
> He snatches up the Kaiser's spear,
>> And kills him then and there.

> It's current here in Gloucestershire
>> That thus the Kaiser was caught,
> And let us hope that it is true,
>> Though official it is not.

The techniques are also varied. Literary allusions and plays on words abound,
and, in the stories, there is a conscious development of plot, often with a carefully
thought-out climax. The family's interest in the theater is evident in the use of
dramatic devices, including a great deal of dialogue (for "the sound of sense"),
irony, humor, and one-act plays.

We know that the Frosts brought to England an interest in painting and drawing and that Elinor Frost worked with her children to develop their artistic talents.
While Lesley, Carol, and Marjorie would go on to become writers of one sort or
another, Irma longed to become a sculptor. As long as the family still resided
together—as they did in England and, briefly, in Franconia, New Hampshire—
all four children loved to do artwork for *The Bouquet.* In one issue, Carol included a description of "clever paints," using green lichen from old wood, blackberries from over the back fence jammed up in a cup, petals of dandelions in a
cocoa-can cover, and sand mixed in an old tobacco box: "That made the paint
very sandy," Carol lamented, "because sand doesn't melt, and after we painted
with it and it had dried it all rubbed off."

The illustrations for *The Bouquet,* however, are far more successful. The profusion of pencil and watercolor drawings (some with protective tissues), submitted
by each contributor, the use of cream wove paper, paperboard covers (at one time
sewn with string or ribbon or secured with metal clasps), when added to Lesley's
typed manuscript, give each issue of *The Bouquet* a finished, professional look.
The children's artwork, including drawings sent by the outside contributors, are
scattered generously throughout the six issues. Lesley seems to have preferred
mood pieces, such as her "Stormy Days," with its sailing ship in a rough sea
surrounded by fog-shrouded cliffs; Carol and Merfyn produced amusing carica-
tures or line drawings of animals, like the "Weasel" and "Hedgehog"; and all the

contributors to the magazine prepared surprisingly detailed pencil and watercolor illustrations of various flora and fauna, such as the "Hawthorne," "Everlasting Peas," "Yew," "Tassels," "Rose," "Potato Blossom," "Wild Honeysuckle," "Blackberries," "Holly," "Poppys," "Horses," and an "English Robin." In all these efforts, we can see signs of the children's careful observation—under their parents' tutelage—of their natural surroundings, in general, and of plant life, in particular.

In keeping with the children's love of fairy stories, Irma made a color drawing of "Fairy Folk" for *The Bouquet,* and Lesley, in a light vein, includes her "My Story of a Fairy (Before I forget it)" in another issue. The illustration of anthologized verses was a particularly satisfying pastime for Lesley, and it reinforces what we know about her youthful preferences in literature. We are not surprised to find an illustrated transcription of the first and last verses of William Allingham's "The Fairies," with their red caps and green jackets, and, in another issue, a picture she called "Fairies" to illustrate verses from an unidentified poem by R. Buchanan. Other watercolor illustrations by Lesley, absent a text, appear to be inspired by some unidentified literary source: "Gareth," depicting King Arthur's nephew, and "The Three Queens of Avillion," standing in a rowboat on a moonlit night. With still other color illustrations—of verses recalled from the family's anthologies—Lesley has written out a few lines appropriate to the picture. Some verses are not identified by author—such as

> Lougharema, Lougharema
> It lies so high among the heather
> A little lough, a dark lough
> Its waters black and deep

—but we can identify the ballad of "The Count Ornaldos" by Longfellow, where Lesley has painted the Count watching pass "a fair and stately galley" with a seabird "poised upon the mast" to hear the helmsman; and we can recognize the lines from Walter de la Mare's "The Listeners" below her drawing "The Traveler":

> "Is there anybody there?" said the Traveler,
>   Knocking on the moonlit door;
> And his horse in the silence champed the grasses
>   Of the forest's ferny floor.
> And a bird flew up out of the turret
>   Above the Traveler's head:

Lesley's pencil and watercolor drawing of "The Little Grey Church on the Windy Hill" carries with it the lines from Matthew Arnold's "The Forsaken Merman":

> Come, dear children, come away down.
>   Call no more.
> One last look at the white-wall'd town,
> And the little grey church on the windy shore.
>   Then come down.

And her picture of "Spring" accompanies some verses by Alfred Noyes I have been unable to locate:

> When Spring comes back to England
> And crowns her brows with May
> . . . .
> She throws a rose to Italy
> A fleur-de-lis to France.

The illustrations and literary allusions in *The Bouquet* were, in one sense, examples of the liberal use of journalistic flourishes—ads, promotions, ciphers, puzzles, riddles, serial stories, bylines about contributors, and parodies—intended to hold the interest of the subscribers.

Each of the surviving issues of *The Bouquet* features "advertisements" such as the pen and ink drawings of Stephens' blue-black writing fluid, Danes' finest tennis racket, and Vim for hardwood floors. Puzzles and riddles were a favorite enticement to the reader. For Merfyn Thomas's "The Cypher," offering a twenty-five-cent prize, and Lesley's "Puzzle," asking the reader to connect the dots to form a sentence, *The Bouquet* promises answers and the names of the winners in the next issue. Because the May 1915 issue is missing, we learn only that the winner of the puzzle is Master Carol Frost. Other teasers were riddles, such as "When is a door not a door?" or: "The blind fiddler had a brother. The blind fiddler's brother died. The brother that died had no brother. What relation was the blind fiddler to the brother that died?" Can *you* solve them?

To whet the reader's appetite still further, the children occasionally prepared an elaborate backpiece:

> You gentlemen and sportsmen where
>   ever you be,
> All you that love hunting draw near
>   unto me,
>   and
>
> BE SURE AND CONTRIBUTE TO OUR MAY NUMBER.
> EXCITING story of an encounter with a BEAR
>   by the authoress, IRMA FROST.

INTERESTING article by our WAR EXPERT.
More IMAGINATIVE stories by the rising
    authoress, Miss MARJORIE FROST.
MANY FINE ILLUSTRATIONS.
VARIOUS THINGS by MERFYN THOMAS and
    CAROL FROST. BOTH famous authors
    AND artists.
ILLUSTRATIONS by the world-famous
    ARTIST, LESLEY FROST
NEW CONTRIBUTORS will be HEARTILY
    WELCOMED.
ENLIST NOW.

It will come as no surprise to the reader that Robert Frost, as father, teacher, and poet, is revealed through the pages of *The Bouquet* and other writings by the Frost children. As in the Derry journals, RF's lifelong quest for the philosophical or psychological origins of things—often combined with the direct observation of natural phenomena—is reflected in his children's notebooks and their little magazine.

At times, we run across touches of pure Frostian outlook and wry humor. After trying to guess which way the wind was blowing—like the kite, toward the east—Carol tells Marjorie (in his piece called "The Weather-reports") that he has a more exciting idea:

> We were in the kitchen and the soup was cooking when I said, "Lets go out and prophesy the stars." (It was a starry night.) The first thing I prophesied was that two stars were going to bump. (But that was all nonsense). We didn't both agree to that. We had to prophesy the same thing, and Marjorie prophesied that the world was going to end tomorrow. (That did make me shudder. It was silly of me). And the next thing we prophesied was that a shooting-star would come down our chimney. We both agreed to that and went in (for something scared us) and had our supper. (June 1914)

Two of Robert's passions were astronomy and the mysteries of the universe in the stars, interests Lesley develops in her journals. In her notebook, "On the Road to Fleuraclea," she includes a poem, "The Two Cords," the ones God used to tie the universe: "the milky way" and the outer one too far out to see, but, she adds, "I would say it was tied with Heaven. / And you?" In another poem, "The Plaides" [sic], the constellation is "a group of eight gold stars . . . like a bunch of purple grapes." On the blackest night she can see two more in the group—"dim but there." A third poem in the notebook, "On the Mountain's Side," once again pits Lesley against a wild Nature to which she responds in late Victorian fashion, but with touches of direct observation. It conveys, as do many of her father's poems, a curiosity about the universe (far-off stars) and nature close at hand (snowberries wet with dew). Lesley is standing "Up among the mountain's stunted trees" beside a shadow-filled bog ("mere") as the wind bends the reeds:

> The mere's three shadows were clouds of jet
> And reeds and grasses trembling but clear
> Its reflections stars, and a moon that was new
> That among the clouds was climbing the sky
> And it whitened a path that twisted by
> And showed six snowberries wet with dew.
>
> (October 8, 1913)

Frostian touches are everywhere, as we find in Lesley's more thoughtful entries. In *The Bouquet,* she includes a poem, "Fame," that may be a comment not only on her own battle with the Muse but her father's "cold fits" as well:

> They gave me of ink, and some sheets of
> the paper so white.
> And they sat me down in the world and
> they told me to write.
> But they said I was famous for what I
> wrote in the past,
> And that I must write more, and as good,
> to make my fame last.
> The ink had dried up on my pen, the sheets
> moulded away,
> E're I thought of a word that was good
> enough ever to say.

In another poem, "Winter," found in Lesley's untitled, red-covered notebook (Beaconsfield, 1912–1913), the third stanza is suggestive of the click of ice and pane of glass in "Birches" and "After Apple-Picking," written at this time:

> The woodbine stems are coated thick
> With ice all tempting, smooth and cold
> And if you bend it, with a click
> The ice will bend and flake like gold
> And fall from off its long slim vines
> That look through ice like a candle wick.

From days on the Derry farm, we know of the Frost children's fear of the dark—in the woods and in an unoccupied or unlit house at night. Their parents had taught them to confront such fears through poetry. Compare, then, Lesley's poem

"Fear" (from the same notebook and dated January 20, 1913) with her father's narrative verse, "The Fear" (*North of Boston,* but first published in Harold Monro's *Poetry & Drama,* December 1913), and, especially, "The Hill Wife: II. House Fear" (*Mountain Interval*) that concludes, "They learned to leave the house door wide/Until they had lit the lamp inside":[25]

> When all the house is dark at night
> Save where the family sit in light
> Fear comes up the rainy steps,
> And enters through the gloomy halls.
> It creeps along the darkest walls.
> It goes through cracks of bedroom doors,
> And hovers near the dusky floors.
> It cowers under every bed
> With eyes of gleaming dragon red,
> It makes the windows creak and knock,
> As if someone were at their lock.
> It floats around the ceiling[']s edge
> Like fringe of trees around a ledge.
> It hides itself in ev'ry wrap,
> And dark dim coatsleeves seem to flap.
> It writhes itself about the posts,
> And turns them into standing ghosts.
> On doors it sprinkles magic dust
> Until their hinges squeak with rust.
> Fear, though, leaves us in the morn,
> And each grey post and coat and door
> Resumes the life it led before.

The blank verse lines in Lesley's "The Shepherd to his Flock," which read "I have gone with you home through the rocks, / I have let you wend homeward alone . . ." remind us of "Reluctance" from *A Boy's Will,* that begins "Out through the fields and the woods / And over the wall I have wended; . . ."

RF often spoke of kinesthetic images, dreams, and the like, areas of exploration he probably derived from William James's *Principles of Psychology,* mentioned earlier as a textbook he used in the classroom at the Plymouth Normal School in 1911–12. We can assume that James's theories and RF's opinions were discussed with the Frost children at home, usually tempered by a wry, self-deprecating humor that pervades their writings. On a variety of topics in their journals, the Frost children seek—often awkwardly—the philosophical angle or moral implications of their observations, as well as the underlying psychological reality. One senses in these efforts an empathetic way of looking at things—

different moods and thoughts being mined by their developing Muses and shared with one another and the rest of the Frost family late into the evenings.

One clear example of this symbiotic relationship is Lesley's recurring treatment of memory as it relates to the senses, a frequent Jamesian topic explored by her father. In "The Fire-flies Lights" (from *The Bouquet*), Lesley describes a sunset and the psychological influence on her perception of the natural phenomenon: "I could see the pink air around me like a mist. . . . Here and there were floating webs of air of a darker pink like frayed silk . . . All about hundreds of fire-flies were flying, black specks in the pink air." When a drop from a cloud descends on her, she is surprised: "It was cold, like the wind on the mountain, but because I expected it to be hot the cold drop seemed to burn and I shook my hand to shake it off as one does when a drop of hot fudge splashes on your hand."

Also from *The Bouquet* is Lesley's short essay on "Wandering Thoughts." Sitting on the ground contemplating a little grass-beetle climbing a stem by winding instead of in a straight line to the top, she observes "How thoughts wander" before being wrenched back. From the red-covered notebook, her poem "Dust" describes the selectivity of our thoughts (like gold dust, grains are missing or cast aside in the mills):

> It's just the same with our thinking.
> From dust our thoughts are wrought . . .
> . . . .
> So from our thoughts when done
> Some of the grains have vanished.

Especially striking for its parallels with her father's (and William James') thinking is Lesley's essay on "Memory" (from her red-covered notebook), in which the author explores the kinesthetic relationship between the body and one's emotions. "When I think of tennis or climbing trees," she wrote (on January 21, 1913), "I feel a tensioning of the muscles in my arms and legs that are used in these plays. When I think of seasickness a horrible sinking feeling sweeps over my stomach and when I think of anything sour like vinigar [sic] or anything rough a shiver starts at the end of my teeth and goes down my back. . . . These feelings we would not have unless the body had something to do with memory and not entirely the mind."

On the cover of her notebook entitled "On the Road to Fleuraclea" (Dedicated to Papa on Christmas morning, December 25, 1913), Lesley has written "This book is thought of, written, typewritten, approved of, published, worried about, and given away by the author Lesley Frost." Put together with obvious care, the poems and stories cover a range of emotions and literary styles, displaying irony, humor, parody, and make-believe (or metaphor), anchored by realistic detail. Her Christmas gift to her father (she would have made something else for her mother) suggests a growing closeness between Robert and his eldest daughter as conspirators of the imagination. More than in her other notebooks, Lesley experiments with form and language, hoping, I am sure, to win her father's approval.

From this specially-prepared notebook, in her essay "Some Place to Somewhere," Lesley treats the vagueness of memory in describing a walk "which was taken many years ago" on the side of a mountain. There are "blanks" in her memory as she wanders through valleys, all of which "are too much alike." She remembers leaving the road to pick some flowers, arriving at a dairy barn, and passing through "a queer white gate of some kind to somewhere, and this is all I seem to remember," she concludes.

A poem she calls "Knowing Without Seeing" explores a related concept. She traces the path of a sparrow as it lands and takes off from the "casement rosebine" by its effect on its surroundings:

> The bird was not in view,
> But every where he hopped
> The place I knew.
> At last away he flew.
> As all was still again
> I knew that too.

Not only a fellow conspirator with her father, Lesley had also learned well how to pass the idea through the prism of the intellect.

(113)

People	Chandlers.
Gardners	Oldfields, Ledington
Farm Cornor, Tadworth	Ledbury
Surry, England.	Herefordshire, England
Mairs	Woods
14 Campden Hill Gardens	Henberrows, Ledington
Kensington. W.	Ledbury
	Herefordshire, England.
Smiths	
20 Braid avenue	Farmers
Morningside, Edinburgh	Glyn Iddens
Scotland.	Leadington, Ledbury
	Herefordshire
Gibsons	England
The Greenway	
Dymock, Gloucestershire	Haines
England	St Helier, Hucclecote
	Gloucester
	Gloucestershire, England.

"People" on the Frost children's list of family contacts. ("An Important Year"—1913)

Different Feelings.

Excited! If we children were
not excited the last week or two
before we left "The Cottage, No 8
                    Highland Ave.
                    Plymouth, N.H."
I don't know who ever gets excited.
It seemed all like a dream. First
came moving's share of deciding,
then packing, getting information
about England and a hundred other
things, then saying goodby to Plymouth
friends, finally getting dressed the
last morning after a tossing night
on mattresses on the floor, and going
to the train. At last all was over though
and we rolled out of the Plymouth
station, maybe forever.
                    Out into the blazing

"Different Feelings," at the moment of departure from Plymouth (August 1912) by Lesley Frost. ("An Important Year"—1913)

blossoms sailed.

And other flowers of other colors flowered in that swamp
And every time I rode that road the road to
Fleuraclea
I stopped to pick a calapogan, rush or fleur-de-lis
                    Lesley Frost.
                    November 6, 1913.

The Far-off Whistle.

Over the roofs of the houses
Through the night of the city
Comes the long-drawn far-off whistle
Of a train on its airy journey
It awakens a feeling within you
As mysterious as that far-off cry.
                    Lesley Frost
                    December 2. 1913.

"The Far-Off Whistle" by Lesley Frost. ("On the Road to Fleuraclea")

A Game of Cards

Scene. a sitting room in an English
Bungalow. Two large chairs confront the
fireplace. One of wood and cloth. The other
of wicker and cloth. Papa sits in the wooden
one. Mama sits in the wicker. In wooden
dinning chairs which are scattered about
sit Irma, Carol, Lesley, and Marjorie.

Papa begins the conversation.

Papa. "I'll play a little game of card
    tonight if you want to children".
Different pesonages. "Suve","yes", "Alright".
Lesley. "Where are the cards."
Mama "Look in the drawer."
Table drawer is opened. Shuffling of paper
    and books ensues. Mama and papa talk
I rma. "Found them"?   (together)
    Two or three no follow!
Lesley. "Who had them last."

"A Game of Cards" (fragment) by Lesley Frost. ("An Important Year"—1913)

With the seasprayed gale
Your little red legs
Tucked up for a sail.
                Lesley Frost.
Monday, June 23, 1913.

"The Seagull," extract of poem with watercolor by Lesley Frost. ("An Important Year"—1913)

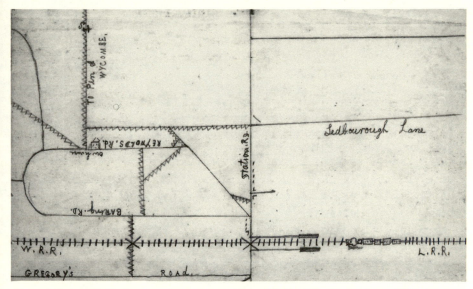

Map of Beaconsfield showing the cottage on Reynolds Road by Lesley Frost. ("An Important Year"—1913)

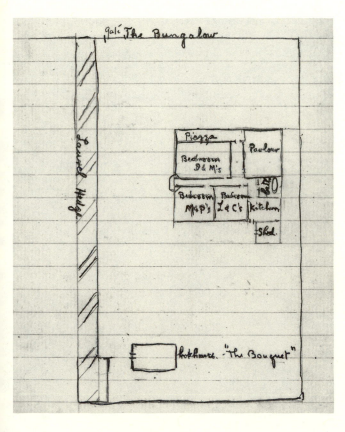

Floor plan of The Bungalow by Lesley Frost. ("An Important Year"—1913)

What A Swallow Must Be.
By Lesley Frost.

I think somebody's bow and arrow must
have flown away together. I never look at a
swallow but what I think so. Some little
child with a very tiny bow, like these I
used to make for Marjorie out of the limbs
off my large bow. I really think it must
have been Marjorie who made the first swallow. She was probably down in the meadow below our farm, and laid the arrow on the bow
so that it stuck, and they both flew off
across the brook leaving her empty handed.
Funny she never mentioned it! Anyway I advise you to try catching your arrow on the
bow that way next time you have one. But do
it when you are alone as Marjorie seems to
have. Only you tell what the consequences
are.

@ @ @ @ @ @ @ @ @ @ @ @ @ @ @ @
End.

"What a Swallow Must Be" by Lesley Frost. (The Bouquet—July 1914)

A POEM.   (Adjectival)
By Amy Smith.

Down by the water where the oozy pools
Are speared by brown-tipped reeds, and
    where the bog
Spreads quacking over miles of wasted
    moor,
There lies a shelving ridge of grey-ribbed
    rock,
There sits, 'neath vaulted skies of dark-
    est dye
Where banshees flit and wraiths intangible
And formless voices float upon the wind -
Strange Night: she clasps her arms about
    her knees,
And looks with magic glinting in her eyes,
Up into space, upon the yellow moon,,
That tosses on a hoary sea of cloud.

"A Poem. (Adjectival)" by Amy Smith. (The Bouquet—June 1913)

Locked Out.

Always when we lock up at night
We lock the garden flowers outside
Cut off from even window light.
To think! - the night the door was tried
And brushed with buttons upon sleeves,
The flowers were out there with the thieve
Yet nobody molested them.   (s
We did find one nasturtium
Upon the steps with bitten stem.
I always blamed myself for that:
I always thought it must have been
Some flower I played with as I sat
At dusk to watch the moon down early.
                                   Anon.

Robert Frost

"Locked Out" by Robert Frost. (The Bouquet—September 1914)

Nettles.
                         By Edward Thomas

Tall nettles cover up, as they have done

These many springs, the rusty harrow, the ploug
Long worn out, and the roller made of stone:
Only the elm butt tops the nettles now.

This corner of the farmyard I like most:
As well as any bloom upon a flower
I like the dust on the nettles, never lost
Except to prove the sweetness of a shower.

                 END.........

"Nettles" by Edward Thomas. (The Bouquet—June 1916)

The *"Bouquet House,"* pencil drawing of the summerhouse at The Bungalow by Irma Frost. (The Bouquet—*September 1914)*

The little grey church on the windy hill.
Come, dear children, come away down.
    Call no more
One last look at the white-walled town
And the little grey church on the windy shore
    Then come down.   Arnold.

"The little grey church on the windy hill," pencil and watercolor illustration by Lesley Frost of Matthew Arnold's "Forsaken Merman."

"Poppys," watercolor by Marjorie Frost. (The Bouquet—April [1915])

"A French gun in action," pencil drawing by Merfyn Thomas. (The Bouquet—June 1915)

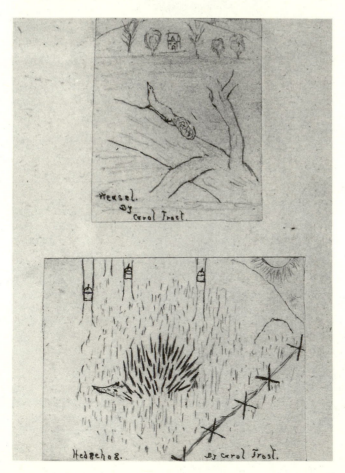

"Weasel and Hedge-hog," pencil drawing by Carol Frost. (The Bouquet—June 1915)

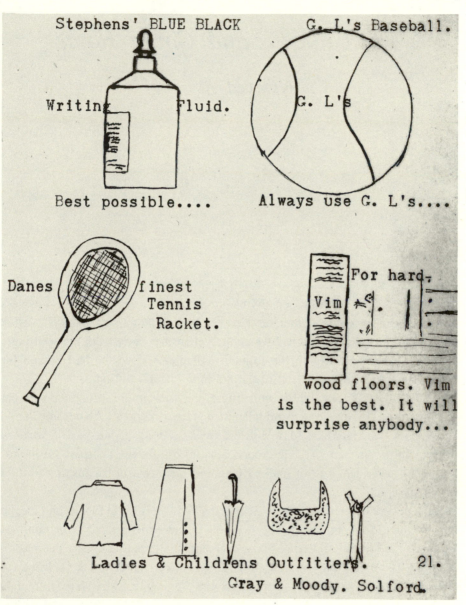

Advertisement. (The Bouquet—June 1914)

8

The Gallows and Going Home

"It Grieved My Soul"

*I*n Beaconsfield, Robert especially had been torn between the serious business of writing, on the one hand, and, on the other, the exhilaration of being with other poets and their families. He had wanted to get further away from the seemingly artificial literary coteries in the London coffeehouses, yet he had longed for companionship with his artistic peers in a more natural setting.

At first, Little Iddens and the gathering of the poets in the spring and summer of 1914 seemed idyllic. Walks and talks with Haines, Thomas, Abercrombie, and Gibson and their families; May Hill; the river Leadon; the success of *North of Boston;* and, above all else, the companionship of Edward Thomas: "1914 was our year. I never had, I never shall have another such year of friendship," Robert would proclaim.[1]

But, one month after the war broke out, the Frosts left Little Iddens and moved in with the Abercrombies at The Gallows to cut expenses for both families. Although the reviews of *North of Boston* (including three by Edward Thomas, in the *Daily News,* the *New Weekly,* and the *English Review*) that made their way to Gloucester and Little Iddens throughout the summer months were extremely favorable, Robert was being shunned by his publisher: "Mrs. Nutt is against me in the matter of my selling to magazines. She seems jealous of my getting cold cash for anything that in book form is so unprofitable," he complained.[2]

Only with a nudge from Robert's sister Jeanie had Robert received $150 from the trustees of his grandfather's estate, which, together with a small payment from Harriet Monroe at *Poetry* and a loan (of $25 or $50) from Sidney Cox, had made possible the move to Gloucestershire in early April. Sources of income had been exhausted. To make matters worse, by the end of August, with the outbreak of the war, the Frosts found themselves isolated and under suspicion as German spies.

Naturally, they were grateful when, having been asked to leave Little Iddens, the Abercrombies invited them to move in with them at The Gallows. Robert explained to Haines, "Our landlord wanted the house on Ledington Hill for hired help so we have come to the Abercrombies for the winter."[3] For Elinor, besides the obvious benefit of cutting expenses, the dream of living under thatch, disappointed at Little Iddens—which they had rented sight unseen—would be realized by the move.

Lascelles Abercrombie's sister had noticed the refurbished pair of thatched cottages in the Ryton/Dymock region, and, in 1911, arranged for her brother and his wife, Catherine, to rent them from Lord Beauchamp:

> Attractively surrounded by lofty elms and backed with an uphill stand of firs, the place was called The Gallows because it stood on the high ground where, centuries earlier, a locally celebrated character known as Jock of Dymock had been hanged for poaching the king's deer. Abercrombie rented it . . . with permission to wander at liberty over all the farm and woodland which comprised this part of the [Beauchamp] estate. . . . The older of the two cottages was the smaller; a "black and white" structure, half-timbered, with white plaster covering the brick walls and thatched roof steeply pitched so that the straw at the eaves was only shoulder high. . . . They called this older cottage The Study because Lascelles did his writing in the main downstairs room. The Abercrombies used the upstairs bedrooms for themselves and their two small children [David, born at The Gallows in April 1911, and Michael]. . . . From The Study there was a passage into the larger cottage, solidly built of red sandstone native to the region.[4]

While Catherine Abercrombie would recall nostalgically the idyllic rusticity of her surroundings, conditions at The Gallows were primitive: no hot water, oil stoves for cooking, and no bath except for a sort of shower, which Eddie Marsh described as "a shed out of doors, with a curtain instead of a door, a saucer bath which you fill by means of an invention of Lascelles' (who was a scientist before he was a poet), a long tube of red india rubber, with a funnel at the end, which you hang on a pump at the other side of the path—cold water, alas!"[5]

In a reminiscence written in 1947 not long before his death, Wilfrid Gibson tried to capture the friendship in poetry that was known at The Gallows:

> While, nigh the old thatched cottage the wind tossed
> The branches of the elm-tree boisterously,
> Beside the Gallows' hearth I sat one night
> With Lascelles Abercrombie, Robert Frost
> And William Davies, dreaming in the glow
> Of the logs' leaping light:
> . . . .

> It flashed into my mind
> That it was the magnetism of poetry
> Of elemental inspiration served to draw
> Together such dissimilar men
> In an intuitive fellowship, and bind
> Their lives inevitably
> In mutual aspiration . . .[6]

Gibson's flat, sentimental recollection, from which all texture of conflicting personalities has been erased, stands in sharp contrast with Robert's contemporaneous and powerfully introspective poem, "The Thatch"; it is a dark, brooding tribute to The Gallows, remembered on a cold, rainy night, before the cottage fell into ruin:

> But the strangest thing: in the thick old thatch,
> Where summer birds had been given hatch,
> Had fed in chorus, and lived to fledge,
> Some still were living in hermitage.
> And as I passed along the eaves
> So low I brushed the straw with my sleeves,
> I flushed birds out of hole after hole,
> Into the darkness. It grieved my soul,
>
> . . . .
>
> They tell me the cottage where we dwelt,
> Its wind-torn thatch goes now unmended;
> Its life of hundreds of years has ended
> By letting the rain I knew outdoors
> In onto the upper chamber floors.

Whatever the recollection of the thatched cottages—sentimentalized or brooding—there is no question but that the onset of war quickly altered the lives of all the poets: the summer idyll was past; and, in many senses, the poets' illusionary vision turned as bleak as the winter that soon descended upon them at The Gallows.

Before moving to Gloucestershire, Robert had expressed his sensitivity to the complexities of rank and status dominating rural life in England at the time. "The poor, I have made up my mind, have a hard hard time here, with no houses to live in and no wages to buy common food with," he wrote Silver from Beaconsfield. He itemized the cost of eggs, milk, corn, and other staple goods, citing the extremely low wages ("from 20 shillings down to 10 a week"), and observed women and children at work in the fields picking up stones. "But the worst of it is not this. These people are allowed to call only a small part of their soul their own. . . . The fortunate monopolize too much here. The fortunate are very delightful people to meet, they afford so many of the virtues and graces. But one can't help seeing the unfortunate who may afford a virtue or two but not one grace."[7]

In her dissertation on the *Georgian Poets and the Land,* Jan Marsh develops Robert's thesis. Farm laborers, she notes, were as badly off as during the time in the 1880s depicted in Hardy's *Tess of the D'Urbervilles.* The laborer was hounded by farmer and gamekeeper if he tried to add to his meager diet rabbits and pheasants—and even nuts and berries in some places. The villagers were discouraged by the landowners from using gardens for pigs or chickens; the cottages were damp and crumbling, the plumbing in disrepair. "But the greatest disadvantage suffered by the agricultural labourer," Marsh points out, "was the invisible but powerful one of class inferiority and servility. . . . This invidious position was part of the whole British class system, but it was aggravated in the villages by the constant, daily, visible reminders—touching one's cap to the 'gentry,' not speaking until spoken to, and so on."[8]

In sum, the deadweight of custom and tradition was oppressive in the countryside. Hardy's pessimism, rooted in deep documentary knowledge, contrasted sharply with the view of the Georgian poets, which often manipulated the grim economic reality to suit their poetic purposes. Abercrombie in *Deborah* and Gibson in *Daily Bread* seem shallow in their knowledge. Marsh concludes, "Robert Frost was horrified by this indifference—and his indignation on behalf of the poor cottager was apparently a source of amusement to his Gloucestershire neighbours, Gibson and Abercrombie, who were perhaps not so much indifferent as congenitally tolerant towards the immemorial British class system that so often shocks outsiders. But Frost had come from a community of independent people in New England, and the degradation and servility continued to shock him."[9]

Much of the Georgian verse presented an optimistic, even rosy view of the cultivated English countryside. The Ryton/Dymock region of The Gallows had experienced only gradual change, a less catastrophic decline than elsewhere during the depression. Socially, the villages were stagnant. The landowner and patron was Lord Beauchamp, who sold the estates in 1919 after years of depression. He did not live on his estates, but was a civil and conscientious landlord. His employees, a bailiff and a gamekeeper, were less pleasant, and it was with these that the ordinary people of Dymock had to deal.[10]

With the move to The Gallows, the tensions and misunderstandings between the poets grew as the effects of the war spread across from the continent into their homes. Although the Abercrombies were away a great deal of the time, visiting friends and awaiting the birth of their third child, Ralph, the Frosts were apprehensive about the future. Their natural anxieties and those of their hosts are reflected in an interview with Catherine Abercrombie (recorded in 1965). She has nothing but praise for Robert as conversationalist-poet-philosopher, and as a man whom she found pleasant, gentle, and humane. Her description of Elinor and the children, on the other hand, is rife with condescension:

> And his little wife Elinor was a charming little woman, quite an ordinary little woman, rather shy person; and their children, older than my children rather, and the children didn't like me. Well it was rather difficult to know what to do with the children because they would not try to mix with the natives. You see, we lived in the remote country, where there were only other farm children; there was nobody else for them to meet. But they would insist that these farm children chased them and threw stones at them, which is perfectly unbelievable because they're frightfully kind people, the Herefordshire/Gloucestershire people, and I have never found a concrete case. But they got so that the children wouldn't leave the house. I mean they wouldn't leave the grounds and garden. They refused to go out on walks at all. Well then their father had to take them out walking in the woods and fields, and he came up against the gamekeeper of the [Beauchamps], and Robert fell out with them very badly, so I don't know whether it was their Americanism showed very much as something strange and foreign, or what it was, but they weren't having it, unless we all went out in a bunch. . . . But it was all very trying.[11]

Accounts such as this, offered to the public some fifty years after the stay at The Gallows, are interesting and suggestive, but like those of Helen Thomas and Eleanor Farjeon, not very reliable. While some suffer from an excess of nostalgia or sentimentality, others are flawed by natural bias or jealousy or simply by the selectivity of faulty recollection.

The problem of mixed perceptions is particularly apparent when we approach the climactic weeks prior to the Frosts' departure from The Gallows and from England for America and what came to be known locally as the "gamekeeper incident." The aftermath affected the mood of the entire Frost family and may have hastened their departure.[12]

At the time of the incident, in late November 1914, their hosts, the Abercrombies, were away, and Edward Thomas had stopped by to visit the Frosts en route to London from Wales. Most accounts agree that Robert and Edward were walking alone through the heavily wooded preserve near The Gallows that belonged to the Lord of the Manor in Ryton (William, seventh Earl of Beauchamp). Those perceived as "gentry," such as the Abercrombies and the Gibsons, were allowed open access to the preserve for walks, picnics, berrying expeditions, and the like. The head gamekeeper, named Bott, reported to the Albrights, a family of farmers living adjacent to The Gallows. A bully by reputation, Bott carried a shotgun, and had been known to threaten adults and children alike in enforcing the rules against trespassers. On the occasion in question, he came unexpectedly upon

Robert and his guest after they had emerged from the woods onto the main road. Insults were exchanged, and Robert was called "a damned cottager," in keeping with the class system of the day. While Robert's temper flared, Edward retreated in fright. There may have been an earlier incident with the Frost children, as the interview with Catherine Abercrombie suggests, which would help explain Robert's quickness to anger and the children's reluctance to wander far from The Gallows's orchard. In any event, as the two men continued their walk, Robert decided to return in pursuit of the gamekeeper, tracking him to his house, where he threatened to beat him up if he ever harassed him or his family again. The gamekeeper stepped inside and grabbed his shotgun, pointing it at Edward, who had tried to stay out of the fracas. The next day, Robert was issued a summons by the local constable in response to the gamekeeper's charge that he had threatened bodily harm.

In Abercrombie's absence, Robert turned to Gibson for help, and was horrified by Wilfrid's unwillingness to intervene on his behalf, an unwillingness Robert attributed to a fear of offending the local gentry. Two letters from Lascelles Abercrombie, mailed to Jack Haines from the Trevelyans (The Shiffolds) on December 1 and 4, respectively, seeking legal advice, only recently surfaced. Providing as they do new insights into the dynamics of a confused situation, they are included here in their entirety:

> Frost, I hope, has by this [time] put before you his trouble with Albright's keeper. I am trying to get at Albright personally, but don't know yet what the result will be. And if he won't keep his keeper in order, I am determined to bring the law in if it *can* come in. As to the affair in the wood, we can, of course, do nothing; but when the keeper takes to threatening Frost *in the road,* the affair is obviously intolerable and must be put a stop to. Preferably, as I say, by getting directly at Albright; for I still think there must be some misunderstanding. But I should like to know whether the fellow's brutal behaviour does make him liable to a summons. I understand Frost has Thomas as a witness. Sorry to trouble you! Yours in haste Lascelles Abercrombie

The Albright referred to in the December 1 letter was a farmer living near The Gallows believed to have some authority over the gamekeeper. We do not have Haines's prompt reply, or Thomas's version of the event, which he appears to have shared with Abercrombie, but Abercrombie's December 4 letter places the incident in the woods (rather than on the road). Like Gibson, he defends the right of the gamekeeper to protect the preserve and shifts at least some of the blame to Robert:

> Many thanks for your most sensible letter. My sole reason for writing to you was on account of the alleged insult in the road, which, if true, was clearly intolerable and to be put a stop to somehow or other. Thomas's description of it, however, scarcely

bears out Frost's, and I now believe he has rather exaggerated the incident in a way which he is a trifle inclined to: I mean he is peculiarly sensitive to anything remotely resembling insult or deliberate annoyance to himself. This is not the first time he has been aggrieved. —As to the wood incident, he had, of course, no right there. I have permission, but that does not imply permission to my friend. The strange thing was that the keeper, knowing where Frost was staying (so Frost says) should have been so unpleasant. If you can see Frost it would be a great advantage. I believe the secret of the whole thing is that Frost does not know how to talk to such folks as keepers. . . . I have asked my sister to interview Albright.

Clearly, the story went through a series of transformations following this contemporaneous and somewhat confusing exchange.

And it did not end there. Once Abercrombie, perhaps through his sister at Much Marcle, had gathered what facts he could, he seems to have contacted Lord Beauchamp, who got the charges against Robert dropped, and sent a personal note of apology to the American. Later, Robert learned from the constable that Lord Beauchamp had chastised the gamekeeper and told him that "if he wanted so much to fight he had better enlist."[13]

Robert and Edward soon were heard making light of the confrontation. In a mock rivalry, Robert wrote Harold Monro at the Poetry Bookshop from The Gallows shortly after the incident that he had had a "little war of my own down here with a bad game keeper who attacked me for going where he allowed the Gibsons to go as gentry. Me he called a 'damn cottager.' *Now* who will have the better claim to the title of the People's Poet? Thomas says it is the best testimonial I have had and I must get my publisher to use the game keeper in advertising me—that is, if I survive my war with the brute—and even if I don't—."[14]

Back in Franconia, writing to his friend Haines, Robert asked him not to mention Gibson—"a coward and a snob not to have saved me from all that." He gave credit to Abercrombie for settling the dispute: "I have never had one penny or one word of accounting from Mrs. Nutt," he wrote Lascelles, "and I should like nothing better than just to cry Havoc and let you loose on her. I wish you could settle her for me by yourself the way you settled the gamekeeper."[15]

Robert may not have realized that Haines and Abercrombie, and perhaps even Thomas, faulted him for exaggerating the incident and for not knowing how to talk to a gamekeeper. It seems Gibson was equally unaware of (or impervious to) these differences when he wrote, in November 1915, asking Robert to contribute to the *Annual of New Poetry* despite Mrs. Nutt's opposition: "and blow Mrs. Nutt!" he wrote. "And why do you speak as if *she* were English? That Gamekeeper, too, was doubtless a German spy!" While, for Robert, the incident highlighted Wilfrid Gibson's social snobbery, he seems to have excused the others—Abercrombie, Haines, and Thomas—who shared to some degree Gibson's reluctance to accept a more democratic view of the mingling of the classes and who, unlike Robert, accepted a social hierarchy that branded as trespassing any incursion into the Beauchamps woods by those not passing as gentry.

Robert continued, in a humorous vein, to associate his war with the gamekeeper with his ongoing battle with Mrs. Nutt. But Edward seems to have internalized the incident quite differently. Although there is absolutely no evidence to suggest that Robert accused Edward of cowardice in his conduct, his introspective and self-deprecating friend seems to have blamed himself for failing to intervene in Robert's defense.[16] Edward had begun writing poetry in late November or early December 1914, and he makes specific mention of the gamekeeper in "An Old Song":

> I roamed where nobody had a right but keepers and squires,
> and there
> I sought for nests, wild flowers, oak sticks, and moles,
> both far and near
>
> . . . .
> Since then I've thrown away a chance to fight a gamekeeper;
> And I less often trespass, and what I see or hear
> Is mostly from the road or path by day: yet still I sing:
> 'Oh, 'tis my delight of a shiny night in the season of the year[17]

Except for a passing reference to the gamekeeper in a May 1915 letter (in which Edward Thomas says, "I dread [editors] as much as that keeper"), the subject is not mentioned in the correspondence between Robert and Edward until Edward is preparing to leave for the front. Describing his efforts to ride a motorcycle and the need some find to face realities, he asserts: "So-and-so can't face more than he was born to, I expect: nor I. So that I worry less and less about that gamekeeper."[18]

The gamekeeper incident, and its relevance to Edward Thomas's personal need to face the horror of war with courage, surfaces again as he describes the observation post to which he is assigned overlooking No Man's Land. He finds himself unable to climb the chimney: "It was just another experience like the gamekeeper—but it lies far less on my mind, because the practical effect of my failure was nil."[19]

With Edward's death and the passing of the years, it would become almost impossible to determine the "sound of sense" in these attributions: to what extent were the participants making light of the incident, to what extent were they taking the matter to heart?

The gamekeeper incident had become closely associated with the other war, the war against the Germans and the fear in England of an imminent invasion. "We are away in the country," Robert wrote home, "where you wouldn't think we would have any part in the excitement of war. But we haven't escaped being taken for spies. As writers we are a little mysterious to the peasant kind. They have had the police busy about us—about Abercrombie, too, in spite of the fact that he is well connected in the 'country.'"[20]

The incident with Edward Thomas in the woods not only exacerbated the neighbors' suspiciousness but also stirred tensions between and among the poets. Despair set in as any hope of finding a market for their work seemed to evaporate overnight, and the always nagging financial worries loomed ever larger. Robert understood the impact of the war on the "literary game." It was time to return home: "I have two fervent hopes," he wrote. "One is that the Germans may not sow the Western Ocean with mines before I cross with the family and the other is that I may find something to do to make up for lost money when I get across."[21]

The direct effect of the declaration of war was delayed in reaching Gloucestershire, however. Only Rupert Brooke had confronted the serious possibility of war, and his prophetic *1914* sonnets appeared in the fourth and final issue of *New Numbers* (put on hold until February 1915 to accommodate Brooke's submission); having enlisted in the Royal Naval Division, he would soon go off on the ill-fated expedition through the Dardenelles to his death on April 23.

But the indirect effects were devastating. Delays in the publication of the third and fourth issues of *New Numbers,* as well as of *Georgian Poetry* II, forced Catherine Abercrombie, expecting her third child, to continue her clerical job as her confinement approached. Income from reviewing ceased abruptly, and Lascelles became despondent, leaning on Eddie Marsh to use his influence with the Royal Literary Fund to procure a small stipend. Although his books, *Borderlands* and *Thoroughfares,* did not sell well, Gibson remained fairly cheerful, aware of his wife's independent means and of the success of his poems in America. Brooke's fellow Georgian poets—Abercrombie, Gibson, and Drinkwater—were as yet unaware that it was the war that would bring Brooke a modicum of fame, while they would be forgotten, paradoxically benefiting from the not insignificant bequest of income from his *New Numbers* poems that has continued unabated. And Robert and his family, out of money and seemingly out of luck, had no way of knowing what the future held for them as they fled the war zone for home.

Sailing from Liverpool on the SS *St. Paul,* February 13, 1915, the Frosts (accompanied by Edward and Helen Thomas's son, Merfyn) were shaken by the proximity of the blockade and the uncertainty of war and their own future in America, an uncertainty heightened by the suddenness of their departure.

In pitch darkness and rain, with the SS *Lusitania* nearby, the *St. Paul* was escorted by two battleships out into the Atlantic. Lesley's college composition describes the harrowing scene:

> Standing in a fine cold grey rain that blew down the Mercy river from the sea, we watched our boat, the St. Paul, come slowly in to the wharf, rubbing against the great buffers. They lowered a gangplank. A hard-faced official took our passports, glanced at them swiftly with hard eagle eyes, and pushed us on board. For the next two hours we stood about on deck watching the Lusitania anchored near, and waiting for us, as two battleships were going to take her and the St. Paul around the coast of Ireland in the night. Night came and we sailed. It was so dark we could see nothing through the sifting rain but a few twinkling shore lights and the long restless rays of two searchlights that felt of us again and again, as with fingers. The next morning we were far out in the Atlantic.[22]

Shortly after the Frost family was settled in New Hampshire, Robert sent Lascelles Abercrombie a more humorous description of

> an inspector at the gangway in Liverpool who was for keeping us in England till our greatness ripened a little more. Very well says I, maybe you know more about what's good for me than I do myself. I like England and I'm willing to stay if some one else will take the responsibility. But I give you fair warning: if I dont go now I wont go at all. I shall become a British subject and "run for" the Laureateship. That seemed to make him think. He let us go on board—muttering.[23]

Abercrombie and his wife "chuckled mightily" as Lascelles read aloud Robert's description of the interview with the "Inspector at Liverpool" to his friends and family in Gloucester.[24] Like Lesley, Robert told his English friends how they had withheld their speed "and didnt sail till dark, and we had when we did sail two battleships with us all down the Irish Sea—to pick us up I suppose if we got into the water for any reason. But we didn't get undermined and we didnt get torpedoed—else you would have heard of it before this. We got kicked about a deal for nine whole days and seasickened and discouraged from ever crossing again."[25]

Bidding farewell to such friends as Thomas, Smith, Abercrombie, Haines, Monro, even Gibson and their families had been painful. Last-minute notes from Robert to Monro and Flint (the latter written on shipboard but never mailed) betray Robert's mournful mood.[26] But in his letter to Abercrombie the following month, he is nostalgic but upbeat: "If I forget England!" he wrote. "My thanks for all you did to make her what she is to me. Now go ahead and win the war." He sent his love "and especially to the little boy [David] I taught while he was young and there was yet time, a way to make a big splash with a small object and a small splash with a large object. Ask him if he remembers."[27] Haines wrote Robert that his letter from Liverpool "made us quite miserable. You must have been pretty miserable when you wrote it. What on earth you felt it necessary to apologize for, as to the manner of your going, we utterly fail to understand." He conveyed in his letters to Robert the praises of Gibson and Abercrombie, adding how he and his wife Dorothy (Dollie), and his son Robin, feel "quite lost without your family circle, you were like a breath of fresh air and filled us with all manner of new ideas and now we feel all 'stuffy' again."[28]

The first order of business in New York—where the Frosts landed on February 22—was to gain the release of Merfyn from Ellis Island, where he had been detained by immigration officials for five days, according to Robert's contemporaneous account to his children. "Poor Merfyn had to be all alone most of the time," he wrote the children from New York, "and he was in the realest danger of being sent straight back in the boat he came by. There was one man down there who shot himself while we were there rather than be sent back. And there were mad people and sad people and bad people in the detention rooms. I don't know how I ever got Merfyn out of it." Lawrance Thompson's version of the Ellis Island affair reduces the number of nights of Merfyn's confinement to *one*, claiming that Robert placed Merfyn on a train the very next day for East Alstead (where he was to be met by the Russell Scotts).[29]

Remaining behind in New York, Robert took time to confer with his publishers, travel by train to visit his sister Jeanie where she was teaching, in the remote coal-mining town of South Fork, Pennsylvania, and stop over in Lawrence, Massachusetts, before joining his family on the farm of the John Lynches in Bethlehem, New Hampshire.

We know that, upon his arrival in New York, Robert had written immediately to Ernest C. Jewell, his friend from the Lawrence High School days, announcing plans to spend several nights in Lawrence on his way north.[30] William, the late son of Ernest and Elizabeth Jewell, remembers Robert coming to Lawrence and leaving the fifteen-year-old Merfyn with his parents for almost a week, while Robert was being lionized by Amy Lowell and others in the Boston area. He said it upset his mother to be left with the boy, "with heavy thermal underwear expecting a very heavy winter in New England. . . . It was a mild winter and the boy was so homesick and so depressed he just sat in his room and stared out the window and perspired nearly to death." William was about nine, and he and his sister tried to entertain the teenage boy. Frost returned and William's mother said "*Where* have you been?" and Frost recounted the excitement of his reception in Boston.[31]

Myfanwy Thomas, in her memoirs, recalled her brother's stay on Ellis Island as *three* days:

His journey to the States was a muddle, for the fifteen-year-old boy had spent three days in primitive conditions on Ellis Island with a number of doubtful characters who were awaiting unlikely permission to land. They were kind to the shy English boy and tried their best to make him feel at ease, among other things teaching him the three-card trick, "Find the Lady." I think that must have been where Merfyn learnt the expression "Snow again, sonny, I don't catch your drift," which amused his father so much. He loved salty speech.[32]

Once safely ensconced with the Scotts in East Alstead, however, Merfyn made light of the whole adventure, signing himself as "ex-convict" in a letter to Lesley. The first weeks of his stay, finding himself surrounded by snow and ice, he was unhappy and lonely, but by early spring he began to get used to his surroundings: "The ice on the lake is melting ever so fast now," he wrote Lesley. "To-day it has rained a little! Hurrah! It reminds me of England." He took classes with a neighbor, Herman Chase, with whom he was building a model sawmill on a nearby stream (but who, according to Merfyn, would not be contributing to *The Bouquet,* "and he can't draw"); "I am getting quite used to the life here now," he wrote, "and I don't find it so lonely."[33]

By early summer his father reported to Robert that Merfyn's letters home were "cheerful." When he visited the Frosts in Franconia, Elinor was too ill to have responsibility for another child: "Elinor is so sick day and night as to affect the judgement of both of us," Robert explained in a letter to Edward. Although the plans originally called for Merfyn to remain with the Scotts for a period of two years "for his education," his parents now wanted him back in England by Christmas, so that he might see his father before he shipped out to the front. Father and son had been estranged, and shortly after his return home (on the SS *St. Louis,* December 10, 1915), Merfyn was apprenticed by his parents to a friend at a school in Coventry for a year to prepare him for going into engineering works. Edward and Merfyn arranged their Christmas holidays to coincide, and this final family gathering brought some peace to Edward on the eve of his departure for France.[34]

Merfyn would enlist on his seventeenth birthday (January 12, 1917), with the understanding that he would not be called up for another year. It was at this time that Robert wrote Helen wondering "if it would be too much trouble for Merfyn to write a pretty little note to Frederick Howe, Commissioner of Immigration, Ellis Island New York to thank him for the glimpse he gave him of these United States and to tell him that he is safely back in his own country and promised as a soldier when his country shall want him? I have meant to ask Merfyn myself. I had a nice letter from him awhile ago."[35]

Upon landing in New York, the Frosts discovered that, as Robert himself reported to Haines, "they were hailed by one or two intelligent people as a poet and family."[36] Although Florence I. Holt (Mrs. Henry Holt) had written Robert months earlier of her interest in *North of Boston,* and correspondence had begun between her husband's firm and David Nutt and Co., the Frosts were pleasantly surprised to find in New York a publisher willing to take on the fierce widow Nutt for the American rights to Robert's books. Alfred Harcourt and the Holts, Robert happily announced, were "going to be a father" to him.[37]

By the time the Frosts had made their way to Bethlehem, New Hampshire, however, they realized the precariousness of their situation. Spring still seemed far away, and no money was coming in; as Elinor's health deteriorated, the nostalgia for what was left behind in England intensified: "I am coming back to you someday," Robert confided in Haines, "after I am forgotten over here and you shall pour sherry by the open fire in Hucclecote and comfort me for what I have had only to lose. I'm talking myself sadder and sadder." Like Segismundo, he couldn't believe what was happening was real, that he might awaken as from a dream. Even when he boasted to Edward that he had earned "by poetry alone in the year and a half about a thousand dollars," he felt compelled to add that "it can never happen again."[38]

9

War

"For Children Too"

$\mathcal{N}$ews of the impact of the war on the lives of the Frosts' English friends soon made its way across the Atlantic. From Jack Haines, who kept in touch with the poets and sent word of their doings, the Frosts learned that Harold Monro had joined the army, leaving Alida Klemantaski in charge of the Poetry Bookshop; Ford Madox Hueffer was reported to be back in England with shell shock; and Wilfrid Gibson and Lascelles Abercrombie had failed the physical. Gibson reported that he had been rejected three times and that, "thank God!" they wouldn't even take Lascelles into the reserve. Dorothy Haines wrote that her husband, although accepted for service, "is in the very last group of all." Some writers like Gordon Bottomley, W. H. Davies, Walter de la Mare, and John Fletcher, continued to publish; but Catherine Abercrombie complained that her husband, despite reasonably good health, is so distressed he "cannot write poems or letters and hardly ever reads."[1]

Although Robert was still annoyed with Wilfrid Gibson over his role in the gamekeeper incident, and his estimation of him as a poet had plummeted, they continued to correspond. Gibson confessed to Robert that, out of a sense of duty, he had brought out a book of patriotic verse, titled *Battle,* which he did not want to share with him, "as I thought you might dislike it. I had to publish it," he wrote, "as I felt I must make my little protest, however feeble and ineffectual— so don't be too hard on me." The following year, he would mention his plans to come to America. With a generous assist from Ezra Pound, he had agreed to do a series of readings in the United States, despite mounting trepidations: "I am literally terrified of America," he wrote. "It would be so appalling if I should fizzle, though the money is guaranteed—but the most awful part of all is leaving

Gerald and Audrey for so long."[2] He did, finally, make the trip, in December 1916. While visiting the Browning Society in Philadelphia, he shared the platform with Robert, and is believed to have further irritated his fellow poet by receiving a higher fee.

For the members of the Frost family—whose lives in America were colored by their experience in England and their love of Edward Thomas, his family and friends—dealing with the war was a constant source of anxiety.

In his early poems, Robert seemed to accept the need for war in certain circumstances. "La Noche Triste," "A Dream of Julius Caesar," "Caesar's Lost Transport Ships," and "The Traitor"—from the 1890s and uncollected—are examples of Robert's preoccupation with heroic verse. "In Equal Sacrifice" (previously "A Heart in Charge") tells the story of Douglas (carrying the heart of Robert the Bruce), who, faced with certain death in Spain, on his way to the Holy Land, gives his "heart to the hopeless fight / (The more of right the more he loves)." From the same period is "The Lost Faith," a seventy-seven line poem composed for the fourth annual banquet of the Men's League of the Central Congregational Church in Derry Village (February 21, 1907) but never published in its entirety. The poet regrets that the faith that moved the Union soldiers to heroic acts in the Civil War appears lost,

> No less a dream than of one law of love,
> One equal people under God above!
> . . . .
> A dream so deathless, we to forget it thus
> I do not know; we saw it fade from sight.[3]

Only a year before her father composed "The Lost Faith," then seven-year-old Lesley had written in her Derry journals "About War":

War is a good thing if you have a good reasen for it, but if you think you dont like a country wheather they like you or not then it isn't right to go to war with them. But when theavs dome somthing to you or doing something to you then it is right to stope them. The best reason we have for a war in this country was the reasen for the civel war the reasen to free the slaves. The one between the french and inglish. The french just fort because they didn't like the inglish. June 1, 1906

In philosophical terms, Robert had concluded that "War represents what faith we wont be laughed or reasoned out of."[4] It has to be more than sentiment; a nation has to be directly threatened, like Belgium was. On their return to America, the Frosts found that "no one is as much against Germany as he is against the war."[5] Robert tried to explain to his English friends his country's attitude once war broke out in Europe. He wrote to Edward Thomas:

Every Yankee in America (practically) wants England to win—England and France. They all think you will win, but perhaps not this year. But few consider the war any affair of ours. No one goes into a war on general grounds of humanity. We extend sympathy on general grounds of humanity. We fight only when our material interests are touched. Yours were when Belgium was invaded; ours weren't. Damn the Germans.[6]

And he tried to explain his country's attitude to Jack Haines, slipping into some unpublished lines written before the turn of the century (shortly after he left San Francisco, he said):

Some day the war will end one way or the other (decisively I trust) and then you will come to see us. I wonder what you will say to our cheerful self-sufficiency as a nation. You'd think

> Europe might sink, and the wave of her
> > Sinking sweep
> And spend itself on our shore and we should
> > Not weep,
> Our cities would not even turn in their sleep.

We don't really care what happens over there. It doesn't touch us nearly enough. At least we can't see that it does. We stand lost in sentimental contemplation. Not one nation in the whole fight is out for anything but its own interest. We tell ourselves that the one thing we would not go to war for is self-interest. The fact of course is that that is the only thing we would go to war for. We are only able to hold the high opinions of ourselves we do because our interests are not touched. You can't make it our war any way you look at it. *We* can't by trying. If we look uncommonly foolish at the present moment, it is from trying overhard to enter into the spirit of a row we weren't prepared for and don't understand. I believe the Germans have written of *us* as having done our part to drive them to desperate measures by the step we took outward into world politics when we went to the East Indies. But we are blissfully unconscious of having done anything to make an enemy by a simple act of business expediency. We may have heard of the Germans' view, but we suspect them of being too philosophical and of looking for the bottom of things that haven't got a bottom or a bottom worth looking for. . . . Be careful to distinguish between what I say as speaking for the country and as speaking for myself. You know the views I hold. I like the Germans, but they must excuse me if I want to see them exterminated.[7]

The news from the front has been rotten and Robert feels angry, "an Englishman's anger that after all the talk of what Ki[t]chener's army was going to do in the spring you should let the Germans be beforehand with you in opening the spring campaign. . . . Rotten news. I'm sick of it. And SO ARE MY CHILDREN. We threaten to have our paper stopped. . . . What I long for is certainties where I have fixed my heart."[8]

With the sinking of the SS *Lusitania* on May 7, 1915, Robert and Elinor both boiled over in anger. The next day Robert wrote John Bartlett in disgust: "I'm sick this morning with hate of England and America because they have let this happen and will do nothing to punish the Germans. They can do nothing. I have no faith in any of them. Germany will somehow come out of this war if not completely victorious at least still formidable and needing only time to get wind for another round. Dammit."[9] Even when thinking of his own personal success as poet, Robert's mind is on the war: "But it's hard in these times not to think nationally and owe my gratitude to England instead of to any man or men of England," he wrote Edward Garnett:

> We sailed from Liverpool on February 13 but we left our hearts on the other side at least for the duration of the war. We have tried to wish the States into the war. But we cant talk to our neighbors. They are too indifferent to please us. Here on the edge of it all the fight shades off into a sort of political argument no more rancorous than we are used to at election times. The Yankee will go his joking way till something hits him harder than the loss of the lives on the Lusitania. That's not to say that a very large majority of us are not on your side. I think I can explain our state of mind. We are just near enough to the Civil War to remember that we fought it and just far enough from it to have cooled off and forgotten our reasons for fighting it. We have come to doubt if we ever had any reasons. We doubt if any nation ever had any reasons for any war. So passionate reasons always evaporate. But—there is this: in passion they can be renewed. Give us time to warm up. There is no hurry. The war won't be over for some years yet.[10]

When Harold Monro sought Robert's permission to include several of his poems in a chapbook, Robert reminded him of the widow Nutt's refusal to grant permission because he is "of a nation not represented on the firing line in this war. So she puts it and it sounds patriotic. But I havent failed to discover that her real grievance against me is that I wont write war letters to the papers to get my name before the public and help her sell books." Still, Robert was encouraged by the thought of poetry going on in England "in spite of the war—or is it because of the war? I shouldn't like war if it were incompatible with poetry as some seem to think it is incompatible with Christianity."[11]

Elinor shared her husband's views of the war, but she was writing few letters because of the frequent illnesses of the children and her own poor health. In a letter to Lascelles Abercrombie, whose wife, Catherine, was recovering from breast surgery, Robert conveyed their worst fears: "Elinor is altogether out of health and we are in for our share of trouble too. It is the old story: what she has been through so many times [pregnancy]. But we are not as young as we once were. I'm sure I don't know how it will be with her. The doctor frightens me about her heart. But this is something you mustnt mention in your letters."[12]

Elinor was "unspeakably sick" for three months but miscarried in late November 1915: "We are still six in the family, no more and, thank God, no less," Robert wrote Lascelles.[13] Elinor wrote Dorothy Haines the following year a caring and affectionate letter (that only recently came to light), sharing details of her domestic worries, the health of family members, and her own anxieties about the war and its toll on the families in England:

I want to tell you how . . . glad for your sake [we are] that Jack was rejected [for military service] definitely. I can imagine so well what such a parting would mean to me, that my heart aches for those who have to bear it. I am afraid Mrs. Thomas is not standing it any better than I would, and I am so sorry for her. His training is all over, and he is expecting to be sent to France any time. It's all too dreadful to think of. With anxiety and grief for personal loss, as well as worry over the outcome of the war, I can understand what you say, that you are never quite light hearted, and wonder if you ever will be again. I often wish we had gone into the war when the Lusitania was sunk. I think there was a horror and rage felt at that time which would have burst into flame under the right leadership, and by this time we might have had several million men ready to help on the Western front. I am afraid England and France are not going to be quite strong enough to force Germany to give up much of the territory she has won, much less crush her as I would like to see her crushed.

We, over here, are so busy raising money to help the wounded and homeless, that there is not much energy left for anything else. This week there is a great Bazaar being held in Boston for the benefit of the Allies. Preparations have been going on for several months and it ought to add thousands of dollars to the various funds. Strange to say, I believe that *consumers* are suffering financially here as much as over there. So much of our produce has been sold out of the country that prices have risen enormously, and we are told that it will soon be still worse. Some things have doubled in price, and many things are a third higher. Of course, *producers* of many commodities have grown rich, especially those who have money invested in munitions factories, and that makes it appear as is if we were very prosperous, but it doesn't help those who are living on small salaries or incomes.[14]

Elinor tells Dorothy the children are well, Carol having recovered from what was diagnosed as incipient tuberculosis, and she thinks "Lesley will take her college examinations next June." She promises to get the publisher to send a copy of Robert's new book, *Mountain Interval,* which was just out.[15]

Edward Thomas, on his way out to France as an officer, realizes that Helen "is not often happy now. She is tired and anxious." He writes Elinor that he wants to go to France *and* come to see them in America; but he cannot think of "the evening now . . . Helen is going to find it lonely," he writes; "she does not stand these times very well." While the Thomases have been able to move to a home closer to Merfyn, they have had to put Bronwen in a cheaper school.[16]

Lesley, too, understood the sacrifice of those families whose sons, husbands, and fathers went off to war: "In a way," she wrote in her college composition, "war is harder to bear for those who stay at home than for those who go. . . . Mental suffering is always more unendurable than physical."[17] And Marjorie included, in the June 1916 issue of *The Bouquet,* a piece on the sinking of the SS *Lusitania* (entitled "The wreck of the War"), in which a friend who was rescued from the torpedoed ship was praised for helping others. "So you see," her story concludes, "its best not to howl and cry but save other people."

From the exchange of letters between Dorothy Haines and Lesley, which had begun even before the Frosts left England, we learn more about the daily routine and anxieties in wartime. Besides such mundane matters as the unpredictability of the weather, the difficulties in getting the scarlet runners (beans) to grow, and painting the house and cleaning Jack's books, to his annoyance, there is always the war. Dorothy had taken exams to become a voluntary nurse, "so that by the time the Germans get here," she explained, "I shall know how to patch up a little in case there are no doctors near. It is just as well to be prepared for the worst even if one does not expect it."[18]

At Christmas 1915, Dorothy asks Lesley to "Give all your sisters (as if there were so many of them!) and Carol my love and tell them I wish they would all fly over one night and come to supper with me. I have several plum puddings and lots of etc.—but it takes young people to appreciate them." She imagines that if Lesley were there she

> would be like every other unattached maiden—either nursing or cooking, or clean-ing in a Red Cross Hospital. We who have babies and cannot give very regular spare time go when we can to a Red Cross Depot and make bandages, swabs, plugs and other medical appliances for 'poor broken soldiers' as Robin calls them. Knitting has rather gone out of favour. The younger women got tired of it last winter especially when they heard that the sock that had cost them a month's hard labour had been used by some man to clean his boots with because there was not enough room for his big toe.[19]

In apparent response to Lesley's questions, Dorothy describes the qualifications for nurses, distinguishing between the volunteer and the properly trained hospital nurses. As a volunteer, she had taken two quick and easy sets of lectures on first aid and home nursing. Because of home responsibilities, however, she had not practiced since.[20]

Visiting her family home in Clifton (near the sea at Bristol), Dorothy writes Lesley about *her* childhood education, not too different from that of the Frost children: "I had Doctor's orders as a child not to be sent to school, so except for short and desultory lessons at home in the morning I was allowed to run wild on the Downs here till I was thirteen. I have done nothing ever since but thank my lucky star for giving me such good fortune." Quickly rising to the top of her class in high school, she realized that she had "lost nothing by all those years of freedom and gained something of infinite value to myself." Now her three-year-old son, Robin, is enjoying the Downs, where "at last he has found plenty of room to run about in without even any nasty hedges to make him want to crawl through," and Jack "goes botanizing on the Downs."[21] She sent a postcard to the other Frost children from the family homestead. The one to Carol said, "I suppose you do not ever want to come back here again, after all one's home must be best. This place is my home when a child"; and to Marjorie she wrote: "These downs are about 5 miles square I should think so at last we have found something big enough for Robin to go seeking adventures in."[22] Each letter to Lesley brought news of little Robin: his rides in the "push chair," his trips to the zoo (where he liked the tigers, monkeys, and lionesses, but "went wild with joy over a cage of rabbits," which were familiar to him and at his level on the ground).[23]

The letters from Dorothy also brought news of the Abercrombies, who remained in the Gloucester area until 1918, when they moved to Liverpool. Catherine soon recovered from the surgery (although she would have another scare, this time a nonmalignant tumor, in 1918) and would visit the Hainses with their sons David and Mikey. But, according to Dorothy, Catherine "does not seem very satisfied with herself. Still, knowing what an energetic woman she is I think she couldn't possibly get well quickly enough to please herself."[24] The Abercrombies were positively cheerful, however, when Lascelles was rejected for military service, although "Lascelles is not writing at all, isn't it sad," Dorothy observed. By contrast, when Edward Thomas came for a night he looked "thin and strung up—not at all happy and anything but peaceful. He is writing a great deal tho' isn't he?" And there were tidbits about others, like Eleanor Farjeon, who had begun publishing verse for children, and Walter de la Mare, who was away from his family lecturing most of the time.[25] Dorothy's letters tapered off after 1916; Robert and Jack continued to correspond intermittently until their final visit in 1957 in Gloucester.

It was the war, more than any other subject, that prompted the letters from the Frosts' English friends, especially the Gardners, Smiths, and Mairs. Although correspondence with the Gardners was infrequent after the Frosts left England in 1915, Delphis wrote Lesley about her school experiences under the constant fear of the Zeppelins. In 1916, she was awaiting the return of her father from Salonica, and her sister Phyllis was doing war work as an engineer. Following the Armistice, Mary Gardner wrote to Lesley, announcing that her husband had been asked to go on a lecture tour in the United States and worrying over whether or not she owned any dresses "smart enough to admit of my accompanying him. . . . I never got that letter that your mother was going to write," she added. "Dutiful mothers get barraged into looking after their families. It is only the prospect of crossing the Atlantic at an early date that forces me to write, as if I do come I want to see all the Frosts. . . . And we admire President Wilson top hole. Did you know my name was Wilson (née Wilson, as they say in the papers)." There is no record of Professor Gardner's tour having taken place or of the two families making contact in the United States.[26]

James C. Smith also made unrealized plans to get away from the war zone with his family. In spite of the difficulty of wrenching his wife away, he hoped to accept a professorship of English literature in Toronto: "I have a craving to get the girls away to America, and myself to get back to literature and teaching, which I love," he wrote Robert. He returned in his letters to his worry over his family: "Whatever happens in the war, life will be very hard for girls in poor auld Scotland." He would like to trade places with his American friend: "Do you remember how, as we walked down Baird Avenue, I said I would gladly change places with you? And I was right. You have gone back to freedom and fame," although not to wealth.[27]

In the Mair family, it was Lucy (J. C. Smith's niece) who corresponded with Lesley during the war years. Besides acknowledging Lesley's cards and letters from Franconia—"They're the nicest I've ever seen, especially the one of sunset above the clouds. . . . I like the old man of the mountain next"—and congratulating Lesley for being president of "your Literary Society, and editor of the school magazine too [at Amherst High School]," she wrote about her parents' wartime activities: "Mother [Jesse Mair] told me to tell your mother that she's very sorry she hasn't written, but she's working at the Ministry of Munitions, and she never gets time for anything. Father [David Mair] is working at the Admiralty just now, translating German newspapers." The war dominated her thoughts. As the threat of the Zeppelins subsided, the Germans were being checked on all borders, and Lloyd George was predicting ultimate victory, she doubted America would enter the war: "Wilson seems to be quite content with writing endless notes," she wrote. As the war progressed, Lucy's mother took a position in the Ministry of Food, as Will Beveridge's private secretary; because her Uncle Jim [James C. Smith] was working at the Ministry of Munitions, the Smiths had moved nearby in London, and Amy and Hope could attend school together at St. Paul's: "They are always together out of school" and invented a war game called "Aeronautics."

By 1918, the Smiths were back in Edinburgh (where Lucy forwarded cards addressed to them from the Frosts), and Lucy's mother had been made an Officer of the British Empire, "so we are all awfully proud of her." Lucy describes Armistice Day on Campden Hill, and the family's sense of guilt for having survived the war without loss of life. Her father had returned to his old job at the Wages Section, and her mother was still working as Will Beveridge's private secretary at the Ministry of Food, where he had been made First Secretary and knighted. She praises Wilson, who, when his picture appears on the screen, "always evokes immense enthusiasm. King George doesn't count for much you know. It's Lloyd George who matters. The king sends nice little telegrams to generals who win victories and ministers who have the flu, but he has nothing to do with governing." People who saw Wilson go by Buckingham were "immensely struck by the graceful manner in which he waved his hat. . . . Is it true that the Americans are getting rather tired of him? Everyone here admires him like anything." Lucy, meanwhile, was being examined for a possible Classical Scholarship and for Cambridge Higher Local. After the war, except for a brief exchange in 1924 in connection with the launching of Lesley and Marjorie's bookshop, the Open Book, the correspondence between Lesley and Lucy would taper off.[28]

The European conflict was on everyone's mind in America, as well. One troubling consequence: friends and critics looked to Robert Frost the poet in time of war to take a public stand on the political and military issues of the day. A very New England poem, "The Bonfire," was read by Robert at the Harvard Phi Beta Kappa in 1916 and appeared in the first issue of the *Seven Arts* in November; the journal, the brainchild of Louis Untermeyer, was itself a casualty of war: although it tried to avoid politics, it couldn't avoid the European conflict. "The Bonfire," Untermeyer explained, "caused much comment because of a line, 'War is for everyone, for children too.'"[29] Robert protested: "What disheartened me about this Bonfire was that it made everybody think or so many think that it was saying something on one side or the other of a 'question of the day.' Dammit."[30]

Another war poem included in *Mountain Interval* was "Range Finding," but it, too, Robert asserted, was not written with the current war in mind: "Would it amuse you to learn," he wrote Amy Lowell,

that Range Finding belongs to a set of war poems I wrote in time of profound peace (circa 1902)? Most of them have gone the way of waste paper. Range Finding was only saved from going the same way by Edward Thomas who liked it and asked about it now and then and very particularly once in a letter last Spring—he thought it so good a description of No Man's Land. So you see my poems about this war narrow down to The Bonfire and that is more of New England than of what is going on over yonder.[31]

In another poem from this period, "In the Home Stretch," praised by Edward from the front, the saddened wife looks out the kitchen window and hears the sounds of war:

> . . . for we. are not young now.—
> And bang goes something else away off there.
> It sounds as if it were the men went down,
> And every crash meant one less to return
> To lighted city streets we, too, have known,
> But now are giving up for country darkness.

Two other poems, "To E.T." (first in the *Yale Review,* April 1920, and in *New Hampshire,* 1923), and "Iris by Night" (*A Further Range,* 1936), written after Edward's death, express the pain of loss of an "elected friend." A more direct reflection of the war, however, are "Not to Keep" (probably written in England but first published in the *Yale Review,* January 1917, before Edward's death, and in *New Hampshire)* and "A Soldier" (*West-Running Brook,* 1928).

Through 1916 and into 1917, the Frosts experienced ups and downs in their spirits as the fortunes of war ebbed and flowed. As hope increased so did the nostalgia for their times in England: "They are off," Robert wrote Haines,

and my heart's with them with all the love I bear England for the time I met you or we met you first between the Greenway and Leddington with your canister for tall flowers, for May Hill, for the fern we groped on the little cliff for by the light of a match in your English winter twilight and for the evenings by your books of all the poets . . . , just you and I and your wife together. Old man, I shouldn't have seen you at all if I wasn't going to see more of you. I shouldn't have seen England if I wasn't going to see more of her. You both become an increasing pain as you are. . . . My politics are wholly American. I follow my country in regions where the best of us walk blind. I suppose I care for my country in all the elemental ways in which I care for myself. My love of country is my self-love. My love of England is my love of friends. That may be the higher kind of love, but it is not the kind to make me dangerous. Which is the point. But I want you to win—now!—on this drive—come on!—and be done with your troubles, so that you and I can sit down and talk again in peace of mind either here on a White Mountain or there on a Malvern among old fortifications where your race long ago perhaps extended itself in every faculty as desperately as they are straining today. Carol says "In Berlin tomorrow!" All backward to the German Rhine! How is it the German song goes?[32]

Robert longed to see and talk to Edward Thomas: "I am simply down on the floor kicking and thrashing with resentment against everything as it is. I like nothing, neither being here with you there and so hard to talk to nor being so ineffectual at my years to help myself or anyone else."[33] A year later nothing had changed: "My whole nature simply leaps at times to cross the ocean to see you for one good talk," Robert wrote. "I had a thought of you trying to induct me into clay pipes and all the old days swept back over me. I can never live here any more without longing for there, nor there without longing for here. What kind of a predicament do you call that? But as I said, what's mine is yours. . . . We shall be waiting for you."[34]

Robert, who desperately wanted the war to end soon in victory, had come to believe that nothing would save the English but Lloyd George "and a good deal of him."[35] "Lloyd George is a great man," he wrote Edward:

> I have wanted to do something for your cause if it came my way to. I thought of writing to the papers, but everybody was taking all the space and drowning everybody else out. I did my first material bit the other day when I read to a small audience for "the wounded in France"—*not* for the Red Cross. A collection of a hundred dollars was taken up. I'm to read twice more within a week for the same cause. I only mention this in self-defense. I believe the money reaches its destination through Edith Wharton our novelist who is living in France.[36]

And Robert called on Lloyd George in another attempt to cheer his despondent friend:

> I began to think our positions were reversed—that you had got well-minded from having plunged into things and I had got soul-sick from having plunged out of them. Your letter shows you can still undertalk me when you like. A little vaccination and a little cold and you are down where it makes me dizzy to look in after you. You are so good at black talk that I believe your record will stand unbroken for years to come. . . . But look at Lloyd George. You may be down-hearted and I may be with you. But we have to admit that it is just as well to be able to say things and see things as courageously as he is. I say that quite for its face value. Lloyd George is one of the very great men.

He conceded to his friend that he was "nobody to cheer anyone else when I can't cheer myself of late. And winter's coming on."[37]

Robert defended the vote (November 1916) that would put Wilson back in the White House, defeating Hughes, for whom he had little use. Wilson and the Americans, he asserted, while they supported the war, did not want to get involved in the fighting. Yet he admitted that there was shame: "Talk is almost too cheap when all your friends are facing bullets. I don't believe I ought to enlist (since I am of course an American). . . . I did set myself to wish this country into the war. I made a little noise on the subject, but soon found I wasn't half as good at the noise as some who cared less. . . . Words won't make the shame less."[38]

From the time, in February 1915, the Frosts were settled back in Franconia,

New Hampshire, with Merfyn nearby in East Alstead, Robert had pressed Edward Thomas to join them. By June, he sensed he would not fulfill his wish: either to bring Edward over as a lecturer in a literary camp they would organize or to collaborate in an anthology of verse they would call *The Old Cloak*.[39] "You begin to talk as if you weren't coming to America to farm," he wrote his friend:

> We have gone too far into the wilds for you or something. . . . You may be right in coming over in your literary capacity. Elinor is afraid the rawness of these back towns will be too much for you. You know I sort of like it. The postmaster asked Lesley yesterday "How's Robert?" He's a nice old nasal organist who thinks God has given him the freedom of your heart and mind. I should say it wasn't fair to assume that you couldn't stand him. . . . He doesn't chew tobacco—he is a good Baptist—but many do here. And shoes aren't shined. It is really the Hell of a country. The postmaster for instance traces his descent from someone named somewhere in 500 A.D.[40]

No doubt Robert was remembering his war with the gamekeeper and the effect of the British class system on his friends in poetry!

In his reply, Edward described a dream in which they are parted: "A month or two ago," he wrote Robert, "I dreamt we were walking near Ledington but we lost one another in a strange place and I woke saying to myself 'Somehow someday I shall be here again' which I made the last line of some verses":

> Over known fields with an old friend in dream
> I walked, but came sudden to a strange stream.
> Its dark waters were bursting out most bright
> From a great mountain's heart into the light.
> They ran a short course under the sun, then back
> Into a pit they plunged, once more as black
> As at their birth: and I stood thinking there
> How white, had the day shone on them, they were,
> Heaving and coiling. So by the roar and hiss
> And by the mighty motion of the abyss
> I was bemused, that I forgot my friend
> And neither saw nor sought him till the end,
> When I awoke from waters unto men
> Saying: "I shall be here some day again."[41]

Robert realized that Edward had pulled back from plans to join him in America, but he shared his friend's agony, and both men still dreamt of meeting again in either New Hampshire or Ledington. Even after Edward enlisted, Robert clung vainly to the hope that his friend would not be called upon to make the ultimate sacrifice, that his country "may not ask of you all that you have shown yourself ready to give," he wrote Edward. "I don't want you to die (I confess I wanted you to face the possibility of death): I want you to live to come over here and begin all the life we had in St. Martin's Lane, at Tyler's Green, at White Leaved Dale, and at Balham. Use should decide it for you. If you can be more useful living than dying I don't see that you have to go behind that. Don't be run away with by your nonsense."[42] In these and other letters to Edward, Robert went out of his way to praise his friend's bravery and the "exquisite" pain he has made of it.[43]

Edward Thomas had, indeed, agonized over the decision he finally made; the unfortunate incident with the gamekeeper, while it assumed emblematic proportions in his indecision, could not have affected the inevitability of the outcome. His essay "This England" comes closest perhaps to explaining what for him was the overriding call of country. He describes his walks and talks with Robert in and around the hamlets of Ledbury, Ryton, and Dymock, across the Leadon valley, on May Hill, pausing to talk at stiles and beneath the trees in the Little Iddens orchard.

He and Robert had walked together "nearly regardless of footpaths, in a long loop," so as to end at one lodging or the other. The orchards and meadows were sometimes lined with elms, or an ash "rising out of an islet of dense brambles; many had several great old apple or pear trees. . . . More than one meadow was trenched, apparently by a dried watercourse, showing flags, rushes, and a train of willows." They would pause at gate or stile to talk—"of flowers, childhood, Shakespeare, women, England, the war"—or they looked at a far horizon, which occasionally disclosed, as through a window, the broad dome of May Hill, six miles distant. They knew, having been there in their walks, that the summit, between a few old Scots firs, commanded the Severn and the Cotswolds on the one hand, and on the other "the Wye, the Forest of Dean, the island hills of North Monmouthshire, dark and massive, the remote Black Mountains pale and cloudlike, far beyond them in Wales."

Edward leads us across fields and orchards to the essay's climax, the war, and his decision to enlist. He sees a thatched cottage, "sending up a thin blue smoke against the foliage, and casting a faint light out from one square window and open door. It was cheerful and mysterious too. No man of any nation accustomed to houses but must have longed for his home at the sight, or have suffered for lacking one, or have dreamed that this was it." And then the sight of a new moon, "a stout orange crescent, hung free of cloud near the horizon," carries his thoughts to France and the war:

All I can tell is, it seemed to me that either I had never loved England, or I had loved it foolishly, aesthetically, like a slave, not having realized that it was not mine unless

I were willing and prepared to die rather than leave it as Belgian women and old men and children had left their country. Something I had omitted. Something, I felt, had to be done before I could look again composedly at English landscape, at the elms and poplars about the houses, at the purple-headed wood-betony with two pairs of dark leaves on a stiff stem, who stood sentinel among the grasses or bracken by hedge-side or wood's-edge. What he stood sentinel for I did not know, any more than what I had got to do.[44]

After much soul-searching, Edward would enlist on July 14, 1915. As the war dragged on, he was commissioned as a 2d Lieutenant in the Artillery, volunteering for service overseas. He would carry with him to France a copy of *Mountain Interval,* handed to him by Jack Haines on his last visit to Gloucester. From the front, Edward wrote frequently to Helen, to Eleanor Farjeon, and to Robert. Robert, who longed to see his friend in person, wrote less frequently. In what may have been his last letter to his enlisted friend, he lamented the impasse of the war. Sick and sad, he included a poem "Suggested by Talk of Peace at This Time":

> France, France, I know not what is in my heart.
> But God forbid that I should be more brave
> As watcher from a quiet place apart
> Than you are fighting in an open grave.
>
> I will not ask more of you than you ask,
> O Bravest, of yourself. But shall I less?
> You know the extent of your appointed task,
> Whether you still can face its bloodiness.
>
> Not mine to say you shall not think of peace.
> Not mine, not mine. I almost know your pain.
> But I will not believe that you will cease,
> I will not bid you cease, from being slain
>
> And slaying till what might have been distorted
> Is saved to be the Truth and Hell is thwarted.[45]

These despairing lines were written just months before Edward was killed by the blast of a shell at the beginning of the Battle of Arras (April 9, 1917).

For these two brothers of the spirit, Edward's noble choice transformed their walks-talking into the evanescent and ethereal stuff of myth and nostalgia. In a letter to Eleanor Farjeon, Edward had marveled at a rainbow he saw in Robert's company: "Mine that I saw with Frost seems like the first that ever was except that I knew it was a rainbow. . . . Mine was too much of a pure rainbow, a new toy discovered by Apollo, for anyone to paint. It was more for a mythologist clad in skins."[46]

After Edward was gone, Robert knew he had to compose a poem that did justice to the depth of his feelings for his fallen comrade. In a more conventional tribute, "To E.T.," he eulogizes the soldier-poet; no longer able to unburden himself to his brother, he knows that, for him, the war could not be over "If I was not to speak of it to you / And see you pleased once more with words of mine?" More successful is the beautiful recollection of the rainbow they shared as "elected friends" in "Iris by Night":

> One misty evening, one another's guide,
> We two were groping down a Malvern side
> The last wet fields and dripping hedges home.
> There came a moment of confusing lights,
> Such as according to belief in Rome
> Were seen of old at Memphis on the heights
> Before the fragments of a former sun
> Could concentrate anew and rise as one.
> Light was a paste of pigment in our eyes.
> And then there was a moon and then a scene
> So watery as to seem submarine;
> In which we two stood saturated, drowned.
> The clover-mingled rowan on the ground
> Had taken all the water it could as dew,
> And still the air was saturated too,
> Its airy pressure turned to water weight.
> Then a small rainbow like a trellis gate,
> A very small moon-made prismatic bow,
> Stood closely over us through which to go.
> And then we were vouchsafed the miracle
> That never yet to other two befell
> And I alone of us have lived to tell.
> A wonder! Bow and rainbow as it bent,
> Instead of moving with us as we went
> (To keep the pots of gold from being found),
> It lifted from its dewy pediment
> Its two mote-swimming many-colored ends
> And gathered them together in a ring.
> And we stood in it softly circled round
> From all division time or foe can bring
> In a relation of elected friends.[47]

Receiving the terrible news of Edward Thomas's death, his friends, at first silent with grief, concluded there was nothing left but to honor the life he left behind. Haines wrote Robert that he, too, was "sick at heart"; he and Abercrombie provided details of the Arras offensive and Edward's role in it. With the Frosts' departure, Haines told Robert, Edward "had largely taken your place with Dollie and me."[48] He was pleased that he had had an extra copy of *Mountain Interval* to give to Edward on his last visit to Gloucester, which, according to Haines, he took with him to France (together with *some* Shakespeare, The English Prayer Book, and A Sentimental Journey) and praised at the end as "excellent"; he especially liked "In the Home Stretch."[49] Haines recalled the "prophetic verses" from "Lights Out," written at the front, and he tried to understand why Edward was driven to go, as the poem states,

> into the unknown
> I must enter, and leave, alone,
> I know not how.

"My own belief," Haines wrote Robert, "is that, from the beginning, he was obsessed with the idea that England had been so much to him that it was a kind of duty he owed to her to sacrifice himself. Pagan perhaps but very Thomas-like."[50]

In his poignant and powerful letter of condolence to Edward's widow, Helen, Robert extolled his "elected friend" for his bravery:

> People have been praised for self-possession in danger. I have heard Edward doubt if he was as brave as the bravest. But who was ever so completely himself right up to the verge of destruction, so sure of his thought, so sure of his word? He was the bravest and best and dearest man you and I have ever known. . . .
> Of the three ways out of here, by death where there is no choice, by death where there is a noble choice, and by death where there is a choice not so noble, he found the greatest way. There is no regret—nothing that I will call regret. Only I can't help wishing he could have saved his life without so wholly losing it and come back from France not too much hurt to enjoy our pride in him. I want to see him to tell him something. I want to tell him, what I think he liked to hear from me, that he was a poet. . . .
> It was beautiful as he did it. And I don't suppose there is anything for us to do to show our admiration but to love him forever. Robert[51]

Robert knew he had lost "the only brother" he ever had.[52] Yet, perhaps better than did her husband, Elinor plumbed the complexities of Edward's choice to enlist and serve at the front, where death was almost certain. She thought money worries had not been a factor. His books were selling the same as usual, she thought; he had saved about $1500, and the government gave him a grant of $1500 after the war commenced. "I think he went in the end," she wrote her daughter at Wellesley, "because he thought as he was physically fit to go, he ought to go. He thought he could be of just as much use as a younger man. Then, too, his anxiety to try himself in danger had something to do with it, after his encounter with the gamekeeper. Papa thinks his unhappiness at home, his irritability with Mrs. Thomas and Merfyn, had a good deal to do with it. It might have given him the *impulse* to go but I don't believe it had much to do with his decision in the end." She sent Lesley a book of Edward's poems, marking the ones she cared most for (we don't know which). She regretted that others had said so little about Thomas's personality, "that he *was* loveable, and had many friends."[53]

In her college composition, written at the time of Edward's death, Lesley echoed her mother's sentiments: "*Then,* when the war broke out, after a long and bitter struggle with himself, his strong sense of duty and love of country, for he loved England with that love that few men in this country ever learn, he enlisted in the Field Artillery Corps and later went to France." After several incidents in No Man's Land—hearing a baby's cry from a house on the front line, and watching "a great grey hawk that had been slowly circling above the clouds of smoke swoop down . . . and pick up a tiny field mouse"—suddenly death came. It was Easter Monday, and Edward was killed instantly by a bursting shell. "The relief found him there, dead, and word was sent home to his wife and three children."

10

Aftermath

"The Tender Grace of a Day that Is Dead"

*R*obert, Elinor, Lesley, Carol, Irma, and Marjorie—all gone now, of course. They had come to face personal tragedies unimagined prior to the outbreak of war in August 1914. Following their return to America from England, members of the Frost family would scatter, and Robert Frost the poet would go on to enjoy a public life unparalleled among modern poets.

Yet the early education by poetry, the great adventure in poetry, helped shape the lives of the Frost children, as it had their parents before them and would the literary families they befriended. From poetry to life and back again to poetry was a way of accepting the uncertainties and tragedies that were to be their lot, of coping with the non-reasons of life. Reading aloud, "playing school," and examining the natural phenomena from a philosophical vantage point were ingredients of their at-home education. The goal: to foster intelligence and courage. Often over a child's head, the words would touch the heart that absorbs unconsciously their meanings and their peculiar rhythm and meter. Through the imagination thing, the metaphor as make-believe, the spirit was shot on beyond its circumstances.[1]

In the Frost family's decision to depart England for America, love of country had prevailed. Shortly after reaching Franconia, New Hampshire, "at the tag end of winter," 1915, Robert wrote Jack Haines in Gloucester, sorry to be "far from all the literary life I had ever known and in the midst of dirtier little misgoverned towns than I seemed to remember flourished in America. . . . The dust and litter gathers in and under the snow for six months to come to view almost in heaps and all at once when the snow goes off in March." In another letter, he told Haines the family had gone into the White Mountains to get away from the squalor and into the wilderness: "We are come home."[2]

Once Robert had accepted a teaching position at Amherst College, he and his family could look forward to a degree of financial security not previously enjoyed. The years in search of recognition, however, continued to affect their lives. They had suffered deprivations because of poetry; they had made important friends in the name of poetry; and their future was altered irrevocably because of those early entanglements.

What remained was the nostalgia, the ache of memory. Both Robert and Elinor—and especially Elinor—clung to the belief that they had led a life "that goes rather poetically." It was out-of-sight recollections of the Derry farm—Elinor's love of the orchis and Hyla brook, the children's excitement over the hunt for wild berries and flowers in the pasture and cranberry bog, and, for all of the Frost family, remembering what courage and imagination had gone into their great adventure—that tied them to the early years in New Hampshire. It would be Edward Thomas who remained a strong emotional link between the Frosts and England.

Since the Frosts' return to America, the letters sent back and forth between the Thomas and Frost family members had been full of the uncertainties of war, family cares, and financial distress. But there had always been the hope that the hostilities would end and that the Frosts and their English friends would meet again on one side of the Atlantic or the other. Although Robert had failed to persuade Holt to consider an American edition of Edward Thomas's *Four-and-Twenty-Blackbirds,* which was published in England in 1915, Edward's poems were beginning, with Robert's encouragement, to appear here and there under his pseudonym, Edward Eastaway.[3]

When news of Edward's death reached the Frosts, Robert told friends that he "hadn't a plan for the future that didn't include him."[4] He asked for their help in getting Edward's poems published in America, and he was instrumental in obtaining favorable appraisals of the English poet in *The Yale Review* and the *North American Review.*[5] The loss deepened the friendship between the Frosts and the Haineses, who had come to share their love for the fallen soldier. "It is hard to speak of [Edward] as I want to yet," Robert wrote Jack Haines. "My love of England is my love of friends," he mourned: "I'm really a person who doesn't want anything in the world but my family and a few friends. And I don't want the friends all dead or in England. I demand sight of them."[6]

Nostalgia for their English friends found expression in verse, in such poems as "Iris by Night," Robert's poem for Edward Thomas, or "The Sound of Trees," in which the stately elms beside The Gallows are "close to our dwelling place" and their swaying, tossing, and tugging suggest the restlessness of the poet about "to set forth for somewhere." Wilfrid Gibson would write Robert (in 1916) about their fate: "*Your* trees at the Gallows, the whole group of elms, and our elm over the shed in the field, were all blown down in the same storm in the spring."[7]

Jack Haines shared his friend's nostalgia, born of their common avocation, botany, associated with their walks together in search of specimens: he remembered receiving from Robert a specimen of the Walking Fern or spleenwort (found on a limestone boulder where it "spans its way along by rooting at the tips")—a symbol for meeting again; being with Dollie and Robin on Cooper's Hill (the Cotswold tip), that he and Robert had negotiated in 1914; having "a festive time eating blackberies and running down the steep slope by the old May Pole thereon"; and spending the afternoon "wandering about the little valley of the Leadon, then full of beautiful unusual, autumn flowers, such as the primrose-leaved mullein, the small teasel, and the spreading bell-flower."[8]

Haines became the contact in other matters as well. The struggle with Mrs. Nutt over the rights to Robert's books continued long after the pirating of the first two volumes—*A Boy's Will* and *North of Boston*—and even after *Mountain Interval*. Realizing their growing worth, Robert sent money to Haines to buy up copies of the English first editions, and he asked his barrister friend to represent him in freeing the English publisher, William Heinemann, from Madame Nutt's contract (signed late in 1912) calling for control over a total of four books: "I gave two books ABW and NOB and in return got nothing, neither royalty nor accounting." All he got from Mrs. Nutt were French shrugs and "Oh poetry, you know, can't be expected to make money," and, "Americans were all money chasers."[9] Robert's poems would not appear in the *Annual,* and *Mountain Interval* was not published in England. However, the *Selected Poems of Robert Frost,* which included the poems from *Mountain Interval,* was published by William Heinemann in 1923, and was reviewed by Haines.

In addition to reviewing the *Selected Poems* (1923), Haines published a series of pieces on the Dymock poets that evoked his relations with the two poets, Robert and Edward Thomas.[10] In a response to Robert's introduction to the English edition of *A Masque of Reason and of Mercy* and *Steeple Bush* (1948), Haines referred again to the symbolic importance of the Walking Fern: "I certainly do not think the gulf in word and idiom between Robert Frost and myself has been seriously enlarged since the day when we saw the Spleenwort growing at Ryton by matchlight, through the years of his absence in America . . . until the present day."[11] But it would be in his celebratory essay, "England," included in *The Recognition of Robert Frost,* that Haines captured both the significance and the sadness of the Frosts' eventual return to England:

The death in France in 1917 of Edward Thomas, on whom he wrote a beautiful elegy, was an immense shock to Robert Frost, and for years he kept away from England and its association; but he did return for a short while, in, I think, 1928, and once again he came to Gloucestershire, and once again we walked the Cotswolds together, and later, sat on Churchdown Hill whilst he expounded the inner origin of his poetical themes, and, once again, we climbed May Hill and gazed round that astounding ring of country from the Brecon Beacons to Shropshire, and from the northernmost Cotswolds to the Channel's rim . . . but the wraith of that dead friend was ever before us, "and the tender grace of a day that is dead" could never come back to us.[12]

The shock of losing Edward Thomas had, indeed, made painful any thought of recrossing the Atlantic. But by the fall of 1922, Robert had begun to express the hope of making the return trip to England with Elinor: "I may as well make up my mind to go to you," he wrote Haines. "You will never come to me. You are afraid of this wild country."[13] Until 1928, however, such pronouncements were only wishful thinking, part of the lingering nostalgia:

Why I don't buy a ticket and hoist sail for England when I long to see you as much as I do! We would have to talk and walk in Leddington and Ryton if I came over. I should probably die of internal weeping. We would call on the ladies. Mrs. Badney across from the Gallows who knocked at our door one dark dark night with the news that the Germans had landed in Portsmouth, and Ledbury was up-side-down. (This was her version of the foolish American Christmas ship bearing gifts to the Germans equally with the Belgian French and English) and Mrs. Farmer next to Little Iddens who was a tree-poisoner as I've heard. . . . She was doing her best to live down her crime. I can't tell you how homesick I am.[14]

Once settled back in America, after 1915, the Frost children would move in and out of schools as their parents searched for a more permanent home and tried to overcome a series of debilitating illnesses and grinding financial worries.

Unlike the others, Lesley—more self-willed and energetic—seemed never to look back. Rapidly completing high school in Amherst, Massachusetts (where her father taught at the college), she took one difficult year at Wellesley College (1917–1918). The following summer and fall, she worked on wooden propellers at the Curtis airplane factory in Marblehead, Massachusetts; Irma was nearby at the Dana Hall School in Wellesley, where she experienced bouts of homesickness. Lesley went on to Barnard College (as a Latin major) the spring of 1918, remaining through the following academic year. She followed her parents to the University of Michigan at Ann Arbor, but she soon returned to New York, and to the writing and editorial work in the book trade she had commenced in the summer of 1920. In 1924, she and Marjorie founded The Open Book in Pittsfield, Massachusetts; by the following summer, she had inaugurated The Knapsack, a caravan bookstore mounted on the back of a Ford truck, which she drove through New England towns and camps during the summers, beginning in 1925. Marjorie, however, was "torn two or three different ways at her age and with her mind," and her father wrote Lesley that "the book store has got to be parttime with her till she sees clearer."[15]

Carol Frost would marry, and with his wife, Lillian LaBatt, move to a farm purchased by his parents in South Shaftsbury, Vermont, where their son, William Prescott Frost, was born in 1924. Carol's sister Irma, after taking courses at the Art Student's League and making an unsuccessful attempt to enter the field of fashion design in New York, married John Paine Cone, a promising architect; their first son was born in 1927.

While it was not unusual for a member of the Frost family to come down with one illness or another—with colds and attacks of grippe that often lasted weeks at a time—Marjorie's health had become an ever increasing preoccupation for her parents.

By the summer of 1928, when it at last seemed feasible to get away from the states for a period of three or four months, only Marjorie was still at home. She had suffered from a variety of illnesses and nervous prostration, requiring lengthy convalescence. In connection with a trip to France planned by Lesley but which had to be canceled, Madame Fischbacher, a friend of the Frosts' neighbor in Arlington, Vermont, Dorothy Canfield Fisher, had offered hospitality to members of the Frost family if they should reach France. Marjorie was anxious to learn French, which Lesley had studied before her, and the thought of staying with Madame Fischbacher in Sèvres for a few months appealed to her.[16]

In light of Marjorie's precarious health, her parents agonized over the decision: "We didn't dare to make this expedition with Marj as she is," Robert wrote a friend in Amherst, "and we didn't dare not to make it. The second fear won."[17] With the tickets in hand, and only then, did Robert write to Jack Haines in Gloucester:

> The only thing that can keep me from walking a path with you this year will be the failure of Margery to come up to the mark on sailing day. She is not right. . . . We will have to think a good deal of her while over. . . . Don't set your heart too much on seeing us, and I will try not to set my heart too much on seeing you. I will bring Elinor to your house inside of a few weeks now, though, if it in me lies. You dont care how old we look. Wont it be astonishing to find ourselves again with the three of you.[18]

On the day the three Frosts departed from South Shaftsbury, Robert wrote Lesley: "Marjorie seems so-so and we are off on the Flyer for Queens Hotel Montreal this afternoon (Friday, [3 August 1928]). The [SS] Montnairn starts us down stream at three tomorrow. Too bad we werent educated against sea sickness by being lowered suddenly a lot when babes in arms."[19] Elinor recounted the last-minute uncertainties:

> You don't know anything about the hard time we had just before leaving home. On getting out of bed one morning, Marjorie sprained the sacro-iliac joint in her back, and had intense pain for several days, in her back, and this somehow induced a series of sick headaches. . . . We had a wonderful trained nurse for her—so wondeful that she managed to get Marjorie on her feet and in some sort of condition to take the railway journey to Quebec, and get on board, though we had practically given up going. I had written to the Baltimore doctor, and he advised taking her if we could possibly manage it. Fortunately, her back improved in time for her to walk on deck a lot, and the voyage did her good. She was seasick only a little one morning. I was sick for three days, and as I was nearly a wreck when we started, you can imagine what a state I was in when we reached Paris. Robert was not sick at all.[20]

Having caught the train from Montreal to Quebec, the Frosts boarded the SS *Montnairn* at three o'clock the next afternoon. The first two days on the St. Lawrence seaway were pleasant enough. They "saw a good sized iceberg, and had a lovely view of Belle Isle going through the strait," but the final three days crossing to Cherbourgh were terrible for Elinor (less so for Robert and Marj); already homesick, she swore that "never again after that will I take an ocean trip as long as I live."[21]

Once in Paris, Marjorie seemed to enjoy the art, including some "pictures of water lillies by Monet who," according to her father, "seems to suit her fastidiousness." The letters home, however, told mostly why the Frosts were eager to move over to England as soon as possible. Robert, unable to speak French, was horrified by "the greedy leer and wink everybody has for us and our money . . . what we are most aware of is not the beauty of Paris, but the deceitful hate all round us." They would stay for Marjorie's sake, he wrote Lesley at home in Pittsfield, and "we'll remember the good things when we look back." At the moment, however, he is worried about both Marjorie and Elinor: "Mama is only so so but stoutly denying it. After this folly, rest. . . . What the Hell am I so far out of my balliwick for anyway. Elinor needs a place of quiet to rest in and I need one to write in. So what's this expedition all about? May be Marj. But she doesnt praise it very highly. We could have bought a farm for the price of it. Aint I going strong?"[22]

With the holdover in Paris, Robert wrote to Jack Haines to explain the delay: "We came to France in the hope that it might improve our invalid Marjorie by awakening an interest in her to learn the French language. That hope has failed and the disappointment has been almost too much for Elinor on top of everything else. . . . I cant tell you how she has lost courage and strength." He asked Haines to help him take care of Elinor once they found a suitable "travelling-companion-nurse" for Marjorie: "She must be put on her feet again before we attempt any going around among people in England."[23]

Leaving Marjorie with Madame Fischbacher, Elinor and Robert made their way as far as London, staying at the Imperial Hotel on Russell Square, next door to the old Premier Hotel, where the Frosts had stayed upon their arrival in 1912. After a few days, when Elinor seemed sufficiently rested, they continued on to Gloucester, where the affectionate attentiveness of the Haineses helped them both regain their strength. "We had a pleasant time in Gloucester," Elinor wrote Lesley. "Robin is a very nice boy of 15." Robert reported on their visit to The Gallows and Little Iddens: "The people at the Gallows are at enmity with the neighborhood and drove us off when we tried to look the old place over," he wrote Lesley. "Probably they were ashamed of the rundown condition of the property—everything overgrown and the thatch rotted and fallen in. The people at Little Iddens were glad to show us in. That place is better than we left it."[24]

Upon their return to the Imperial Hotel—with their two quiet and small but cosy rooms on the court, with large bath (for $6.75 per day, breakfast included)— Robert and Elinor began to do the rounds of old and new English friends. They visited J. C. Squire, poet and editor of *The London Mercury,* who published some of Robert's poems; they spent two nights at the home of John Freeman, a Georgian poet (and head of an insurance company) with whom Robert had had only passing acquaintance in the coffeehouses of London thirteen years earlier, and a night with the De la Mares in Taplow; and they received the John Gould Fletchers at the Imperial Hotel. Robert wrote home, "Some things have disappointed us as much as we were afraid everything might (we were prepared for the worst); but De la Mare, A. E., Squier [Squire], and Freeman haven't a bit."[25]

To Lesley her father wrote about the poets she would have remembered: "The Gibsons live at Letchworth (in Hertfordshire), where the children can have the advantages of the Quaker schools. Gibson's stock as a poet is quoted very low right now. How he lives is a puzzle to his friends. His third of the income from Rupert Brooke's books may still be a big help." Walter de la Mare had emerged as "the prominent one of them all" despite serious surgery; W. H. Davies, still writing his best, nevertheless "suffers his worst pangs of jealousy over de la Mare" and had married "a very young wild thing of no definable class, but partly gypsy."[26]

Elinor was feeling well enough to go with Robert by car to visit Davies. They found him delightful and unchanged, ready to take up the conversation just as it had been dropped in 1915: "The minute Elinor and I got there he rose and presented us with an autographed poem as a 'souvenir of our visit.' He hasnt aged a hair. Still harping on why he isnt read in America."[27] Lascelles Abercrombie, Robert wrote Lesley, was living with his family in Leeds, and doing some lecturing, but "has been too busy and recently too ill to write poetry." He had tried to read one of Lascelles's plays that had been branded as immoral, but quickly gave up on it because of its "stilted vernacular."[28]

By mid-September, Elinor and Robert had received word from Marjorie that, although she had "been through the most hellish part of hell" in trying to understand the French language, she was "feeling surprisingly well" and wanted to stay in Sèvres "until the middle of October, anyway." It was Elinor, however, who was continuing to struggle with fatigue and homesickness. She was prepared to stay until the end of October, if Marj wanted her to, but she did not "think any longer than that."[29]

Under the weather with colds, she and Robert had by now moved from the Imperial Hotel to The Georgian House (at 10 Bury Street). "The Imperial was a very nice hotel, and it was more lively," Elinor wrote home, "but here we have large sitting room, with fireplace, and couch and two capacious armchairs and large bedroom & bath. There is no dining room here, but meals are served very nicely in your room if you wish, more expensively also." With the cold weather, she had to keep "a coal fire in the grate all day. The smell of coal reminds me so much of the old days at Beaconsfield. It moves me more than the *sight* of the place did, somehow."[30]

When it came time for Robert to spend a few days in Ireland, Elinor was still too fatigued to accompany him, staying behind in the hotel in London to rest: "I don't know just what day he will come back," she wrote Lesley. "I am supposed to be resting, but I have been writing letters pretty steadily. . . . What a curse is the obligation to write letters! I was not made with the facility about it that some people have, and I often think that trying to write a lot of letters, in addition to my other tasks, is what has brought me down so the last four or five years. When I don't write them they are like a dead weight on my spirits."[31]

Robert had become acquainted with Padraic Colum shortly after returning to New York in 1915 and had entertained George William Russell ("AE") a few years later in Amherst. He had written Colum from London, explaining that because "Elinor has steadily worn down with the effort of travel . . . [s]he wouldn't be able to come with me to Dublin: I should be alone."[32] During his five days in Ireland, Robert stayed with a friend of Colum's, the poet Constantine P.

Curran, and had one brief and disappointing encounter with W. B. Yeats. He was indeed "introduced to Ireland by the right person."[33]

Back in London, there were awkward encounters with old acquaintances, some barely remembered and with whom the Frosts had lost all contact over the intervening years. John Cournos, for example, was found in a moment of personal crisis: his wife was to undergo surgery the next day, and the family was short of cash. Robert sent a check for fifty dollars and took a bouquet of yellow roses to the hospital.

Although the Frosts did not at first hear from the widow of Edward Thomas, they had seen her book, *As It Was* (1926), and, once in London, had learned that she "has entirely new friends" and that she "plans more books about Edward. Nobody blames her to[o] hard for that first one," Robert wrote Lesley.[34] But sometime after Robert returned from Dublin to London, the Frosts must have heard from Helen Thomas; at least one meeting was arranged, perhaps once with Robert alone without Elinor, and then again the two of them with the Thomas children and Eleanor Farjeon. Both Elinor and Robert thought Helen made Edward look ridiculous in her memoirs, by going into such detail in their marital affairs, and in her portrayal of Eleanor Farjeon, whom Robert thought Helen had hoped to "conquer . . . with magnanimity."[35]

Robert wrote Jack Haines that the meeting with Helen Thomas "ended one passage in our lives."[36] And there is where I believe the Frosts would have wanted to leave it. They had concluded that Helen's sentimental journey in print—which, for Helen, was a retrospective attempt to work off her grief and to give meaning to her life—was an unseemly distortion they considered injurious to what they loved in Edward. They were uncomfortable with Helen's desire to carry on a friendship that had meant so much to her husband when alive.

Helen Thomas would bring out a second volume, *World without End* (1931), in which she acknowledged that Robert "loved [Edward], understanding, as no other man had ever understood, his strange complex temperament" and credited him with releasing in Edward "that final and fullest expression of himself which [Edward] now found in writing poetry."[37] The two volumes together, in part because of their more intimate revelations, eased Helen's financial worries and, as she said, "helped Edward in all sorts of indirect ways, . . . [hastening] a wider acknowledgment of him & interest in his work."[38]

With this embarrassing episode behind them, Elinor and Robert tried to make the best of it in London. Although they hadn't "looked up plays yet," they spent an evening seeing "one of the Russian dances—a fantasy called the Nightingale and the Rose." One afternoon they went to tea at the Mairs'; "Lucy is the only child at home," Elinor wrote Lesley. Elinor was still hoping to accompany her husband to Leeds "to spend a day or two with the Abercrombies, and probably on further to Edinburgh to see the Smiths." They had had no communication with the Gardners, however, "or heard anything about them."[39]

Because the Frosts had postponed their trip to England so many times and were reluctant to announce their plans in advance, invitations were slow in coming for Robert to read his poems or to attend public functions in London. The Poetry Bookshop was still a clearinghouse for all the poets, and by 1928 it had moved from its old location at 35 Devonshire Street to 38 Great Russell Street, near the British Museum. Robert had not yet entirely forgiven the dour Harold Monro for failing to appreciate Edward Thomas's poetry until after his death; he also thought that Monro had treated him "very shabily" and that he "always resented my being."[40] He was therefore pleasantly surprised to find Monro more open and friendly than he had been in 1914. Monro soon arranged for Robert to meet a number of the poets, including, for the first time, T. S. Eliot, and he persuaded him to give a reading of his poems at the Bookshop, which he had been too timid to do in 1914.

Among those receiving the Bookshop announcement of the reading, scheduled for October 18, was Wilfrid Gibson, whom Robert had studiously ignored since 1915. Gibson invited the Frosts to visit his home, where they could see Gerald and meet their children: Audrey (12), Michael (10), and Joselyn (8). "Do come," he wrote Robert. "Life is so short at best: and the years race by (I was fifty yesterday!) and there may not be too many more chances of meeting."[41] Robert and Elinor made their way (one hour by train from Kings Cross station) to Hertfordshire. There the two families reminisced about Gloucestershire, Gibson indulging in his usual sentimentalities.

The Frosts and Gibsons did not see each other again in England. But within a few days, Wilfrid would compose a poem, "Reunion—To Robert Frost" (October 6, 1928), commemorating their reunion, which he mailed to the Frosts in America. The thirty-three-line poem in blank verse calls up their gatherings in Gloucestershire,

> Before war overwhelmed our world, and scattered
> As sparks before the wind, our little circle
> Of friendly spirits broadcast . . .
> > Fourteen years
> Of silence lie between us . . .

The poem then moves to the present, recounting how they

> sit at peace,
> Talking once more together, as we talked
> With Abercrombie, Brooke, and Thomas then . . .

And, finally, "the hour of parting nears," to be separated by the Atlantic, "for how long, who knows?"

Once back in the States, Robert sent Gibson a copy of *West-Running Brook* (1928); Gibson returned the favor with a letter of praise, followed by a copy of his latest book of poems, *Hazards* (1930), which included the poem "To Robert Frost." Wilfrid continued to write Robert an occasional letter. By 1934, the Gibsons' income was "dwindling and dwindling" to the point where they contemplated taking in "student paying-guests" to help support their teenage children. Wilfrid wrote Robert that "Lascelles has been very ill" and that he and Catherine "looked as if life had been too much for them." He sent condolences when Elinor died in 1938; and when Lascelles died the following year, he asked Robert to provide a verse or prose tribute in memory of his poet-friend. In rejoicing over Robert's success as a poet, Gibson lamented his own fate: "I am one of those unlucky writers whose books have predeceased him."[42]

In another painfully sentimental tribute to the fellowship of the poets before World War I, Gibson wrote "The Magnet," describing how

> . . . the magnetism of poetry
> Of elemental inspiration served to draw
> Together such dissimilar men
> In an intuitive fellowhip, and bind
> Their lives inevitably
> In mutual aspiration, as, in kind
> They shared the universal ecstasy
> Of nature-lovers; and their hearts were stirred,
> Like mine, to rapture, as they heard
> The West wind sweeping over Gloucestershire
> And flourishing the branches of the tree;
> While, with enkindling eyes, they saw
> The leaping flames of fire;
> And, though they spoke and wrote so variously,
> A kindred instinct quickened their desire
> To voice in words their sensibility."[43]

Elinor was hoping, with help from the Haineses in Gloucester, to go "into an inn in one of these Cotswold villages" where she could rest for a week or two until they sailed, perhaps by the end of October.[44] Unfortunately, she received troubling news from Madame Fischbacher in Sèvres that Marjorie was not well. She insisted upon going on her own to join Marj in France; it was agreed that Robert would follow in a few days, with plans to sail home from Le Havre by the middle of November. The number of engagements for readings and the like had begun to pile up, and Elinor understood the need for her husband to stay behind and meet his obligations.

Among the invitations was one from Jessy Mair, who arranged for Robert to speak on October 25 before a student group at the Literary Society of the London School of Economics, where she was Secretary (and William Henry Beveridge, her future husband, was Director). Word also came from Robert's old Scottish friend, J. C. Smith, who had learned, probably through the Mairs, that he was in Britain. Upon hearing from his American friend, Smith expressed relief, adding that he "should have taken it very much amiss" if the Frosts had gone back to America without coming to see him and his family.[45]

It appears that Robert traveled alone, first to Edinburgh, spending just one night with the Smiths before returning by way of Leeds, where he honored a promise he had given Lascelles Abercrombie to read his poems at the University of Leeds in Yorkshire. Abercrombie, a diabetic and by now a chronic invalid, could talk of little else besides his insulin treatment, Robert recalled. Catherine, he said, "made matters worse by saying that if Lascelles had had any luck he would have 'beaten' Frost in reputation and fame." So far as Robert could see, "there had never been any spirit of competition between them."[46]

While Elinor was away, Robert found time to renew another old friendship, with the poet F. S. Flint, and Flint, in turn, arranged an evening with the critic Edward Garnett.

Before hearing from Elinor that Marjorie was stronger than first word had indicated, Robert wrote to Haines (from London), blaming himself for his predicament. Having asked Haines to help him cash a check for five hundred dollars (in pounds), he went on to explain why in all likelihood they would not get back to Gloucester before sailing: "I wish I could promise to see you again," he wrote. "But it wouldnt be honest as things are. I've made Elinor unhappier keeping her on than I think I ever made her before. She's too sick for a jaunting party and I shouldnt have dragged her out of her home." He urged the Haineses to "come to America to our house . . . any time you get ready—only make it soon. . . . These closing rites (writes) are mournful. Never mind, we arent women and children."[47]

By early November, Elinor had sent word that she would bring Marjorie over to England "because she wanted to see some of the places she remembered as a child."[48] They all three met back at the Imperial Hotel on Russell Square: "Marjorie and I came over to England Saturday," Elinor wrote Lesley. "The Channel was glorious—a sky with billowing black clouds, with patches & streaks of light near the horizon, and steely dark water. It wasn't rough, though, and Marjorie and I stood in the bow of the boat the whole hour of crossing without a single qualm of seasickness, and enjoyed it, immensely." Although Marjorie had made "a big gain in French . . . she really hasn't any ear for it, and she says it would take her 5 yrs to learn to talk and understand." She found Robert had "been getting too tired. Now he has a bad pain in his temples, either neuralgia or sinus and a peculiar hoarseness. . . . He should have a two weeks complete rest, at least, but we are badly situated for that—with many engagements he has made for the week. He cannot seem to stop and I don't know just what to do. We *may* sail on the Olympic, the 14th [of November]."[49]

Neither Elinor nor Marjorie were well enough to see people and go about, and it was just a matter of fulfilling several promised engagements before making their way to Cherbourgh and home. Dinners at the PEN Society and the English Speaking Union had been arranged by the Irish-American poet Norreys Jephson O'Conor and his wife, Grace, whom Robert had known back in New England. Both engagements had to be canceled when Robert became ill, and he was forced to decline an invitation to dine with the Eliots and the Yeatses at the home of Edith Sitwell. He was able to fit in a tea with Poet Laureate Robert Bridges in Oxford, having traveled there alone (on November 8). Just before leaving, he joined his wife and daughter in visiting a few more of the sights in London Marjorie remembered from childhood.[50]

Robert, Elinor, and Marjorie sailed together from Cherbourgh aboard the SS *Olympic* (White Star Line) on November 14, all three Frosts fighting fatigue and stress. Before reaching New York, four days out in the Atlantic, Robert wrote John Freeman to explain their abrupt departure:

> The abruptness made it easier to break with you all. . . . We ran right out of Cherbourgh into a hundred-and-fifty mile gale that knocked her nose in and brought us to a standstill for three hours a thousand miles from anywhere among some of the biggest waves they say you ever see. . . . It scared the sea sickness out of us to be so mysteriously dead in those wind-played hills and hollows. . . . We all relapsed into sea-sickness from the depressing effect of sustained thinking. All that was days ago. We are now knowtting along at the rate of 500 a day about off Nova Scotia and shall soon be on the farm in Vermont with a falalalala. It will be too late to see my water lily leaves before they go under water for the winter. That is a good deal your fault old man and you will have to answer for it by coming over to see us soon in the Richest County and bringing with you all the family. Seriously you must. We know how to talk to each other. You bound me to England with new ties for some of the old that proved to have broken.[51]

Traveling alone by air, the by-now widowed Robert Frost would return to England (with a brief stopover in Ireland) in May 1957, to receive honorary degrees at a number of universities, including Oxford and Cambridge. I would join my grandfather in London on June 1, from Madrid, where I was employed in the American Embassy.

RF had been invited to make this arduous journey, late in his life, as part of the United States Department of State's Educational Exchange: American Specialists Program. Harold E. Howland, in the State Department at the time, explains the circumstances of his mission:

> When we in the State Department discussed our desire to invite Mr. Frost to take on this cultural "mission" we debated in our own minds whether we should ask this distinguished and venerable man to undertake the arduous task of lecturing and traveling throughout England. Our experience with much younger men on these cultural lecturing tours had provided us with ample evidence that these assignments could be taxing ones, indeed. The "stakes were high," however. . . .
>
> It was our belief that we needed someone, not in politics, not in government, but rather from "our people" who was loved and respected by both England and America, to remind the British people of our mutual aspirations and hopes. Mr. Frost's greatness as a poet was discovered in England even before our country recognized his abilities. . . .
>
> So we called on Mr. Frost and discussed with him our desire for him to go, but also our especial concern over his age and his well-being. I shall never forget his words: "I was re-reading recently the life of Voltaire. You will recall that Voltaire, in 1778, left the serenity of his village residence in Ferney, Switzerland to again appear with the crowds of Paris. It was a stren[u]ous visit and he died on that trip. His age then was, as is mine now, 82. Nevertheless, if my country believes I can be of any use in reminding the British people of our own warm affection and strong friendship, why, of course, I'll go. I don't want to be an unguided missile, however; don't spare me. Tell me where you want me to go and when. I'll be ready."[52]

That he was ready, and that he was successful, may be attested to by the abundant acclaim, honors, and tributes he received throughout the British Isles.

A few days after I arrived in England, at Oxford University, we would listen to the Oration delivered in Latin to "one who has loved his Virgil from his schooldays onwards."[53] On the drive back to London, accompanied by reporters from *Life* magazine (and by me as the only family member), we called on the now nearly blind Jack Haines, who was living with his son Robin in Cheltenham. We spent the night, giving the two elderly men an opportunity to meet alone for several hours, recalling their time together in 1914 with Edward Thomas and the other poets, and with Elinor and Dorothy on his return visit in 1928. "We are not as sentimental about anything as we used to be unless it is friendship," Robert told Haines as the trials of a long life were coming to an end.

"I shall have less to say," Robert's English poem had proclaimed, "but I shall be gone."[54]

The next day, the official party, led by the *Life* reporters, stopped at The Old Nailshop at the Greenway (where W. W. Gibson and his wife had resided in 1914) and Little Iddens (where the Frosts had lived the months before the outbreak of war).[55]

In his book *Dymock Down the Ages,* the Reverend J. E. Gethyn Jones describes the memory-charged moment as Robert entered The Nailshop:

> Slowly he entered the "Golden Room" where, in the distant past, he had held the silent circle spellbound. Within that room, the central meeting-place of their fellowship, Frost was strangely silent. Did the shades speak to him? Did a laughing voice echo across land and sea from the Aegean Isle where Brooke's body rests? Did Frost hear again the measured phrase of Thomas from the Vimy Ridge [Arras]? In his imagination were they all there, those whom he knew so well and loved so dear? Who knows?[56]

Moving on, our small caravan stopped across from Little Iddens in a field of young green oats, and Robert hesitated to enter the home where Elinor had once held sway: "How his fortune had changed since first he viewed that half-timbered cottage backed by the cherry trees on Henberrow bank!" Reverend Jones recalled. "Elinor and the children had been with him when first he came. In 1957 a grown up grand-daughter stood by his side, but the older generation had passed within the 'veil.'" The *Life* photographer captured the American poet as he stood in the field of young oats—Little Iddens in the distance behind him—his hand covering his eyes in ache of memory. Here in this place he and Elinor and their four children had experienced the joy of poetry in motion—in Nature as in their natures. Here he and Edward had known the "easy hours" of talks-walking and friendship. And here he had savored, for the first time, overwhelmingly favorable reviews of his poems (in *A Boy's Will* and *North of Boston*). The cares of a lifetime weighed heavily on him now, but the resolve, hope, and expectations from those early years gave way to the demands of the heart. As I look now at my grandfather's picture from that day together, I can hear his measured voice recite the lines from his "Wild Grapes":

> The mind—is not the heart.
> I may yet live, as I know others live,
> To wish in vain to let go with the mind—
> Of cares, at night, to sleep; but nothing tells me
> That I need to learn to let go with the heart.

An emotional moment, of course, but Robert approached the poor, cramped cottage quietly, touching the low box hedge and water pump by the kitchen door and remarking that they were there "when we were here."[57] Making his way up the narrow staircase and through the upstairs rooms, he was relaxed with the current occupants, chatting with their young son; out one of the windows he could catch a glimpse of May Hill.

With the press of photographers and onlookers, we did not stop at Oldfields, where the Thomases had stayed through August 1914, although we could see it easily across the pasture from Little Iddens. We drove on to The Gallows, which had been deteriorating rapidly when Robert last visited the Dymock region in 1928. Now there was stark ruin: "The Gallows of the Abercrombies had gone. One wing alone, and that hidden by undergrowth and ivy-covered, remained to give shelter and to remind one of a house that once had rung with laughter and had seen great days."[58]

By the time I arrived in London on June 1, my grandfather had already caught a glimpse of Edward Thomas's widow, Helen (and her daughter Bronwen), at a reading at the University of London, where he also saw his friends Eleanor Farjeon and F. S. Flint. Plans made for us to travel with Eleanor Farjeon to Helen's home in Lambourn, a good three hours away in the Embassy car, had to be canceled when Robert's health became more unstable on what was the eve of his all-important trip to Oxford.[59]

Among the numerous social functions, sometimes as many as three in one day, RF had attended a sherry party with Amy Smith Pantin (the wife of Professor C.F.A. Pantin and daughter of J. C. Smith of Edinburgh) in Cambridge, and would have tea at her home before the conferral of the honorary degree.[60] He had also seen Jessy Mair, widowed (in 1942) and remarried to Lord William Beveridge, and her daughter, Lucy, at a luncheon in the House of Lords; he would lunch with them again at University College (Oxford) a few days later.[61] Robert had met T. S. Eliot for the first time in 1928. On this trip, he dined with the Eliots at their home and was toasted by Eliot at a dinner at the English Speaking Union.[62] He had tea at The Westbury with Mrs. Lascelles (Catherine) Abercrombie and Mrs. Ralph Abercrombie, her daughter-in-law, and the following day had tea at the home of Eleanor Farjeon at Perrins Walk (Hampstead).[63]

Eleanor Farjeon had taken me to see Shakespeare's *Antony and Cleopatra* at the Old Vic. Later, during my grandfather's visit to her wooden hayloft (where Eleanor worked), she produced a copy of *Kings and Queens,* a collection of witty biographical poems she and her brother Herbert ("Bertie") had published with lavish illustrations, which she inscribed: "To [Lesley] Lee with love from Eleanor Farjeon in memory of our evening at the Old Vic here are more Kings than even Shakespeare wrote of, and as much of English History as anybody needs to know. June 10th 1957"; for Robert, she inscribed a copy of Edward Thomas's first volume of poems (London, 1917, using his pseudonym, "Edward Eastaway," and the first book ever dedicated to Robert Frost): "To Robert from Eleanor June 1957 (*October 1917*)."[64]

Seeming to understand not only the problems of illness and logistics but the overriding momentousness of the occasion as well, Eleanor Farjeon concluded her account of her final meeting with my grandfather (at her hayloft on Whit Monday): "We did not meet again, and we did not write. The friendship that stretched from the day I met Robert Frost in 1914 to the day he died in 1963, remains as unbroken as in those forty-two years of silence. We do not lose our friends when they die, we only lose sight of them."[65]

Robert and Elinor Frost Family Chronology

1844 Oct 2	RF's mother, Isabelle Moodie, born at Leith, seaport of Edinburgh, Scotland; she sailed to America in c. 1853 and became a schoolteacher in Columbus, Ohio; died Nov 2, 1900.
1850 Dec 27	RF's father, William Prescott Frost, Jr., born at Kingston, New Hampshire; after graduating Phi Beta Kappa from Harvard College in June 1872, he served as headmaster of Lewistown Academy in Lewistown, Pennsylvania, where he married Isabelle Moodie on March 18, 1873; died May 5, 1885.
1873 Oct 25	Elinor Miriam White born in Acton, Massachusetts; died March 21, 1938, in Gainesville, Florida, following cancer surgery and heart complications.
1874 March 26	Robert Lee Frost born in San Francisco.
1876 June 25	RF's sister, Jeanie Florence Frost, born in Lawrence, Massachusetts, died September 7, 1929.
1885 May	Upon the death of RF's father, Isabelle Moodie Frost and her two children, Robert and Jeanie, moved back to New England, settling in Salem, New Hampshire.
1890	RF wrote and published (in the Lawrence High School Bulletin) his first poem, "La Noche Triste."
1892 June	RF and Elinor White were graduated from Lawrence High School and shared valedictorian honors.
Sept	Elinor White began studies at St. Lawrence University; RF attended Dartmouth College for three months. RF began two-and-a-half year sequence of occasional jobs as teacher, millworker, and newspaperman.
1894	RF had first book of poems privately printed; the only "edition" of *Twilight* consisted of two copies.
Nov 8	"My Butterfly: An Elegy" published in *The* (New York) *Independent*.

1895 Dec 19	RF and Elinor White were married in Lawrence, Massachusetts.
1896 Aug 20	RF published second poem in *The Independent:* "The Birds Do Thus."
Sept 25	First child born to RF and Elinor, a son named Elliott; died July 28, 1900, of *cholera infantum.*
1897 Jan 13	RF published a third poem in *The Independent:* "Caesar's Lost Transport Ships."
April 30	RF published a poem entitled "Greece" in the Boston *Evening Transcript.*
Sept	RF began attending Harvard College; withdrew March 31, 1899, and returned to Lawrence, Massachusetts.
Sept 9	RF published a poem entitled "Warning" in *The Independent.*
1899 April 28	Birth of RF's and Elinor's second child, Lesley; died July 9, 1983.
1900 Oct	The Frost family moved to Derry, New Hampshire, and settled on a farm purchased by RF's grandfather, William Prescott Frost; willed to RF (with an annuity) upon his death on July 10, 1901.
1901 June 27	RF published a poem, "The Quest of the Orchis," in *The Independent.*
1902 May 27	Third child born to RF and Elinor, a son named Carol; committed suicide on October 9, 1940, in South Shaftsbury, Vermont.
1903 June 27	Fourth child born to RF and Elinor, a daughter named Irma; died April 12, 1981.
1905 March 29	Fifth child born to RF, a daughter named Marjorie; died May 2, 1934.
1906 March 9	RF published a poem, "The Tuft of Flowers," in the Derry *Enterprise.*
March 16	RF published a poem, "Ghost House," in *Youth's Companion.*
Spring	RF began teaching part-time at Pinkerton Academy; in September the position became full-time.
Summer	The Frosts began spending summers in Bethlehem, New Hampshire, with John and Margaret Lynch.
Oct 11	RF published a poem, "The Trial by Existence," in *The Independent.*
1907 March	RF published a poem, "The Later Minstrel," in the Pink-

	erton *Critic* and another poem, "The Lost Faith," in the Derry *News*.
June 18	Sixth child born to RF and Elinor, a daughter named Elinor Bettina; died two days later.
Oct	RF published a poem, "A Line-storm Song," in *New England Magazine*.
1908 March 26	RF published a poem, "Across the Atlantic," in *The Independent*.
1909 May	RF published a poem, "Into My Own," in *New England Magazine,* and another poem, "The Flower-boat," in *Youth's Companion*.
Sept	The Frosts left the Derry farm and rented an apartment in Derry Village.
Oct	RF published a poem, "A Late Walk," in the Pinkerton *Critic*.
1911 Sept	Having completed his teaching duties in June, RF moved with his family to Plymouth, New Hampshire, where he taught at the State Normal School for one academic year.
1912 Aug 24	Having sold the Derry farm, the Frost family sailed on the SS *Parisian* from Boston to Glasgow, traveling by train to London on September 3 and spending the first days in England at the Premier Hotel, Russell Square.
Sept 10	The Frost family arrived at The Bungalow in Beaconsfield.
Oct 3	RF published a poem, "October," in *Youth's Companion*.
Oct 26	MS of *A Boy's Will* accepted for publication by David Nutt and Company, London.
Nov	RF published a poem, "My November Guest," in *The Forum,* and another poem, "Reluctance," in *Youth's Companion*.
Christmas	Irma Frost presented "Many Storys" to her parents.
1913 Jan 8	RF attended opening of the Poetry Bookshop in London. Met F. S. Flint.
	"An Important Year by Four Children" dedicated to their parents by the Frost children.
April	*A Boy's Will,* RF's first trade book of poetry, published in London by David Nutt.
Aug	The Frost family went by boat to Leith, Scotland; spent two weeks in the coastal village of Kingsbarns, Fifeshire, on the Firth of Tay.

Oct 6	RF introduced to Edward Thomas by Ralph Hodgson in London.
Dec	Harold Monro's *Poetry and Drama* includes two poems by RF: "The Fear" and "A Hundred Collars."
Christmas	"On the Road to Fleuraclea" presented to her father by Lesley Frost.
Christmas	"Our Old Farm" presented to his father by Carol Frost.
1914 April	The Frost family moved from Beaconsfield to London, taking rooms above Harold Monro's Poetry Bookshop.
May	The Frost family moved from London to Gloucestershire, remaining in the country (at Little Iddens and The Gallows) for nine months, until their departure for the United States.
May 15	*North of Boston* published in London by David Nutt.
June	First surviving issue of *The Bouquet*. The issues for July and September 1914, [Jan] and April 1915, and June 1916 have also been preserved.
July	RF met Jack Haines at Little Iddens.
Aug	The Thomas family and Eleanor Farjeon joined the Frosts, Gibsons, and Abercrombies at Ryton/Dymock. Declaration of war.
Sept	RF and Lesley traveled to Edinburgh to visit J. C. Smith and his family.
late Nov	RF and Edward Thomas involved in the "gamekeeper incident" near The Gallows.
1915 Feb 13	The Frost family, bringing with them Edward and Helen Thomas's son Merfyn, sailed on the SS *St. Paul* out of Liverpool, arriving in New York on February 22.
Feb 20	*North of Boston* published in New York City by Henry Holt and Company.
April	*A Boy's Will* published by Henry Holt and Company. RF arranges to purchase a farm in Franconia, New Hampshire.
1916 Nov	RF's *Mountain Interval* published by Henry Holt and Company.
1917 Jan	RF began a relationship with Amherst College that would continue, intermittently, for nearly a half-century.
Sept	Lesley attended Wellesley College for one year.
1918	Lesley worked at Curtis airplane factory in Marblehead, Massachusetts, during summer and fall.

Fall	Irma attended Dana Hall School, Wellesley, Massachusetts.
Winter	Lesley commenced year-and-a-half of studies at Barnard College (Latin major).
1920 Summer	Lesley undertook writing and editorial work in New York.
Fall	The Frost family made gradual move from Franconia to South Shaftsbury, Vermont. Irma studied at the Art Students League in New York and made unsuccessful attempts to enter the field of fashion designing. Carol continued his life as poet-farmer.
1921 Sept	RF began first of three one-year stints in residence at the University of Michigan, returning to Amherst in 1926.
1923	RF's *Selected Poems* published. Carol Frost and Lillian LaBatt married. RF's *New Hampshire* published; awarded Pulitzer Prize.
1924	Lesley and Marjorie founded The Open Book in Pittsfield, Massachusetts.
1925 Summer	Lesley inaugurated The Knapsack, a traveling adjunct to the Pittsfield bookstore.
1926	Irma and John Paine Cone married. Two sons: John Paine, Jr. (b. 1927) and Harold (b. 1940).
1928	Lesley and James Dwight Francis married. Two daughters: Elinor Frost (b. 1929) and Lesley Lee (b. 1931).
Aug 4	RF, Elinor, and Marjorie sailed from Quebec on the SS *Montnairn* for Cherbourgh (France). Leaving Marjorie in France, RF and Elinor continued on to England, where they remained until Marjorie was fetched to London just prior to their departure for home.
Nov 14	The three Frosts sailed for New York from Cherbourgh on the SS *Olympic*.
1929	Marjorie entered nurse's training in Baltimore.
1930	RF's *Collected Poems* published; awarded Pulitzer Prize.
1931	Marjorie entered TB sanitarium in Boulder, Colorado. Carol and his family moved to California, where Lillian LaBatt Frost was treated for TB.
1932	Lesley divorced.
1933	Marjorie married Willard E. Fraser.
1934 April	Carol and his family returned to Vermont. Marjorie became ill with childbed fever following the birth of her and Willard's daughter, Robin. RF and Elinor rushed to Bill-

	ings, Montana, to be with her, and followed her to the Mayo Clinic in Rochester, Minnesota, where she died on May 2.
Sept	Lesley began two-year residence at Rockford College (Illinois) as teacher and director of Maddox House, its cultural center.
1936	RF's *A Further Range* published; awarded Pulitzer Prize.
1938	After death of Elinor, RF moved to Boston. Later appointed to the Harvard University Board of Overseers and participated in the Bread Loaf Writers' Conference in Ripton, Vermont.
1939	RF's *Collected Poems* (enlarged edition) published. Appointed to the faculty of Harvard University, where he remained until 1943, purchasing a home at 35 Brewster Street, Cambridge, Massachusetts, and the Homer Noble Farm in Ripton, Vermont.
1940	Construction began on "Pencil Pines," a winter retreat in South Miami, Florida.
1942	RF's *A Witness Tree* published; awarded Pulitzer Prize.
1943	RF began an affiliation with Dartmouth College, where he remained until 1949, when he returned to Amherst College with a life appointment.
	Lesley began four years' service with the Office of War Information and the State Department (in Washington, D.C., and Madrid, Spain).
1945	RF's *A Masque of Reason* published.
1947	RF's *Steeple Bush* published.
	Irma and John divorced; Irma committed.
1949	RF's *Complete Poems* published.
1952	Lesley and Joseph W. Ballantine married.
1957 May 21	RF left New York by plane for London to make a "good will mission" under the auspices of the U.S. Department of State: he received honorary degrees at Oxford and Cambridge Universities (England) and National University (Ireland).
1958	RF named Consultant in Poetry, Library of Congress.
1961 Jan 20	RF took part in inauguration of President John F. Kennedy; named "Poet Laureate of Vermont" by action of the state legislature.

1962   RF's *In the Clearing* published.
1963 Jan 29   RF died at Peter Bent Brigham Hospital in Boston follow-
                     ing surgery. His ashes were interred (together with those
                     of his family) at the cemetery of First Congregational
                     Church, Old Bennington, Vermont.

[Small unresolved discrepancies in dating may be noted in comparing Lawrance Thompson, the Frost family headstone, and the "Frost Family Chronology" in *The Family Letters of Robert and Elinor Frost.*]

Notes

The following abbreviations are used throughout the notes to indicate locations of primary source material:

ACL	Amherst College Library
BUL	Boston University Library
DCL	Dartmouth College Library
TUL	University of Texas Library
UVL	University of Virginia Library
PCL	Plymouth State College Library

Introduction: Education by Poetry

1. The professor was Dr. José A. Balseiro, a scholar, musician, poet, and politician, who taught at a number of American universities before retiring to his native Puerto Rico; he was the best professor I ever had.

2. William Ernest Henley's *A Book of Verses* was first published in London by David Nutt in 1888 and may have inspired RF to take his first two volumes to that particular firm. In the first edition of Henley's volume, which I own, the poem "Invictus" is untitled.

3. See RF, "Education by Poetry: A Meditative Monologue," in *Robert Frost, Poetry and Prose,* ed. Edward C. Lathem and Lawrance Thompson, 329–40. The quotes are from pages 304, 413, and 439.

4. In *The Jameses: A Family Narrative* (New York: Anchor Books, Doubleday, 1993), R. W. B. Lewis notes how RF, entering Harvard College in 1897, anticipated studying under William James, who, unfortunately, was spending the year in England. He studied with Hugo Münsterberg instead. Besides the philosophical attraction to *The Will to Believe* and *Essays in Pragmatism,* RF used *The Principles of Psychology* (abridged version) in his classes at Plymouth Normal School. The Jamesian approach to the "braving of difficulties" clearly influenced the maturing poet and teacher.

5. RF, *Poetry and Prose,* 316.

6. RF, "The Poet's Next of Kin in a College," a talk of October 26, 1937, in *Poetry and Prose,* 374.

7. The author's articles on various aspects of the Frost biography are listed in the Selected Bibliography.

8. RF to Harold G. Rugg, December 4, 1936, *The Selected Letters of Robert Frost,* ed. Lawrance C. Thompson, 433; Elinor Frost to Edith H. Fobes, January 21, 1936, ibid., 425; Elinor Frost to Margaret Bartlett, c. July 3, 1913, ibid., 78.

9. RF to Louis Untermeyer, November 17, 1917, *The Letters of Robert Frost to Louis Untermeyer,* ed. Louis Untermeyer, 63.

10. See also Donald G. Sheehy, "The Poet as Neurotic: The Official Biography of Robert Frost," *American Literature* 58.3 (Oct. 1986): 393–410.

11. Lawrance Thompson, notes for a lecture to the Literary Fellowship in October 1968. Quoted in Sheehy, "The Poet as Neurotic," 393. The selective method used in the biography had been used in the *Selected Letters* (see Stanley Burnshaw, *Robert Frost Himself*) and would be used, to a lesser extent, in *New Hampshire's Child*. Besides the choice of letters to include and passages to omit, obvious examples are in the indices to these volumes, where seemingly negative qualities of personality, taken out of context, are listed by category.

12. RF to Lesley Lee Francis, December 30, 1953, *Family Letters of Robert and Elinor Frost*, ed. Arnold E. Grade, 266–67.

13. Eleanor Farjeon, foreword to *You Come Too*, 7–8.

14. "A Soldier," *The Poetry of Robert Frost*, ed. Edward C. Lathem, 261–62.

15. Lesley Frost, "Our Family Christmas."

16. "The Tuft of Flowers," *Poetry of Robert Frost*, 23.

1. A Literary Family on the Verge: Derry and Plymouth

1. *Robert Frost, Poetry and Prose*, ed. Edward C. Lathem and Lawrance Thompson, 321.

2. Lesley Frost, *New Hampshire's Child: The Derry Journals of Lesley Frost*, ed. Arnold E. Grade and Lawrance Thompson.

3. Meredith Reed, *Our Year Began in April* (New York: Lothrop, Lee and Shepard, 1963), 83–85, 86.

4. Ten-step was a game played with two lines of players; each line attempted to kick-catch the ball before it hit the ground, and thereby gained ten steps toward the opponent's goal. In RF's poem "In the Home Stretch" (*Mountain Interval*), we find the lines: "We drop our eyes or turn to other things, / As in the game 'ten-step' the chidren play."

5. I have drawn the student opinions cited in this section from letters written in 1968 in response to Miss Marcia Pushee by former students at Pinkerton Academy and the Plymouth Normal School. The letters are in the PCL.

6. John E. Walsh, in *Into My Own: The English Years of Robert Frost*, and RF's daughter-in-law, Lillian LaBatt Frost (Mrs. Carol Frost), in letters to Sandra Katz, challenge Thompson's conclusion that the Frosts experienced serious marital difficulties while at Derry. The incident cited most frequently to bolster such an interpretation—my mother being dragged from her bed to witness her father threatening her mother with a revolver—is refuted by both Walsh and Lillian Frost: they believe that in all likelihood my mother dreamed the uncorroborated incident during one of her not infrequent nightmares mentioned in her journals.

7. The Reverend Lorenzo Dow Case, quoted in Lawrence Thompson, *Robert Frost: The Early Years, 1874–1915*, 529.

8. Arnold E. Grade in *Family Letters of Robert and Elinor Frost*, 275.

9. Lesley Frost, Introduction to *New Hampshire's Child*.

10. Charles Sullivan, ed., *Imaginary Gardens: American Poetry and Art for Young People* (New York: Harry N. Abrams, 1989), 92. Lesley's poem "Rock 'N' Roll," from *Going on Two*, was included in another anthology, Charles Sullivan, ed., *America in Poetry* (New York: Harry N. Abrams, 1988), 168.

11. Brian Wilks, *The Brontës: An Illustrated Biography* (New York: Peter Bedrick Books, 1986), 26.

12. Quoted in Wilks, *The Brontës*, 49.

13. Wilks, *The Brontës*, 48–54; see also Rebecca Fraser, *The Brontës: Charlotte Brontë and*

Her Family (New York: Crown, 1988), and William Stanley Braithwaite, *The Bewitched Parsonage: The Story of the Brontës* (New York: Coward-McCann, 1950).

14. A description of the magazine, with an excerpt that appeared in *Little Women,* is found in Martha Saxon's biography, *Louisa May: A Modern Biography of Louisa May Alcott* (New York: Houghton Mifflin, 1977), 338–41.

15. Quoted in Madelon Bedell, *The Alcotts: Biography of a Family* (New York: Clarkson N. Potter, 1980), 299. The book features a bibliographical note in which the author lists important works on the subject of the American family and recommends, among others, Arthur W. Calhoun's *Social History of Family Life,* Nancy F. Cott's *Root of Bitterness,* and Ann Douglas's *The Feminization of American Culture.*

16. Jane Begos, *Diarist's Journal,* n.d., 19–21. Ms. Begos concludes with a comment I hope to address: "As far as I know, Lesley Frost did not go on to a literary career, but became a wife and mother. I have no information on whether or not she continued to keep journals."

17. Lesley Frost to Arnold E. Grade, October 11, 1966, quoted in Arnold E. Grade, "A Chronicle of Robert Frost's Early Reading, 1874–1899," 616. Grade points out that "at the age of eleven, Frost began writing a serial story which bears a striking resemblance to one portion of a four-part serial published in *St. Nicholas* that year."

18. RF to editor of *The Companion,* c. December 1912, BUL.

19. Lesley Frost, "Robert Frost Remembered," 15.

20. *New Hampshire's Child* 3:50.

21. RF Notebook (1912 and before), BUL. Margot Feldman and John Ridland have worked extensively with the early notebooks, and John Walsh includes a selection as an appendix to his *Into My Own.*

22. Bruno Bettelheim, *The Uses of Enchantment: The Meaning and Importance of Fairy Tales* (New York: Alfred A. Knopf, 1976).

23. RF Notebook (1912 and before), BUL.

24. RF, *Stories for Lesley,* ed. Roger D. Sell.

25. For further discussion, see Walsh, *Into My Own,* 128. An entry in the Dartmouth notebook from this period includes a list of "Subjects for Lesley":

> Best things in life
> Absent-mindedness of elders
> She must furnish set of subjects first.
> Killing things
> Pleasure of writing verse—what is it.

2. The Trip: The SS *Parisian*

1. RF to Susan Hayes Ward, December 19, 1911, *The Selected Letters of Robert Frost,* ed. Lawrance C. Thompson, 43; Lesley Frost to David Tatham, received May 24, 1969, published in Tatham, *A Poet Recognized.*

2. Lawrance Thompson, *Robert Frost: The Early Years, 1874–1915,* notes, 583.

3. See *Family Letters of Robert and Elinor Frost,* ed. Arnold E. Grade, 62, for information about the life of the Frosts' typewriter: a "visible writing machine," one of the first truly portable, purchased c. 1900, and still being used by Carol Frost in 1919, when he had it "all in pieces" cleaning it. The typewriter was used in England (primarily by Lesley) to type her father's manuscripts and the text for the in-house magazine *The Bouquet.*

4. Thompson, *The Early Years,* 391, has the gangplank going up.

5. Tatham, *A Poet Recognized.*

6. Elinor Frost to Margaret Lynch, October 25, 1912, *Selected Letters,* 53–54.

7. Lesley Frost's college compositions are in the University of New Hampshire Library. The two cited here are dated November 21, 1917, and April 15, 1918.

8. Elinor Frost to Margaret Lynch, October 25, 1912, *Selected Letters,* 53.

9. RF to Harold Brown, January 7, 1913, *Selected Letters,* 63.

3. Beaconsfield: "At a Christmas Window"

1. See RF, "This Is My Best: A Choice of Sixteen Poems," in *Robert Frost, Poetry and Prose,* ed. Edward C. Lathem and Lawrance Thompson, 378.

I was with my grandfather in June 1957 when, accompanied by several reporters from *Life* magazine, we stopped in Beaconsfield on the return trip from Oxford and Ryton/Dymock, but the party was unable to locate The Bungalow on Reynolds Road. The cottage where the Frosts lived from September 1912 until March 1914 should have been easy to identify. Set back on a rectangular property of just over a quarter-acre on a semicircular section of the road that is virtually unchanged, the cottage is still one of the tallest with one of the largest frontages, distinguished from the other houses in the area by its light tan walls of a rough, pebbly grout. But it was the end of a long, physically and emotionally draining day for the 83-year-old poet, and he was anxious to return to his hotel and to be free of the press entourage. In the prologue to his book *Into My Own: The English Years of Robert Frost,* John E. Walsh (who spent two months in The Bungalow in the summer of 1985) surmises that RF failed to identify the cottage on this occasion because of psychological distress brought on by family tragedies in later years.

2. Elinor Frost to Margaret Lynch, October 25, 1912, *The Selected Letters of Robert Frost,* ed. Lawrance C. Thompson, 53–54. For a general description of the town, see Walsh, *Into My Own,* 18.

3. Sometime after her tenth birthday in June 1913, Irma contributed this entry, and Lesley's transcription of this as well as other, although not all, entries is suggested by the placement of a sprinkling of phonetically misspelled words—such as *fernercher*—in quotation marks. "Our New House" was cited out of its correct context by Elizabeth Shepley Sergeant, *The Trial by Existence,* 93, and Walsh, *Into My Own,* 21.

4. RF to Susan Hayes Ward, September 15, 1912, *Selected Letters,* 52; RF to Harold Brown, January 7, 1913, ibid., 63; and Walsh, *Into My Own,* 19.

5. Frances N. Ellis, "Robert Frost in England, 1912–1915," 11. See also Elinor Frost to Margaret Lynch, October 25, 1912, *Selected Letters,* 53–54. RF to John Bartlett, c. November 5, 1913, *Selected Letters,* 99.

6. Elinor Frost to Mrs. Harold Brown, October 25, 1912, *Selected Letters,* 53.

7. RF to Susan Hayes Ward, September 15, 1912, *Selected Letters,* 52.

8. Ibid.

9. Elinor Frost to Margaret Lynch, October 25, 1912, *Selected Letters,* 54. For a general discussion, see Gorham B. Munson, *Robert Frost: A Study in Sensibility and Good Sense.*

10. Robert Francis, *Robert Frost: A Time to Talk,* 16.

11. On November 19, 1912, Robert had written to the Portland, Maine, publisher Thomas Bird Mosher in the midst of the negotiations: "I have three other books of verse somewhere near completion, 'Melanism,' 'Villagers,' and 'The Sense of Wrong,' and I wanted to be alone with them for a while. If I ever published anything, I fully expected it would be through some

American publisher. But see how little I knew myself. . . . I have signed no contract as yet. . . . I am nearly the worst person in the world in a muddle like this" (*Selected Letters,* 55–56). He soon discovered, as others had (see Sir Stanley Unwin, *The Truth about a Publisher* [New York: Macmillan, 1960], 127), how impossible this obsessive and bitter woman was in the endless negotiations. Madame Nutt, whose autobiography, *A Woman of Today,* was being published by the Nutt firm at the same time as *A Boy's Will,* was scornful of social institutions, including motherhood, and dwelled on theories of genetic perfection through sound heredity. She may or may not have heard from Mosher in America or from John Drinkwater in England about Robert's potential as a poet, but she never let on who, if anyone, had expressed an interest in his poetry. Her determination to hold the aspiring American poet to four books, and her refusal to provide him with any royalties or an annual accounting, opened the way for Robert's first two volumes to be pirated by Henry Holt and Co. and contributed to the bankruptcy of her publishing firm and her apparent impoverishment and unheralded death in France. But none of this unsuspected outcome intruded upon the Frost family's joy and celebration come Christmas 1912, with the signing of the contract. Robert was already planning a third book (of plays), and he did not think the contract burdensome.

12. Lesley Frost, lecture notes.

13. RF to Harold Brown, January 7, 1913, *Selected Letters,* 63–64. Brown was an assistant to Henry Clinton Morrison, state superintendent of public instructions in New Hampshire from 1904 to 1917. Morrison had played an important part in helping RF climb from a teaching post at Pinkerton Academy to the faculty of the New Hampshire Normal School in Plymouth.

14. Elinor Frost to Margaret Lynch, October 25, 1912, *Selected Letters,* 54, and Elinor Frost to Sidney Cox, July 10, 1913, ibid., 82.

15. Lesley Frost to David Tatham, May 24, 1969, in Tatham, *A Poet Recognized.*

16. Elinor Frost to Mrs. Harold Brown, October 25, 1912, DCL.

17. Elinor Frost to Margaret Bartlett, c. July 3, 1913, DCL.

18. Elinor Frost to Sidney Cox, July 10, 1913, *Selected Letters,* 83.

19. Elinor Frost to Marie Hodge, May 6, 1913, BUL.

20. Elinor Frost to Margaret Bartlett, March 18, 1913, DCL.

21. Elinor Frost to Marie Hodge, May 6, 1913, BUL.

22. RF to John Bartlett, February 26, 1913, *Selected Letters,* 66; Elinor Frost to Margaret Bartlett, c. July 3, 1913, DCL.

23. RF to John Bartlett, February 22, 1914, *Selected Letters,* 114.

24. RF to Susan Hayes Ward, May 13, 1913, *Selected Letters,* 73; Lesley Frost to Beulah Huckins, n.d. [winter 1913–1914 from Beaconsfield], PCL; RF to Susan Hayes Ward, May 13, 1913, *Selected Letters,* 73.

25. RF to Sidney Cox, May 2, 1913, *Selected Letters,* 71–72; Elinor Frost to Margaret Bartlett, c. July 3, 1913, ibid., 77–78.

26. Lesley Frost to Beulah Huckins, n.d. [winter 1913–1914], PCL.

27. John E. Walsh, *Into My Own: The English Years of Robert Frost,* 21.

28. RF to Frank S. Flint, December 10, 1913, UTL, 154.

29. Irma Frost to Beulah Huckins, n.d., PCL.

30. RF to John Bartlett, December 8, 1913, *Selected Letters,* 101.

31. Sergeant, *Trial by Existence,* 100.

32. Lesley Frost, "Our Family Christmas," 97.

33. Walsh, *Into My Own,* 154–55. See Lawrance Thompson, *Robert Frost: The Early Years, 1874–1915,* 430, concerning the Fabians, W. W. Gibson, and this poem.

34. "Robert Frost's Poetry Written before 1913: A Critical Edition," ed. Andrew John Angyal, 103. See also Thompson, *The Early Years,* 430–31.

Lesley's single memory of her older brother, Elliott, was when he was four years old (shortly before his death), and he entertained her with a little metal train at Christmas; she was going on two. The incident is described in "Our Family Christmas."

35. Sergeant, *Trial by Existence,* 99.

4. London and the Poetry Bookshop

1. Elinor Frost to Mrs. Harold Brown, October 25, 1912, DCL. Friend and poet John Cournos remembers a similar scene: Waterloo Bridge "with its lorries, 'buses, and the people on top of the 'buses, and the horses pulling drays, and the countless persons streaming along its bordering pavements, to appear like some toy kingdom peopled by silhouettes. . . . How unreal, and how beautiful!" (*Autobiography,* 239)

2. Elinor Frost to Mrs. Harold Brown, October 25, 1912, DCL.

3. RF to Sidney Cox, c. November 26, 1913, *The Selected Letters of Robert Frost,* ed. Lawrance C. Thompson, 100.

4. RF to John Bartlett, c. December 15, 1913, *Selected Letters,* 103.

5. A one-act prose play that first appeared in the February 1917 issue of the *Seven Arts, A Way Out* is republished in *Robert Frost, Poetry and Prose,* ed. Edward C. Lathem and Lawrance Thompson, 272–82.

6. RF to John Bartlett, February 22, 1914, *Selected Letters,* 113. See also Robert S. Newdick, "Robert Frost and the Dramatic," *NEQ* 10.2 (Spring 1937), reproduced in Richard Thornton, ed., *The Recognition of Robert Frost,* 79–88. The two plays, *In an Art Factory* and *Guardeen,* were edited by Roger Sell, *Massachusetts Review* (summer–autumn 1985): 265–340.

7. RF to Harold Brown, January 7, 1913, *Selected Letters,* 63. The event took place on September 26, 1913. In his pocket-size notebook, reproduced in John E. Walsh, *Into My Own: The English Years of Robert Frost,* 218, Robert wrote simply "In pursuit of GBS." W. H. Davies was friendly with the Shaws (Davies, *Later Days,* 68). And in correspondence with Haines, it appears Robert's friend met and conversed with Shaw on May Hill (RF to John W. Haines, September 1914, DCL).

8. Elinor Farjeon, *Edward Thomas: The Last Four Years,* 200.

9. Anne Born, "Harold Monro and the Poetry Bookshop," in particular, page 187; see also George Sims, "Alida Monro and the Poetry Bookshop." For a general treatment, see Joy Grant, *Harold Monro and the Poetry Bookshop.* Monro had a son, Nigel, born in 1904, whose mother, Dorothy Browne, he would divorce during the war so that he might marry the Bookshop's secretary, Alida Klemantaski, half Monro's age; Alida had replaced Geraldine Townshend as secretary when she left to marry Wilfrid W. Gibson in 1913.

10. RF to Frank S. Flint, January 21, 1913, UTL.

11. RF to Frank S. Flint, July 6, 1913, UTL: RF to Frank S. Flint, c. December 1913, UTL.

12. RF to Frank S. Flint, June 26, 1913, and July 1914, UTL.

13. See B. J. Sokol, "What Went Wrong between Robert Frost and Ezra Pound," *NEQ* (December 1976): 521–41; see also Robert A. Greenberg, "Frost in England: A Publishing Incident," *NEQ* (September 1961): 375–79. Many years later, in 1958, RF was able to show his appreciation of Pound's historic contribution to the arts by joining with others in successfully gaining his release from St. Elizabeths Hospital, where he had been interned (as unable to stand trial for treason) at the end of World War II.

14. Harriet Monroe, *Poets and Their Art,* 233, 236.

15. Cournos, *Autobiography,* 237.

16. RF to Sidney Cox, c. September 15, 1913, *Selected Letters,* 92–94.

17. Elinor Frost to Margaret Bartlett, c. July 3, 1913, *Selected Letters,* 78.

18. The line is mentioned by RF in a letter to Sidney Cox, c. September 15, 1913, *Selected Letters,* 93.

19. John Drinkwater (1882–1937), the son of a schoolmaster, had a passion for amateur dramatics, and he later became a professional actor, leaving school and moving to Birmingham, where he took a series of menial jobs in insurance. He soon began to write poetry and became active in the Birmingham Repertory Theatre, doing some acting with the Pilgrim Players. His first book of poems to attract attention was *Lyrical and Other Poems* (1908), published by Samurai Press, an early venture of Harold Monro's that also published W. W. Gibson. Drinkwater gradually extended his activities to include writing and producing. The play productions brought Drinkwater in contact with Yeats in 1910, when they brought a performance of *The King's-Threshold* to London. Drinkwater's shyness evaporated. He became president of the Birmingham Dramatic and Literary Club, and his next book, *Poems of Men and Hours,* was published in 1911 by David Nutt. There is a strong suspicion that Drinkwater favorably reviewed the manuscript of *A Boy's Will* before Mrs. Nutt accepted it for publication. After the war, he developed a national reputation in drama as the author of *Abraham Lincoln.*

20. W. W. Gibson (1878–1962), or Wilfrid Wilson, as he liked to be called, had come to London two years earlier and had been, along with Lascelles Abercrombie, John Drinkwater, and others, a founder and contributor to *Georgian Poetry,* the anthology first edited by Edward Marsh in 1912. It was Marsh who brought the *New Numbers* poets together, allowing the poets to stay with him at his flat in Grays Inn. His elder sister, Elizabeth Gibson Cheyne, was also a poet. He didn't leave the middle-class security of his home at Hexham, Northumberland, until he was thirty-four. He resided briefly in Glasgow, where he was accepted by the Glasgow literary society, in the tradition of the poor but genteel and very promising young poet. His earlier imitative work was in the romantic Victorian style, which soon underwent an about-face toward realism. Returning to Hexham, he published three volumes of poetic dialogues with the title *Daily Bread* (1910), favorably reviewed by Abercrombie and marking the beginning of his fame as a poet. John Drinkwater, who from this time on greatly admired Gibson's work, and unsuccessfully staged one of the dialogues, *The Garret,* urged the diffident Gibson to write specifically for the theater. With advice from Drinkwater, Gibson wrote *Womankind,* but both men soon realized that this was the wrong direction for Gibson to take. By 1911, Gibson, Abercrombie, Drinkwater, and Bottomley were corresponding.

21. Lascelles Abercrombie (1881–1938) was the the son of a well-to-do stockbroker, with a large, happy family, whose brother became the well-known architect Sir Patrick Abercrombie. Educated at Malvern College, he was forced to abandon his studies because of poor health and depleted family fortune. His first volume of verse, *Interludes and Poems,* appeared in 1908 and caught the attention of Rupert Brooke. He married Catherine Gwatkin in 1909, when she was an art student, and gradually took on a series of review assignments for such papers as the *Liverpool Courier,* the *Manchester Guardian,* and the *London Daily News.* After moving to Ryton, in 1911, Abercrombie produced a second volume of poems, *Emblems of Love,* and another pamphlet, *The Sale of St. Thomas.* A play, *End of the World,* was included in *New Numbers* and was produced by Drinkwater in Birmingham in 1914, as the dramatist explains in his two autobiographical volumes, *Inheritance* and *Discovery* (1897–1913).

22. See Lawrance Thompson, *Robert Frost: The Early Years, 1874–1915,* 446, as told to him by Mrs. Abercrombie on June 9, 1957.

23. RF to Gertrude McQuesten, December 1913, BUL. See also RF to Sidney Cox, March 26, 1914, *Selected Letters,* 121, where he states: "I have no friend here like Wilfrid Gibson whom I am going to join in Gloucestershire next week." Gertrude McQuesten, a teacher at Emerson College of Oratory who had known the poet while at Plymouth, shared his interest in dramatic tones in poetry. In his letter, Robert expresses his hope that she will appreciate the two poems, "The Fear" and "A Hundred Collars," appearing in the December issue of *Poetry and Drama,* as well as the dramatic pieces in *North of Boston,* due out in a few weeks.

24. Davies, *Later Days,* 36, 49.

25. RF to Gertrude McQuesten, undated but postmarked December 11, 1913, BUL, quoted in Walsh, *Into My Own,* 157–58.

26. Elinor Frost to Sidney Cox, July 10, 1913, *Selected Letters,* 82–83; RF to Sidney Cox, March 26, 1914, *Selected Letters,* 121. The December 1914 issue of *Poetry and Drama* included four of Robert's shorter poems: "The Sound of Trees," "The Cow in Apple Time," "Putting in the Seed," and "The Smile." Robert thanked Monro for "placing me so well in such a good number of P & D and offering me your spare room when I should come to London" (RF to Harold Monro, December 1914, *Selected Letters,* 143).

27. RF to Sidney Cox, March 26, 1914, *Selected Letters,* 121; Lesley's postcard can be found in the PCL.

28. Geraldine Gibson to Elinor Frost, February 25, 1914, DCL.

5. Scotland: In Memory of Belle Moodie

1. E. A. Gardner was Yates Professor of Archaeology, University College, who later became vice-chancellor; see *Dictionary of National Biography,* 1931–1940, 307–8, and John E. Walsh, *Into My Own: The English Years of Robert Frost,* 246–47.

2. RF to Gertrude McQuesten, n.d., postmarked December 11, 1913, BUL; RF to Sidney Cox, c. September 15, 1913, *The Selected Letters of Robert Frost,* ed. Lawrance C. Thompson, 94–95.

3. Lesley Frost, "Somewhat Atavistic." Emmanuel Swedenborg (1688–1772) was a Swedish philosopher, scientist, and mystic, whose visionary view of God (as infinite love and wisdom) profoundly affected Belle Moodie and through her impressed RF during the formative years.

4. Lawrance Thompson, *Robert Frost: The Early Years, 1874–1915,* 488–96.

5. See Thompson, *The Early Years,* and Arnold E. Grade, "A Chronicle of Robert Frost's Early Reading, 1874–1899."

6. The original manuscript of "A Heart in Charge" is in the University of Virginia Library.

7. Philip Beveridge Mair, in his family reminiscences (*Shared Enthusiasm: The Story of Lord and Lady Beveridge,* 43) describes his mother's "impulsive way" of concluding that Phyllis and Rupert Brooke had come "to exist but for one another"; but, although Rupert Brooke, in a letter to Katharine Cox calls Phyllis the "Romance of My Life" and refers to her "in veiled terms" in his poem "He Wonders Whether to Praise or to Blame Her," the one letter preserved from Rupert to Phyllis, dated March 1914, from Tahiti, shows otherwise. RF, in his comments on the poem as it appeared in the December 1913 issue of *Poetry and Drama,* tells John Bartlett, "We know this hardly treated girl oh very well. Her beauty is her red hair. Her cleverness is in painting. She has a picture in the New English Exhibition" (*Selected Letters,* 104).

8. Elinor Frost to Margaret Bartlett, c. July 3, 1913, *Selected Letters,* 78–79.

9. Mary Gardner to RF, August 3, 1913, DCL.

10. RF to John Bartlett, August 30, 1913, *Selected Letters,* 91.

11. Ibid.

12. RF to Sidney Cox, March 26, 1914, *Selected Letters,* 121–22.

13. For the comment about John Knox and Golf, see RF to Gertrude McQuesten, n.d., postmarked December 11, 1913, BUL; RF to John Bartlett, August 30, 1913, *Selected Letters,* 91; for the comments about Kingsbarns and friends on the beach, see RF to Sidney Cox, c. September 15, 1913, *Selected Letters,* 94. See also RF to Gertrude McQuesten, n.d., postmarked December 11, 1913, BUL, and Walsh, *Into My Own,* 138–43; for comments about the north people, see RF to Cox, c. September 15, 1913, *Selected Letters,* 94.

14. Her father speaks of these visits by the children in a letter to Sidney Cox, c. September 15, 1913, *Selected Letters,* 94–95.

15. Amy Smith to Lesley Frost, September 9, 1913, UVL.

16. Mary Gardner to RF, June 13, 1913, DCL.

17. RF to John Bartlett, August 30, 1913, *Selected Letters,* 90. To McQuesten he added: "We had a jaunt in Scotland in the summer that we could ill afford" (RF to Gertrude McQuesten, n.d. postmarked December 11, 1913, BUL).

18. Walsh, *Into My Own,* 134–37, provides a detailed account of the significance of these findings and the dispute that arose with Robert over the authenticity of "this prehistoric menagerie." In all likelihood, what Robert wrote to John Bartlett "betraying a confidence" overstates the difficulties in the relations between the two families.

19. Mary Gardner to Elinor Frost, December 15, 1913, DCL. There is a suggestion of further contact in the remarks of Edward Thomas, whose home in Steep was about twenty miles from the Gardner home at Tadworth, when he tells Robert he hopes to hear from him that "Mrs. Gardner [has got] a cottage I can cycle or walk to this autumn & winter" (Edward Thomas to RF, September 19, 1914, DCL). Walsh, *Into My Own,* 252, cites this reference but incorrectly concludes, "There is no sign, however, that the two families were ever in touch after 1913."

20. Mary Gardner to RF, June 13, 1913, DCL.

21. Mair, *Shared Enthusiasm,* 43.

22. Lucy Mair to Lesley Frost, September 10 and 12, [1913], UVL. She is, of course, referring to the recently published *A Boy's Will.* Unfortunately, the photos have been lost.

23. University of New Hampshire Library.

24. RF to Ernest Silver, February 23, 1914, *Selected Letters,* 115.

25. RF to Gertrude McQuesten, n.d., postmarked December 11, 1913, BUL.

26. Ibid.

27. J. C. Smith to RF, September 15 and January 31, 1913, DCL. Walsh, *Into My Own,* 137–43, discusses the genesis of "Mending Wall" and Smith's recognition of the source of inspiration from their walks in Kingsbarns and the "stone dykes."

28. J. C. Smith to RF, September 15 and January 31, 1913, DCL.

29. RF to John Bartlett, February 22, 1914, *Selected Letters,* 114.

30. J. C. Smith to RF, August 25, 1914, DCL.

31. Amy Smith to Lesley Frost, October 28, 1913, UVL.

32. RF to John W. Haines, September 30 and October 1914, from The Gallows, DCL.

33. Amy Smith to Lesley Frost, October 27, 1914, UVL.

34. J. C. Smith to RF, February 11, 1915, DCL.

35. J. C. Smith to RF, April 18, 1915, DCL.

36. J. C. Smith to RF, October 3, 1915, DCL.

37. Amy Smith to Lesley Frost, October 28, 1913, UVL.

38. Amy Smith to Lesley Frost, February 4, 1914, UVL.

39. Amy Smith to Lesley Frost, December 20, 1913, UVL.

40. Amy Smith to Lesley Frost, February 10, 1915. Mary Gardner died in 1936; her husband, Ernest Arthur Gardner, died in 1939, predeceased by Phyllis; J. C. Smith died in 1946; Amy Smith, as Mrs. C. F. A. Pantin, gave RF a sherry party on May 23, 1957; and the Mairs (including Jessy, Lucy, and Lord Beveridge) entertained Robert during his 1957 visit to England.

6. Goucestershire: "Elected Friends"

1. The Beauchamp Arms trap was used to meet the Gloucester to Dymock train. See Lascelles Abercrombie to Elinor Frost, November 19, [1914], DCL.

2. In describing the Dymock/Ryton/Ledbury landscape near Gloucester and the relationship between the poets and their surroundings in this period, I have drawn upon—besides the contemporaneous writings of the poets—the dissertation of Jan Marsh, "Georgian Poets and the Land."

3. From Catherine Abercrombie, "Memories of a Poet's Wife."

4. RF to Sidney Cox, May 18, 1914, *The Selected Letters of Robert Frost,* ed. Lawrance C. Thompson, 122.

5. Elinor Frost to Leona White, c. June 20, 1914, *Selected Letters,* 126.

6. "This England" was first published in *The Last Sheaf,* 1928, but is quoted here from a Books for Libraries Press edition, 1972, 215–21.

7. Elinor Frost to Leona White, c. June 20, 1914, *Selected Letters,* 126. I have walked through Little Iddens—once in 1957 with my grandfather and again while on a fellowship in 1986. The descriptions in Lawrance Thompson, *Robert Frost: The Early Years, 1874–1915,* 447, and John E. Walsh, *Into My Own: The English Years of Robert Frost,* 165, provide additional details.

8. Haines was *not* related to Abercrombie, as Thompson and Walsh have stated in their biographies.

9. John W. Haines, "England," in Richard Thornton, ed., *The Recognition of Robert Frost,* 89–97. (The essay was from the *Gloucester Journal* [February 2, 1935], with additions.)

10. John W. Haines, Introduction to the English edition of *A Masque of Reason and of Mercy and Steeple Bush,* 1948, quoted in Haines, "Robert Frost," in *Now and Then: A Journal of Books and Personalities for Autumn 1948,* 9–11.

11. RF to John W. Haines, September 20, 1920, DCL.

12. Haines, "England," in Thornton, ed., *Recognition of Robert Frost,* 92.

13. RF to John W. Haines, c. July 1, 1914, *Selected Letters,* 127.

14. Quoted in Louis Mertins, *Robert Frost: Life and Talks-Walking,* 132.

15. Helen Thomas with Myfanwy Thomas, *Under Storm's Wing,* 229.

16. Eleanor Farjeon, *Edward Thomas: The Last Four Years,* 88.

17. Catherine Abercrombie, "Extract from a recording by Mrs. Abercrombie," May 30, 1965, provided the author by the executor of the Abercrombie Estate, Jeffrey Cooper.

18. Elinor Frost to Leona White, c. June 20, 1914, *Selected Letters,* 126.

19. They had been introduced by Ralph Hodgson on October 6, 1913, in London. Edward had already favorably reviewed *A Boy's Will.*

20. Chief among them are: R. George Thomas, *Edward Thomas: A Portrait;* John Wain, "Edward and Helen Thomas"; Jan Marsh, *Edward Thomas: A Poet for His Country;* and John Lehmann, *Three Literary Friendships: Byron and Shelley, Rimbaud and Verlaine, and Robert Frost and Edward Thomas.*

21. Abercrombie, "Extract from a recording by Mrs. Abercrombie," May 30, 1965.

22. R. George Thomas, Introduction to *The Collected Poems of Edward Thomas,* ed. R. G. Thomas, xv. The quote from RF is from a letter to Grace Walcott Conkling, June 18, 1921, quoted in *Poetry Wales* 13.4 (Spring 1978), 22.

23. *Collected Poems of Edward Thomas,* no. 101. For all subsequent references to poems by Edward Thomas, I have used this edition. On page 160, Thomas states that this poem was written to his mother rather than to Helen, as seems the more likely, and as Wain discusses in *Professing Poetry,* 363 and 365–66.

24. RF, quoted in Mertins, *Life and Talks-Walking,* 135.

25. *Collected Poems of Edward Thomas,* nos. 106–9. Bronwen was born October 29, 1902, died 1975; Merfyn was born January 15, 1900, died 1965; and Myfanwy was born August 16, 1910.

26. *Collected Poems of Edward Thomas,* no. 112.

27. Farjeon, *The Last Four Years,* 327.

28. First printed in the *Atlantic,* February 1926; published in W. W. Gibson, *The Golden Room and Other Poems,* 1928, 172.

29. RF to Ernest L. Silver, February 23, 1914, *Selected Letters,* 116.

30. Helen Thomas, *Under Storm's Wing,* 229.

31. Helen Thomas to RF, [early March 1917], DCL.

32. *Daily Chronicle,* February 29, 1908, quoted in Marsh, *A Poet for His Country,* 106.

33. April 18, 1906, quoted in Marsh, *A Poet for His Country,* 106; *The Letters of Edward Thomas to Gordon Bottomley,* ed. R. George Thomas (London and New York, 1968), 238; RF to John W. Haines, October 1914, DCL.

34. RF to Sidney Cox, May 18, 1914, *Selected Letters,* 123.

35. Ibid.

36. Abercrombie, "Memories of a Poet's Wife," 793.

37. Haines, "England," in Thornton, ed., *Recognition of Robert Frost,* 93.

38. Ibid., 95.

39. Haines, quoted in Mertins, *Life and Talks-Walking,* 132–33.

40. Ibid., 132.

41. Farjeon, *The Last Four Years,* 85.

42. Ibid., 91.

43. Ibid., 93, 94–95.

44. Ibid., 89.

45. Ibid., 89–90.

46. Edward Thomas to RF, March 16, 1916, DCL.

47. *Collected Poems of Edward Thomas,* no. 119.

48. I discuss these relations at greater length in my article, "Robert Frost and Helen Thomas Revisited."

49. Helen Thomas, *Under Storm's Wing,* 228, 229.

50. R. George Thomas, *A Portrait,* 238.

51. University of New Hampshire Library.

7. The Children as Journalists: *The Bouquet* and Other Writings

1. See, for example, "Lob Lie by the Fire" in De la Mare's *A Child's Day* (1912), and Thomas's favorable reviews of De la Mare's prose and poetry.

2. Helen Thomas with Myfanwy Thomas, *Under Storm's Wing,* 252, 285–86.

3. Quoted by Elizabeth Shepley Sergeant, *The Trial by Existence,* 135.

4. The Cohn notebook, quoted in John E. Walsh, *Into My Own: The English Years of Robert Frost,* 224.

5. "The Combe" can be found in a British Museum draft dated December 30, 1914; Edward had started writing verse c. December 3, 1914. The only changes in "The Combe": a comma has been added after *thorn* and before *and briar;* the word *the* has been eliminated between *loves* and *juniper.* "Nettles," collected as "Tall Nettles," can be found in a May 1, 1916, Bodleian manuscript, and, except for the title, there are no changes. "October" is in the Bodleian manuscript dated October 15 and 16, 1915; the only changes from the typewritten draft included with the letter to Lesley are in the first line of the second stanza, which, in *The Bouquet,* reads *"The rich scene* [instead of "The late year"] has grown fresh again and new," and there is a dash in the line "But if this be not happiness,—who knows?" In a letter to Eleanor Farjeon, Edward mentions that the original version of "October" was in blank verse, but quite different. The letter to Eleanor Farjeon is in Farjeon, *Edward Thomas: The Last Four Years,* 169. The letter from Edward Thomas to Lesley Frost is in the UVL; the typewritten draft is preserved with it.

6. Sergeant, *Trial by Existence,* 135. The English critic Andrew Motion disagrees, claiming the simile is an adaptation of Jefferies's remark about hounds: "The sinewy back bends like a bow, but a bow that, instead of an arrow, shoots itself" (*The Poetry of Edward Thomas,* 97–100); he is citing Richard Jefferies, *The Amateur Poacher* (London: Smith and Elder, 1879), 100.

7. Lesley Frost, introduction to *New Hampshire's Child: The Derry Journals of Lesley Frost.*

8. Lesley Frost, "Our Family Christmas." The six issues were given as a gift by Lesley's family to the University of Virginia Library, C. Waller Barrett Collection.

9. See R. George Thomas, *Edward Thomas: A Portrait,* 226.

10. See Lawrance Thompson, *Robert Frost: The Early Years, 1874–1915,* 600–601.

11. J. C. Smith to RF, January 31, 1914, DCL.

12. J. C. Smith to RF, October 3, 1915, DCL; RF to Sidney Cox, May 18, 1914, *The Selected Letters of Robert Frost,* ed. Lawrance C. Thompson, 123.

13. Amy Smith to Lesley Frost, September 9, 1913, UVL.

14. Amy Smith to Lesley Frost, December 30, 1913, UVL.

15. Amy Smith to Lesley Frost, February 4, 1914, UVL.

16. Ibid.

17. Amy Smith to Lesley Frost, September 9, 1913, UVL.

18. Amy Smith to Lesley Frost, October 27, 1914, UVL.

19. Amy Smith to Lesley Frost, June 23, 1914, UVL. The "Ode to Late October" was included in the June 1914 issue of *The Bouquet,* together with her "Poem"; "The Flint Arrow-Head" appeared in the July 1914 issue.

20. Edith Smith to Lesley Frost, July 27, 1914, UVL.

21. The puzzle appeared on page twenty-four of the April [1915] issue of *The Bouquet.* The letters from Merfyn Thomas cited here are dated March 19 and April 3, 1915. The letters from Merfyn to the Frost children are held by the family of Lesley Frost.

22. The letter from Beulah Huckins is dated March 28 [1915]. This and other letters from her are held by the family of Lesley Frost.

23. Delphis Gardner to Lesley Frost, September 13, 1916, UVL.

24. RF to John W. Haines, c. 1920, DCL.

25. "The Hill Wife: II. House Fear" first appeared in *The Yale Review,* April 1916; "The Hill Wife: III. The Smile" was included with "The Fear" in the December 1913 issue of *Poetry and Drama.*

8. The Gallows and Going Home: "It Grieved My Soul"

1. Robert Frost to Amy Lowell, [October 22, 1917], *The Selected Letters of Robert Frost,* ed. Lawrance C. Thompson, 220.
2. RF to Sidney Cox, March 3, 1914, *Selected Letters,* 118.
3. RF to John W. Haines, c. September 1914, DCL.
4. Lawrance Thompson, *Robert Frost: The Early Years, 1874–1915,* 457–58.
5. Catherine Abercrombie, "Memories of a Poet's Wife." See, also, Christopher Hassall, *Edward Marsh: Patron of the Arts,* 242.
6. Wilfrid W. Gibson, "The Magnet," enclosed with letter to Lawrance Thompson, May 24, 1947, UVL.
7. RF to Ernest L. Silver, February 23, 1913, DCL; in *Selected Letters,* 117, with omissions.
8. Jan Marsh, "Georgian Poets and the Land," 198.
9. Ibid., 207.
10. Ibid., 213.
11. Catherine Abercrombie, "Extract from a Recording by Mrs. Catherine Abercrombie," May 30, 1965.
12. For a general treatment of the incident, see Thompson, *The Early Years,* 467 and notes; John E. Walsh, *Into My Own: The English Years of Robert Frost,* 202 and notes; Marsh, "Georgian Poets," 213; and Robert S. Newdick's *Season of Frost,* ed. William A. Sutton (Albany: State University of New York Press, 1976), 298.
13. Thompson, *The Early Years,* 468.
14. RF to Harold Monro, December 1914, *Selected Letters,* 142.
15. RF to John W. Haines, April 2, 1915, DCL; RF to Lascelles Abercrombie, September 21, 1915, DCL.
16. Myfanwy Thomas incorrectly contends in her introduction to *Under Storm's Wing* that Robert "was near to calling him a coward for not squaring up to the gamekeeper" (14). See Walsh, *Into My Own,* 262, where he speaks of Myfanwy's "curiously inaccurate reference to this unfortunate little drama."
17. "An Old Song [1]," *The Collected Poems of Edward Thomas,* ed. R. George Thomas, no. 12, is based on "The Lincolnshire Poacher" and an informed interest in ballads and folk music. See note by R. George Thomas in *Collected Poems of Edward Thomas,* 133.
18. Edward Thomas to RF, January 22, 1917, DCL. See also Edward Thomas to RF, May 23, 1915, DCL.
19. Edward Thomas to RF, April 2, 1917, DCL.
20. Robert Frost to Sidney Cox, September 17, 1914, *Selected Letters,* 136.
21. Ibid., 135.
22. Wellesley College, November 12, 1917. A second view of the war (in Lesley's composition) is of a student who says to her teacher: "But, Mrs. Moore, the patriotic business is quite over now. My father told me last night that all the Liberty Bonds were sold." Lesley comments that this is an example of how "children will get such quaint notions into their heads."
23. RF to Lascelles Abercrombie, March 15, [1915], *Selected Letters,* 157.
24. John W. Haines to RF, April 17, 1915, DCL.

25. RF to Lascelles Abercrombie, March 15, [1915], *Selected Letters,* 157.

26. RF to Frank S. Flint, c. February 13, 1915, *Selected Letters,* 152. The Flint-RF correspondence in the UTL shows there was no rupture between the two, as suggested by the unmailed note and Thompson's biography.

27. During my visit with the Abercrombies in Edinburgh in 1986, David told me how pleased he was by Robert's message to his father.

28. John W. Haines to RF, February 22, 1915, DCL; John W. Haines to RF, April 17, 1915, DCL.

29. *Family Letters of Robert and Elinor Frost,* ed. Arnold E. Grade, 3; Lawrance Thompson, *Robert Frost: The Years of Triumph, 1915–1938,* 4–7; see also *Selected Letters,* 164.

30. RF to E. C. Jewell, February 24, 1915, University of Florida Library. The letter is found in a first edition autographed presentation copy of *North of Boston,* inscribed "E.C. Jewell from Robert Frost." The letter does not mention Merfyn Thomas.

31. From *Friends Remembering Frost,* pamphlet published privately by Phi Beta Kappa (Boston, 1977): 9–10.

32. Helen Thomas, *Under Storm's Wing,* 286–87. Edward referred to this pun as from an actor friend, just back from the states; Myfanwy's version is therefore probably inaccurate.

33. Merfyn Thomas to Lesley Frost, April 3, 1915.

34. The letters cited here are Edward Thomas to RF, June 1 and 15, November 23, and February 1, 1915 (DCL; R. George Thomas, "Six Letters from Robert Frost to Edward Thomas," 52; and *Selected Letters,* 150, respectively). In Edward Thomas to RF, December 31, 1916, DCL, Edward reported enjoying the housework and wood gathering and the forest and a few walks; Merfyn was home. See also *Collected Poems of Edward Thomas,* notes, 162–63. Included here is a quote from Merfyn about his relations with his father: "I did not understand him nor he me, and while I did not appreciate his point of view, he would not or he could not see mine. . . . I have the most happy memories of our life together, of his gentle kindness, of his knowledge and appreciation of the countryside and the simple things of life which he instilled into me." Merfyn served briefly (in 1918, after his father's death) in the Kent Rifle Regiment; during World War II, he served in the REME Corps in the Middle East 1941–1946, attaining the rank of major. He went on to become a highly regarded technical journalist, serving as technical editor (from 1946 to 1965) of various transportation journals. He died on August 2, 1965, six months after his retirement.

35. RF to Helen Thomas, February 6, 1917, *Selected Letters,* 211.

36. RF to John W. Haines, March 15, [1915], *Selected Letters,* 157.

37. Florence I. Holt to RF, August 7, 1914, *Selected Letters,* 130–31; RF to Sidney Cox, c. March 2, 1915, *Selected Letters,* 156.

38. RF to John W. Haines, December 3, 1915, copy in DCL; RF to Edward Thomas, August 15, 1916, Thomas, "Six Letters," 53.

9. War: "For Children Too"

1. Wilfrid Gibson to RF, November 18, 1915, DCL; Dorothy Haines to Lesley Frost, December 16, 1915, UVL; Catherine Abercrombie quoted by John W. Haines to RF, March 7, 1915, DCL.

2. Wilfrid Gibson to RF, November 18, 1915, DCL; Wilfrid Gibson to RF, October 2, 1916, DCL.

3. See "Robert Frost's Poetry Written before 1913: A Critical Edition," ed. Andrew John Angyal, 83–85; see also Lawrance Thompson, *Robert Frost: The Early Years, 1874–1915,* 329–30.

4. Cohn notebook, quoted by John E. Walsh, *Into My Own: The English Years of Robert Frost,* 221.

5. RF to John W. Haines, April 2, 1915, DCL.

6. RF to Edward Thomas, April 17, 1915, *The Selected Letters of Robert Frost,* ed. Lawrance C. Thompson, 166.

7. RF to John W. Haines, July 17, 1915, *Selected Letters,* 183–84; the lines of verse are quoted in "England," in Richard Thornton, ed., *The Recognition of Robert Frost,* 95; see also "Robert Frost's Poetry Written before 1913," ed. Angyal, 56, which places the poem in c. 1892, and includes two additional lines from what was originally a much longer poem, never published: "Our faces are not that way or should not be / Our future is to the West on the other Sea—" lines inscribed to William Meredith in a copy of *A Masque of Mercy.*

8. RF to John W. Haines, April 25, 1915, *Selected Letters,* 170.

9. RF to John Bartlett, May 8, 1915, *Selected Letters,* 173.

10. RF to Edward Garnett, June 12, 1915, *Selected Letters,* 180.

11. RF to Harold Monro, August 7, 1915, *Selected Letters,* 185–86.

12. RF to Lascelles Abercrombie, September 21, 1915, *Selected Letters,* 192.

13. RF to Lascelles Abercrombie, December 1, 1915, *Selected Letters,* 197. See also RF to John Bartlett, December 2, 1915, *Selected Letters,* 197.

14. Elinor Frost to Dorothy Haines, December 7, [1916].

15. Ibid.

16. Edward Thomas to RF, July 29 and November 4 1916, and Edward Thomas to Elinor Frost, November 27, 1916, DCL.

17. Wellesley College, 1917, University of New Hampshire Library.

18. Dorothy Haines to Lesley Frost, March 8, 1915, UVL.

19. Dorothy Haines to Lesley Frost, December 16, 1915, UVL.

20. Dorothy Haines to Lesley Frost, December 11, 1916, UVL.

21. Dorothy Haines to Lesley Frost, July 16, 1915, UVL.

22. Cards postmarked July 29, 1915, UVL.

23. Dorothy Haines to Lesley Frost, July 16, 1915, UVL.

24. Ibid.

25. Dorothy Haines to Lesley Frost, December 11, 1916, UVL.

26. Mary Gardner to Lesley Frost, February 1, 1919, UVL.

27. J. C. Smith to RF, October 3, 1915.

28. The letters cited here, located in the UVL, are from Lucy Mair to Lesley Frost, December 31, 1915; June 16, 1916; January 13, 1917; January 1, 1919; June 7, 1924; and December 30, 1924.

29. Louis Untermeyer, in *The Letters of Robert Frost to Louis Untermeyer,* ed. Louis Untermeyer, 35; see also pages 28 and 36.

30. RF to Louis Untermeyer, undated letter, c. June 1916, *Letters of Robert Frost to Louis Untermeyer,* 36. *Seven Arts* also carried *A Way Out,* RF's one-act play, in its fourth issue.

31. RF to Amy Lowell, [22 October 1917], *Selected Letters,* 220.

32. RF to John W. Haines, July 4, 1916, *Selected Letters,* 205–6.

33. RF to Edward Thomas, November 23, 1915, in R. George Thomas, "Six Letters from Robert Frost to Edward Thomas," 51.

34. RF to Edward Thomas, August 15, 1916, in R. G. Thomas, "Six Letters," 53.

35. RF to Edward Thomas, June 26, 1915, in R. G. Thomas, "Six Letters," 51.

36. RF to Edward Thomas, August 15, 1916, in R. G. Thomas, "Six Letters," 53–54.

37. RF to Edward Thomas, September 28, 1916, in R. G. Thomas, "Six Letters," 55.

38. RF to Edward Thomas, November 6, 1916, in R. G. Thomas, "Six Letters," 56.

39. The title of the collection is from the sixteenth-century anonymous poem about a farmer who has to give up getting a new cloak to provide for his nagging and scolding wife and numerous offspring.

40. RF to Edward Thomas, June 26, 1915, in R. G. Thomas, "Six Letters," 50.

41. Edward Thomas to RF, July 22, 1915, DCL. The poem, "A Dream [Sonnet I]," is in *The Collected Poems of Edward Thomas,* ed. R. George Thomas, no. 81.

42. RF to Edward Thomas, November 15, 1915; the printing, in *Poetry Wales* and again in *Under Storm's Wing,* mistakenly transcribes "Use should decide it" as "We should decide it," a serious distortion of meaning; R. G. Thomas, "Six Letters," 52; original in University College, Cardiff.

43. RF to Edward Thomas, July 31, 1915, *Selected Letters,* 184.

44. "This England," in Thornton, ed., *Recognition of Robert Frost,* 218–21.

45. RF to Edward Thomas, December 7, 1916, in R. G. Thomas, "Six Letters," 58.

46. Edward Thomas to Eleanor Farjeon, May 22, 1915, Eleanor Farjeon, *Edward Thomas: The Last Four Years,* 327.

47. *The Poetry of Robert Frost,* ed. Edward C. Lathem, 315.

48. John W. Haines to Robert Frost, May 19, 1917, DCL.

49. John W. Haines, "Edward Thomas, As I Knew Him," *In Memoriam: Edward Thomas* (Morland Press, July 1919), 17, and Edward Thomas to Robert Frost, January 22, 1917, DCL.

50. John W. Haines to Robert Frost, May 19, 1917, DCL. The poem is from *Collected Poems of Edward Thomas,* no. 139.

51. Robert Frost to Helen Thomas, April 27, 1917, *Selected Letters,* 216.

52. Robert Frost to Edward Garnett, April 29, 1917, *Selected Letters,* 217.

53. Elinor Frost to Lesley Frost at Wellesley, n.d., c. 1917, held by family.

10. Aftermath: "The Tender Grace of a Day that Is Dead"

1. See Lesley Frost, "Somewhat Atavistic."

2. RF to John W. Haines, March 14, 1915, DCL. These observations may have inspired "A Patch of Old Snow," included in *Mountain Interval.* RF to John W. Haines, April 2, 1915, copy in DCL.

3. Some of Edward Thomas's poems appeared in *An Annual of New Poetry* (London: Constable, 1917), for which Edward saw the proofs; in *Six Poems* (London: The Pear Tree Press, 1916); in *Poetry, A Magazine of Verse,* edited by Harriet Monroe (February 1917); and in Selwyn and Blount's collection of his *Poems* (1917), going to press at the time he was killed. His *Collected Poems* would appear under his real name after his death.

4. RF to Edward Garnett, April 29, 1917, *The Selected Letters of Robert Frost,* ed. Lawrance C. Thompson, 217.

5. The articles were by George Whicher and Louis Untermeyer, respectively. See Lawrance Thompson, *Robert Frost: The Years of Triumph, 1915–1938,* notes, 548–49.

6. RF to John W. Haines, July 4, 1916, and January 20, 1921, *Selected Letters,* 206 and 264.

7. Wilfrid Gibson to RF, October 2, 1916, DCL. When Haines told Edward Thomas about the "destruction of some beautiful trees near Lascelles Abercrombie's cottage," Edward replied: "I don't think I shall regret the trees cut down till after it is all over, if I regret anything then" (John W. Haines, "Edward Thomas, As I Knew Him," *In Memoriam: Edward Thomas* (Morland Press, July 1919), 17.

8. See RF to John W. Haines, September 20, 1922, and May 18, 1917, DCL; and Haines, *In Memoriam,* 13.

9. For RF's lack of royalties, see RF to John W. Haines, September 20, 1922, DCL. For RF's recollections of Mrs. Nutt's comments, see RF to John W. Haines, June 7, 1921, DCL.

10. Haines wrote a piece on "The Dymock Poets" that appeared in the *Gloucestershire Countryside* (October 1933); he published "Edward Thomas, As I Knew Him," recalling his and Robert's walks together with their sad, melancholic friend, which was included in *In Memoriam,* 13–18; and his poem about the death of Edward Thomas called "April 1917" appeared in his *Poems* (1921).

11. John W. Haines, *Now and Then: A Journal of Books and Personalities for Autumn 1948,* 9–11.

12. Richard Thornton, ed., *The Recognition of Robert Frost,* 95–96; from the *Gloucester Journal* (February 2, 1935), with additions. The line "and the tender grace of a day that is dead" is from "Break, Break, Break" by Alfred Tennyson.

13. RF to John W. Haines, September 20, 1922, DCL.

14. RF to John W. Haines, July 21, 1925, *Selected Letters,* 315.

15. RF to Lesley Frost, [late fall 1925], *Family Letters of Robert and Elinor Frost,* ed. Arnold E. Grade, 109.

16. Before leaving New York for Pittsfield, Lesley had hoped to spend some time (up to six months) in France. When, in September 1920, plans to go to Europe with a friend fell through—after the young woman, Catherine McElroy, got herself locked into the New York Public Library, and her father said she was too irresponsible to go abroad—Robert and Elinor tried to help Lesley make it to France on her own, or even with her mother or with Marjorie. They soon realized that "it might cost too much for the family purse" if more than one family member went, and, her father wrote, "I'm half scared to have you go alone" (RF to Lesley Frost, October 14, 1920, *Family Letters,* 106).

17. RF to Otto Manthey-Zorn, August [18], 1928, ACL. For a detailed account of the Frosts' trip to Europe, see chapter 23 of Lawrance Thompson, *Robert Frost: The Years of Triumph, 1915–1938,* 328–43. Once again, Thompson appears to hold RF personally responsible for everything that went wrong in RF's family life.

18. RF to John W. Haines, July 29, 1928, DCL.

19. RF to Lesley Frost, August 3, 1928, *Family Letters,* 115.

20. Elinor Frost to Edith Manthey-Zorn, October 4, 1928, ACL; Edith was the wife of Otto Manthey-Zorn, a professor at Amherst College.

21. Elinor Frost to Lesley Frost, [August 1928], from the *Montnairn, Family Letters,* 116.

22. RF to Lesley Frost, [August 23, 1928], *Family Letters,* 119; RF to Lesley Frost, August 21, 1928, *Family Letters,* 117; RF to Lesley Frost, August 23, 1928, *Family Letters,* 121.

23. RF to John W. Haines, August 25, 1928, DCL.

24. Elinor Frost to Lesley Frost, September 20, 1928, *Family Letters,* 126; RF to Lesley Frost, September [1], 1928, *Family Letters,* 123–24.

25. RF to Edward [Ted] Davison, October 11, 1928, DCL.

26. RF to Lesley Frost, [September 11, 1928], *Family Letters,* 124.

27. RF to Davison, October 11, 1928; DCL. Quoted in Thompson, *Years of Triumph,* 336; see also John Freeman to Jack Haines, *John Freeman's Letters,* ed. Sir John Squire (London: Macmillan and Co., 1936), 239, where he mentions that Davies presented Robert "with a new book, duly signed and beamed over . . ."

28. RF to Lesley Frost, [September 11, 1928], *Family Letters,* 125.

29. Elinor Frost to Lesley Frost, September 20, 1928, *Family Letters,* 126.

30. Elinor Frost to Lesley Frost, [September 1928], *Family Letters,* 130; Elinor Frost to Lesley Frost, October 1, [1928], *Family Letters,* 131.

31. Elinor Frost to Lesley Frost, October 1, [1928], *Family Letters,* 130.

32. RF to Padraic Colum, September 18, 1928, *Selected Letters,* 349–50.

33. See RF to Davison, October 11, 1928, DCL, and Thompson, *Years of Triumph,* 337 and 349. Padraic Colum, in "A Yankee Sage," in Thornton, ed., *Recognition of Robert Frost,* 165, and in "Frost in Dublin," *Mark Twain Quarterly* 3.4 (Spring 1940), 11, recounts Robert's efforts in Dublin Castle to trace his genealogy and coat of arms back to the Lincolnshire Frosts and an arms representing a gray squirrel and a pine tree. Although Robert was well aware that the Nicholas Frost family originated in Cornbre Hill, Cornwall, and came to America from Tiverton in Devonshire, he kept the likeness of the coat of arms, signed C'onno Curr'an, among his treasured possessions (as it is now among mine). See Thompson, *Years of Triumph,* notes, 638. In the letter of October 11, 1928, to Davison cited above, Robert mentions a trip he and Squire planned to take "to Iverton where my ancestry came from. I dont know what struck [Squire] this way, but he seemed to like the idea of my having originated in Devon. He says we must make the most of it—celebrate it by going down there and looking up the family records in the regulation American fashion. Maybe I'll find I have a coat of arms. Then it wont matter what I do to earn a living any more." There is no evidence that the planned trip was ever realized.

34. RF to Lesley Frost, September [1], 1928, *Family Letters,* 125.

35. RF to Sidney Cox, October 11, 1928, *Selected Letters,* 351.

36. RF to John W. Haines, October 11, 1928, DCL

37. Helen Thomas, *World without End,* 151.

38. Helen Thomas to Elinor Frost, [October 1928], DCL. One consequence of this distancing from Helen was that Robert canceled his dedication—To Helen Thomas in Memory of Edward Thomas—which had been in his *Selected Poems* since 1923. Although it was too late to have the dedication removed from the 1928 edition, by error it reappeared in the 1934 edition. See Thompson, *Years of Triumph,* notes, 636–37.

39. Elinor Frost to Lesley Frost, September 20, [1928], *Family Letters,* 127; Elinor Frost to Lesley Frost, [October 1928], The Georgian House, London, *Family Letters,* 129. Elinor promised to tell Lesley about the Mair family in her next letter. Unfortunately, the promised description cannot be found. I believe this letter is improperly dated in *Family Letters* as September 1928. The reference in it to the 25th of the month should be October; also, in September they would still have been at the Imperial.

40. RF to Lesley Frost, [11 September 1928], *Family Letters,* 125.

41. Wilfrid Gibson to RF, October 3, 1928, DCL.

42. Wilfrid Gibson to RF, January 3, 1934, DCL, a letter written in response to Robert's annual Christmas poem. For Gibson's condolences on Elinor's death, see Wilfrid Gibson to RF, April 14, 1938, DCL. For Gibson's request for a tribute to Lascelles Abercrombie, see Wilfrid Gibson to RF, February 3, 1939, DCL; Gibson asked again for a tribute to Lascelles in a letter dated May 4, 1939, DCL. There is no record of RF having responded to the request. For Gibson's lament at his lack of success as a poet, see Wilfrid Gibson to RF, May 4, 1939, DCL.

43. Wilfrid Gibson, 1947; sent to Thompson by letter dated May 24, 1947, UVL.

44. Elinor Frost to Lesley Frost, [November 1928], *Family Letters,* 132.

45. Jessy Mair to RF, October 16, 1928, DCL; J. C. Smith to RF, October 26, 1928, DCL.

46. Thompson, *Years of Triumph,* 339; from letter RF to Lawrance Thompson, July 27, 1941, the original of which I have been unable to locate.

47. RF to John W. Haines, n.d., received November 2, 1928, DCL.

48. Thompson, *Years of Triumph,* 339.

49. Elinor Frost to Lesley Frost, November 6, 1928, *Family Letters,* 133–34.

50. Thompson, *Years of Triumph,* 342.

51. RF to John Freeman, November 19, 1928, UTL; a lighter version of this crossing is contained in a letter to J. J. Lankes, December 22, 1928, UTL; quoted in Thompson, *Years of Triumph,* notes, 640. Robert and Jack Haines continued to correspond sporadically after 1928. Robert would send Haines his annual Christmas poem; Haines would send Robert news of his family, occasionally with something he had written about him. In 1936, Robert contributed generously to a memorial for Edward Thomas (John W. Haines to RF, June 3, 1936, DCL). Robin, by now, was following in his father's footsteps as a barrister, and, in 1938, visited Robert in the United States. And thus Jack Haines continued to send the Frosts news of his family and of the poets: of Gibson, Abercrombie (upon his death in 1939), even word from Helen Thomas and the children. And always a word about Little Iddens, The Gallows (fast disappearing), and May Hill.

52. At the time of Mr. Frost's visit to England and in 1959 when this text was written Harold E. Howland was Chief, Special Cultural Programs Branch, International Educational Exchange Service, in the Department of State. The document is located in DCL.

53. Robert also received honorary degrees at Cambridge, Durham, and Dublin universities. Copies of the orations bestowing the honorary degrees at Oxford (June 4, 1957) and Cambridge (June 13, 1957) are in the DCL. Whereas the Oxford oration refers to Virgil, the Cambridge oration included Latin verses of Horace (*Ars Poetica,* 240–42):

> I will create my poetry out of the familiar,
> so that anyone may hope to achieve the same,
> but may sweat and labour much in vain
> if he ventures on the same.

54. RF to John W. Haines, Christmas card, n.d., postmarked January 9, 1952, DCL; "The Sound of Trees," *Mountain Interval.*

55. The visit to the Gloucestershire locations occurred June 5–6; the press coverage resulted in an article, "A Poet's Pilgrimage," *Life,* September 23, 1957, 109–112.

56. Reverend J. E. Gethyn Jones, *Dymock Down the Ages,* 2d ed. (Gloucester: Alan Sutton, 1985), 115.

57. Ibid., 116.

58. Ibid.

59. RF had seen Helen Thomas in London on May 21. The luncheon was scheduled for June 3, 1957.

60. May 23 and June 12, 1957. I have corresponded with Dr. Henry M. Pantin, son of Amy Smith Pantin and Carl Frederic Abel Pantin and grandson of James C. and Edith Smith. He told me that, before her death, his mother threw out papers, "resenting anything that reminded her of happier days." As a consequence, no letters from Lesley to Amy have survived. Dr. Pantin was delighted to learn that his mother wrote poems as a child for *The Bouquet* and he asked to see copies of her letters to my mother cited elsewhere. He is in the process of editing the poems of his aunt, Rose Ann Smith, who, he said, "led a very sad life, which dominates her poetry."

61. May 29 and June 5, 1957. In my search for letters from Lesley to Lucy Mair, I have

corresponded with Peter Mair, grandson of Jessy Philip and David Mair and son of Philip Beveridge Mair, author of *Shared Enthusiasm,* who presented me with a signed copy of his father's memoirs. In *Years of Triumph,* 339, Thompson incorrectly has Jessy Mair widowed and about to marry Lord Beveridge in 1928 (rather than 1942).

62. June 9 and 11, 1957, respectively.

63. June 9 and 10, 1957. See my article "Robert Frost and Helen Thomas Revisited," and Eleanor Farjeon's foreword to *You Come Too* (London: The Bodley Head, 1964).

64. *Kings and Queens* (London: J. M. Dent, 1953) is in my library; *Poems* (together with *The Childhood of Edward Thomas,* London [1938], *The Country,* London [1913], and *Lafcadio Hearn,* Boston [1912], inscribed "E. & R. F. from E. T.") is in the New York University Bobst Library, which holds the poet's personal library, given to NYU by his daughter, Lesley Frost, 1964–1968.

65. Farjeon, foreword to *You Come Too,* 16. Upon learning of my grandfather's death, Eleanor Farjeon wrote my mother: "So he has gone, Lesley, leaving what will live as long as America does. I can't write about him, or my feelings today—no words seem real enough, they are all cliches. Only he, who never used a cliche in his life, could put his finger on the pulse and find its true beat. It isn't grief, or a sense of loss. There's a great deal of gladness in it that such a man was, and is; and that he was and is my friend. It's that I'm sending you. With my love Eleanor" (A letter in my possession, dated January 29, 1963).

Selected Bibliography

Abercrombie, Catherine. "Memories of a Poet's Wife." *The Listener,* November 15, 1956, 793–94.

Anderson, Margaret Bartlett. *Robert Frost and John Bartlett: The Record of a Friendship.* New York: Holt, Rinehart and Winston, 1963.

Barry, Elaine. *Robert Frost on Writing.* New Brunswick, N.J.: Rutgers University Press, 1973.

Born, Anne. "Harold Monro and the Poetry Bookshop." *Antiquarian Book Monthly Review,* April 1980, 184–193.

Burnshaw, Stanley. *Robert Frost Himself.* New York: George Braziller, 1986.

Cook, Reginald. *Robert Frost: A Living Voice.* Amherst: University of Massachusetts Press, 1974.

Cooper, Jeffrey. *A Bibliography and Notes on the Works of Lascelles Abercrombie.* Hamden, Conn.: Archon Books, 1969.

Cournos, John. *Autobiography.* New York: G. P. Putnam's Sons, 1935.

Davies, W. H. *Later Days.* London: Jonathan Cape, 1925.

Davison, Peter. "The Self-Realization of Robert Frost, 1911–1912." *New Republic,* March 30, 1974, 17–24.

Drinkwater, John. *Discovery.* London: Benn, 1932.

Eckert, Robert P. *Edward Thomas: A Biography and a Bibliography.* London: Dent, 1937.

Ellis, Frances N. "Robert Frost in England, 1912–1915." Master's thesis, Columbia University, 1948.

Farjeon, Eleanor. *Edward Thomas: The Last Four Years.* New York: Oxford University Press, 1958.

———. Foreword to *You Come Too,* by Robert Frost, 7–16. London: The Bodley Head, 1964.

Francis, Lesley Lee. "Between Poets: Robert Frost and Harriet Monroe." *The South Carolina Review* 19 (Summer 1987): 2–15.

———. "A Decade of 'Stirring Times': Robert Frost and Amy Lowell." *The New England Quarterly* 59.4 (December 1986): 508–22.

———. "Robert Frost and Helen Thomas Revisited." *Dartmouth College Li-*

brary Bulletin, n.s., 32.1 (November 1991): 10–17. Reprinted in the *Robert Frost Review* 3 (Fall 1993): 77–85.

———. "Robert Frost and Susan Hayes Ward." *The Massachusetts Review* 26.2–3 (Summer–Autumn 1985): 341–50.

———. "Robert Frost and the Majesty of Stones upon Stones." *Journal of Modern Literature* 9.1 (1981–1982): 3–26.

———. "Robert Frost at Harvard: 'Imperfectly Academic.'" *Harvard Magazine* (March–April 1984): 51–56.

Francis, Robert. *Robert Frost: A Time to Talk.* Amherst: University of Massachusetts Press, 1972.

Frost, Lesley. "Certain Intensities." *Ball State University Forum* 15.3 (Summer 1974): 3–8.

———. *New Hampshire's Child: The Derry Journals of Lesley Frost.* Edited by Arnold Grade and Lawrance Thompson. Albany: State University of New York Press, 1969.

———. "Our Family Christmas." *Red Book Magazine,* December 1963, 45, 97–98.

———. "Robert Frost Remembered." *The American Way* 7.2 (March 1974): 12–17.

———. "Somewhat Atavistic." *Ball State University Forum* 11.1 (Winter 1970): 3–6.

Frost, Robert. *Family Letters of Robert and Elinor Frost.* Edited by Arnold E. Grade. Albany: State University of New York Press, 1972.

———. *The Letters of Robert Frost to Louis Untermeyer.* Edited by Louis Untermeyer. New York: Holt, Rinehart and Winston, 1963.

———. *The Poetry of Robert Frost.* Edited by Edward C. Lathem. New York: Holt, Rinehart and Winston, 1969.

———. *Robert Frost, Poetry and Prose.* Edited by Edward C. Lathem and Lawrance Thompson. New York: Henry Holt and Company, 1972.

———. "Robert Frost's Poetry Written before 1913: A Critical Edition." Edited by Andrew John Angyal. Ph.D. diss., Duke University, 1976.

———. *The Selected Letters of Robert Frost.* Edited by Lawrance C. Thompson. New York: Holt, Rinehart and Winston, 1964.

———. *Stories for Lesley.* Edited by Roger D. Sell. Charlottesville: University Press of Virginia, 1984.

Gethyn-Jones, J. E. *Dymock down the Ages.* Rev. ed. Gloucestershire: Alan Sutton Publishing Ltd., 1966.

———. "Robert Frost—6th June 1957." *The Courier,* Syracuse University, Summer 1969, 1–8.

Grade, Arnold E. "A Chronicle of Robert Frost's Early Reading, 1874–1899." *Bulletin of the New York Public Library* 72.9 (November 1968): 611–28.

Grant, Joy. *Harold Monro and the Poetry Bookshop.* London: Routledge and Kegan Paul, 1967.

Haines, John W. "Robert Frost." In *Now and Then: A Journal of Books and Personalities for Autumn 1948.* London: Jonathan Cape, 1948.

Harcourt, Alfred. *Some Experiences* (includes chapter, "A New Magazine *and* a New Poet," about publishing Robert Frost's books of poems in America). Privately published, Riverside, Conn., 1951.

Hassall, Christopher. *Edward Marsh: Patron of the Arts.* London: Longmans, 1959.

Lehmann, John. *Three Literary Friendships: Byron and Shelley, Rimbaud and Verlaine, and Robert Frost and Edward Thomas.* New York: Holt, Rhinehart and Winston, 1983.

Mair, Philip Beveridge. *Shared Enthusiasm: The Story of Lord and Lady Beveridge.* Surrey, England: Ascent Books, 1982.

Marsh, Jan. *Edward Thomas: A Poet for His Country.* London: Paul Elek, 1978.

———. "Georgian Poets and the Land." Ph.D. Diss., University of Sussex, 1970.

Mertins, Louis. *Robert Frost: Life and Talks-Walking.* Norman: University of Oklahoma Press, 1965.

Monroe, Harriet. *Poets and Their Art.* New York: Macmillan, 1926.

Motion, Andrew. *The Poetry of Edward Thomas.* London: Routledge and Kegan Paul, 1980.

Munson, Gorham B. *Robert Frost: A Study in Sensibility and Good Sense.* New York: Haskell House, 1973.

Poirier, Richard. *Robert Frost: The Work of Knowing.* New York: Oxford University Press, 1977.

Pritchard, William H. *Frost, A Literary Life Revisited.* New York: Oxford University Press, 1984. 2d ed. with a new preface, Amherst: University of Massachusetts Press, 1993.

Ross, Robert H. *The Georgian Revolt.* London: Faber and Faber, 1967.

Sergeant, Elizabeth Shepley. *The Trial by Existence.* New York: Holt, Rinehart and Winston, 1960.

Sims, George. "Alida Monro and The Poetry Bookshop." *Antiquarian Book Monthly Review,* April 1980, 262–67.

———. "In Pursuit of Edward Thomas." *London Magazine,* July 1984, 38–51.

Tatham, David. *A Poet Recognized.* Syracuse, N.Y.: Syracuse University Press, 1970.

Thomas, Edward. *The Collected Poems of Edward Thomas.* Edited by R. George Thomas. New York: Oxford University Press, 1978; pbk ed., 1981.

Thomas, Helen. *As It Was*. London: William Heinemann, 1926.

———. *World without End*. London: William Heinemann, 1931. (Reprinted in one volume by Faber and Faber, 1956, and included in *Under Storm's Wing*, with Myfanwy Thomas.)

Thomas, Myfanwy. *Under Storm's Wing*. London: Carcanet, 1988; London: Paladin, Grafton Books, 1990.

Thomas, R. George. *Edward Thomas: A Portrait*. Oxford: Clarendon Press, 1985.

———. "Six Letters from Robert Frost to Edward Thomas." *Poetry Wales* 22.4 (1987): 48–58.

Thompson, Lawrance. *Robert Frost: The Early Years, 1874–1915*. New York: Holt, 1966.

———. *Robert Frost: The Later Years, 1938–1963* (with R. H. Winnick). New York: Holt, 1976.

———. *Robert Frost: The Years of Triumph, 1915–1938*. New York: Holt, 1970.

Thornton, Richard, ed. *The Recognition of Robert Frost*. New York: Henry Holt and Co., 1937.

Wain, John. "Edward and Helen Thomas." In *Professing Poetry*, by John Wain, 335–66. London: Macmillan, 1977.

Walsh, John E. *Into My Own: The English Years of Robert Frost*. New York: Grove Press, 1988.

Index

Permissions

Formal acknowledgment is made as follows to libraries, publishers, and individuals for their kind permission to quote from copyright material and for the use of family photographs:

Amherst College Library: letters from RF to Otto Manthey-Zorn (ms. Frost 154 and ms. Frost 493).

Boston University Library: letters from RF to Gertrude McQuesten; letters from Elinor Frost to Marie Hodge; RF's Notebook (England).

Carcanet Press: letters from RF to Edward Thomas in *Under Storm's Wing* © 1988.

Jeffrey Cooper (Executor of the Abercrombie Estate): unpublished letters from Lascelles Abercrombie to Jack Haines; "Extract from a Recording by Mrs. Abercrombie"; "Memories of a Poet's Wife"; a photograph of the Abercrombies.

Dartmouth College Library: letters from RF to Edward Thomas and from Edward Thomas to RF; letters from W. W. Gibson to RF; letters from RF to Lascelles Abercrombie; letters from RF to Jack Haines and from Jack Haines to RF; letters from Mary Gardner to RF and Elinor Frost; letters from Helen Thomas to RF; letters from RF to Edward Davison; letters from J. C. Smith to RF; letters from Jessy Mair to RF; letters from Elinor Frost to Mrs. Harold Brown; letters from Elinor Frost to Margaret Bartlett; other related materials.

Gervase Farjeon (Executor of the Eleanor Farjeon Estate): *Edward Thomas: The Last Four Years* © 1958; Foreward to *You Come Too* © 1964; photograph of Eleanor Farjeon.

Michael Gibson (Executor of the W. W. Gibson Estate): letters from W. W. Gibson to RF; poems "The Golden Room" and "The Magnet."

Peter A. Gilbert (Executor of the Robert Frost Estate): unpublished letters and other copyrighted materials.

Henry Holt and Company: *The Letters of Robert Frost to Louis Untermeyer* edited by Louis Untermeyer © 1963 by Louis Untermeyer (reprinted by arrangement with Henry Holt and Company, Inc., and the Estate of Robert Frost); *The Poetry of Robert Frost* edited by Edward C. Lanthem © 1975; *Robert Frost: The Early Years, 1874–1915* by Lawrance Thompson © 1966 by Lawrance Thompson (reprinted by permission of Henry Holt and Company, Inc.); *Robert Frost: The Years of Triumph, 1915–1938* by Lawrance Thompson © 1970 by Lawrance Thompson, © 1970 by the Estate of Robert Frost (reprinted by permission of Henry Holt and Company, Inc.); *Robert Frost: The Later Years, 1938–1963* by Lawrance Thompson and R. H. Winnick © 1976 by the Estate of Robert Frost (reprinted by permission of Henry Holt and Company, Inc.); *The Selected Letters of Robert Frost* edited by Lawrance Thompson © 1964 by Lawrance Thompson and Henry Holt and Company, Inc. (reprinted by arrangement with Henry Holt and Company, Inc., and the Estate of Robert Frost).

Jonathan Cape: *The Poetry of Robert Frost* edited by Edward Connery Latham © 1975.

Peter Mair: *Shared Enthusiasm: The Story of Lord and Lady Beveridge* by Philip Beveridge Mair © 1982; photograph of Jessy Mair and her children.

Jan Marsh: *Edward Thomas: A Poet for His Country* © 1978; dissertation, "Georgian Poets and the Land."

University of New Hampshire Library (Lesley Frost Ballantine Collection): Wellesley College compositions by Lesley Frost.

Plymouth State College (Herbert H. Lamson Library): letters from Lesley Frost to Beulah Huckins; photograph of the Frost children at Beaconsfield.

State University of New York Press: *Family Letters of Robert and Elinor Frost* © 1972; *New Hampshire's Child: The Derry Journals of Lesley Frost* © 1969.

University of Texas Library (Harry Ransom Humanities Research Center, The University of Texas at Austin): letters from RF to Frank S. Flint and John Freeman.

R. George Thomas: *Edward Thomas: A Portrait* © 1985.

Myfanwy Thomas (Executor of the Edward Thomas Estate): poems by Edward Thomas in *The Collected Poems of Edward Thomas* © 1978.

University of Wales, Cardiff: photographs of Edward, Helen, Bronwen, Merfyn, and Myfanwy Thomas.